NEW MERMAIDS

General editors:
William C. Carroll, Boston University
Brian Gibbons, University of Münster
Tiffany Stern, University College, University of Oxford

NEW MERMAIDS

The Alchemist

All for Love

Arden of Faversham

Arms and the Man

Bartholmew Fair

The Beaux' Stratagem

The Beggar's Opera

The Changeling

A Chaste Maid in Cheapside

The Country Wife

The Critic

Doctor Faustus

The Duchess of Malfi

The Dutch Courtesan

Eastward Ho!

Edward the Second

Elizabethan and Jacobean Tragedies

Epicoene or The Silent Woman

Every Man In His Humour

Gammer Gurton's Needle

An Ideal Husband

The Importance of Being Earnest

The Jew of Malta

The Knight of the Burning Pestle

Lady Windermere's Fan

London Assurance

Love for Love

Major Barbara

The Malcontent

The Man of Mode

Marriage A-La-Mode

Mrs Warren's Profession

A New Way to Pay Old Debts

The Old Wife's Tale

The Playboy of the Western World

The Provoked Wife

Pygmalion

The Recruiting Officer

The Relapse

The Revenger's Tragedy

The Rivals

The Roaring Girl

The Rover

Saint Joan

The School for Scandal

She Stoops to Conquer

The Shoemaker's Holiday

The Spanish Tragedy

Tamburlaine

The Tamer Tamed

Three Late Medieval Morality Plays
  Mankind
  Everyman
  Mundus et Infans

'Tis Pity She's a Whore

The Tragedy of Mariam

Volpone

The Way of the World

The White Devil

The Witch

The Witch of Edmonton

A Woman Killed with Kindness

A Woman of No Importance

Women Beware Women

NEW MERMAIDS

OSCAR WILDE

AN IDEAL HUSBAND

Edited with notes by Russell Jackson
Allardyce Nicoll Chair in Drama, University of Birmingham

Introduction by Sos Eltis
Fellow in English at Brasenose College, Oxford

methuen | drama
LONDON · NEW YORK · OXFORD · NEW DELHI · SYDNEY

METHUEN DRAMA
Bloomsbury Publishing Plc
50 Bedford Square, London, WC1B 3DP, UK
1385 Broadway, New York, NY 10018, USA

BLOOMSBURY, METHUEN DRAMA and the Methuen Drama logo are
trademarks of Bloomsbury Publishing Plc

This New Mermaid edition first published in Great Britain 2013

Reprinted by Bloomsbury Methuen Drama 2014 (twice), 2015,
2016 (twice), 2017, 2018 (three times)

A catalogue record for this book is available from the British Library.

ISBN: PB: 978-1-4081-3720-8
ePDF: 978-1-4081-3721-5
ePub: 978-1-4081-3651-5

A catalog record for this book is available from the Library of Congress.

Series: New Mermaids

Printed and bound in Great Britain

To find out more about our authors and books visit
www.bloomsbury.com and sign up for our newsletters.

CONTENTS

PREFACE

I am grateful to Merlin Holland, the author's grandson, for permission to quote from unpublished drafts, and to the following institutions for access to materials in their possession: Birmingham Public Library; the Bodleian Library; the British Library; the William Andrews Clark Memorial Library, University of California; the Harvard Theatre Collection; New York Public Library at Lincoln Center; the Theatre Museum, London. Mrs S. Bruce, secretary general of the Women's Liberal Association, responded kindly to enquiries concerning the organisation's early history. I have benefitted from the encouragement and advice of Brian Gibbons, Ian Small and John Stokes, and I am especially grateful to Joel H. Kaplan, editor of the play for the forthcoming Oxford English Texts Edition, for information concerning the recently discovered typescript of the play. My greatest single (and continuing) debt remains that to my wife, Linda Rosenberg.

R.J.
Birmingham, February 1993

This edition of *An Ideal Husband* by Russell Jackson has a new Introduction and Bibliography by Sos Eltis; the edited play text with commentary notes, the sections on 'The Author', 'A Note on the Text', 'Abbreviations' and Appendices, are by Russell Jackson.

INTRODUCTION

Sir Robert Chiltern is the Under-Secretary for Foreign Affairs, a rising politician with a reputation for brilliance and unshakeable integrity. But he has a dark secret in his past, which his adoring wife does not suspect, and which the ruthless Mrs Cheveley intends to exploit to secure the success of her own underhand schemes.

Oscar Wilde's *An Ideal Husband* is one of the most frequently and successfully revived plays of the nineteenth century. Dealing with high-class intrigue, political corruption, blackmail and scandal, the play has puzzled, entertained and challenged audiences and critics since its premiere in January 1895. *An Ideal Husband* drew many of the richest and most powerful figures in society to the prestigious Haymarket Theatre to see and be seen at Wilde's witty and luxuriously staged drawing-room drama. Revolving around questions of public and private morality, con-tested gender roles and women's political involvement, the play left critics divided as to its implications and intent. Was Wilde satirising or flattering the privileged elite? Was the play suggesting that moral probity was politic-ally essential or distractingly irrelevant, that women were to be excluded from the political sphere, or that their contribution was an essential counterbalance to men's self-serving ambition? Modern critics remain more fiercely divided over *An Ideal Husband* than any other of Wilde's plays.

Wilde's arrest and prosecution for acts of 'gross indecency' with young men interrupted the play's successful run, bringing an inescapable personal resonance to a drama which centres on marital secrets, love and the threat of public disgrace. Yet the play's analysis of the tensions between human frailty, political convenience and public reputation applied with equally unsettling accuracy to the scandals which brought down contemporary politicians including the Irish nationalist leader Charles Stuart Parnell and the radical politician Sir Charles Dilke, a man who held the same post as the fictional Sir Robert Chiltern. As sexual and financial corruptions continue to be uncovered at the heart of government, revivals of Wilde's play have struck modern audiences with a relevance that seems almost uncannily prescient when issues of social hypocrisy, political convenience, the power of the press and the connection between social influence and wealth remain as pressingly relevant now as they were over a century ago.

Plot Summary

Act I

Sir Robert and Lady Chiltern greet arriving party guests at their luxurious London residence. A glamorous and uninvited guest, Mrs Cheveley, asks Sir Robert to use his position as Under-Secretary for Foreign Affairs to give government support to the Argentine Canal scheme, a financial speculation in which she has invested heavily. Sir Robert denounces the scheme as a fraud and reacts with outrage to Mrs Cheveley's attempt to bribe him. Mrs Cheveley coolly points out that he launched his political career by selling confidential government information for money and that she holds in her possession the incriminating letter he wrote to seal the transaction. Sir Robert agrees to give his political support in return for the letter. Lady Chiltern, however, on hearing that her husband is planning to back a scheme he previously denounced as corrupt, persuades him to withdraw his support and so preserve the moral superiority for which she admires and loves him. At his wife's instruction, Sir Robert reluctantly writes a letter to Mrs Cheveley, denouncing the scheme as fraudulent.

Meanwhile, another party guest, the exquisite dandy Lord Goring, has found a dropped brooch, and pockets it mysteriously, swearing Sir Robert's younger sister, Mabel, to secrecy.

Act II

Sir Robert confides his secret to his best friend, Lord Goring, who advises him to confess all to Gertrude Chiltern and ask her forgiveness, but Sir Robert insists that his wife will reject him in horror if she learns of his guilt. Mrs Cheveley calls to enquire after a lost brooch. Lady Chiltern's open scorn provokes her into revealing the criminal origin of Sir Robert Chiltern's wealth, and she warns Gertrude that she will ruin him unless he gives the Argentine scheme his political support. Lady Chiltern responds with horror to the revelation of her husband's guilt. Sir Robert angrily reproaches her for idolising him and preventing him from securing the incriminating letter.

Act III

Lord Goring receives a note from Lady Chiltern, taking up his offer of help and support, and announcing her intention to call on him in his bachelor apartments that evening: 'I want you. I need you. I am coming to you, Gertrude'. Goring's father, Lord Caversham, pays an unexpected visit, during which Mrs Cheveley calls and is shown into an inner room – Lord Goring's valet mistakenly believing her to be the expected female guest. Sir Robert arrives, and, when he surprises Mrs Cheveley there, believes his friend has betrayed him. Mrs Cheveley offers to exchange Sir Robert's letter for Lord Goring's hand in marriage, but Goring refuses to sacrifice himself. Learning that the lost brooch was Mrs Cheveley's, he shows how it can convert into a bracelet and clasps it on her wrist. He then tells her he knows that she stole it and threatens to hand her over to the police unless she gives him Robert's letter. She cannot find the hidden catch to remove the bracelet, and hands over the letter in exchange for her release. She then steals Lady Chiltern's letter to Lord Goring and says she will send it to Sir Robert with the implication that his wife is having an affair with his best friend.

Act IV

Lord Goring delights Lady Chiltern with the news that her husband has been saved from disgrace, but she is terrified to learn that her indiscreetly worded letter is in Mrs Cheveley's hands. Sir Robert receives the letter, but mistakenly believes it was addressed to himself, and his wife gratefully takes this as an opportunity for a reconciliation. Lord Caversham congratulates Sir Robert on his stirring denunciation of the Argentine Canal scheme in the House of Commons, and delivers an offer from the Prime Minister of a seat in the Cabinet. Under the watchful eye of his wife, Sir Robert reluctantly declines the seat and announces his resignation from politics. Lord Goring advises Lady Chiltern to forgive her husband and support the political ambitions which are necessary to his happiness, which she promptly does. Lord Goring asks his friend for Mabel Chiltern's hand in marriage, but Sir Robert refuses, believing him to be sexually involved with Mrs Cheveley on the evidence of her presence in his rooms the night before. Lady Chiltern informs her husband that Lord Goring is guiltless and that she herself was the woman he believed was hiding in his rooms. Sir Robert declares his unshakeable faith in his wife's purity, blesses Lord Goring's marriage to Mabel, and receives an assurance from his wife that it is love not pity that she feels for him.

The Background

'I took the drama, the most objective form known to art, and made it as personal a mode of expression as the lyric or the sonnet'; so Wilde boasted in his prison letter, later titled *De Profundis*, laying claim as he had throughout his career to originality and complete indifference to popular taste.[1] In his 1890 essay 'The Soul of Man under Socialism' Wilde disdained the notion that public opinion should exercise any shaping power over art,

---

1 Letter to Lord Alfred Douglas (January–March 1897), *The Complete Letters of Oscar Wilde*, ed. Merlin Holland and Rupert Hart-Davis, Fourth Estate, 2000, p. 729.

criticising the general public for degrading the classics into authorities: 'They use them as bludgeons for preventing the free expression of Beauty in new forms. They are always asking a writer why he does not write like somebody else, or a painter why he does not paint like somebody else, quite oblivious of the fact that if either of them did anything of the kind he would cease to be an artist.'[2] Wilde's championing of artistic autonomy, stylistic innovation and individual expression in 'The Soul of Man' was consistent with his attacks throughout his writing career on any constraints upon artistic freedom. Art, Wilde insisted, was to be judged by aesthetic criteria alone – all others, whether commercial, moral, utilitarian or didactic, were irrelevant and inappropriate. Wilde's provocative assertions of artistic autonomy were interventions in heated contemporary debates on the function, purpose and value of art, which ranged from John Ruskin's and Matthew Arnold's celebration of the morally and socially redemptive potential of art, to Aestheticism's insistence on 'Art for Art's sake', and Decadent writers' experimentation in forbidden subject matter – all these views playing out against the backdrop of a thriving commercial marketplace and the increasing organisation and facilitation of writing as a trade, from new copyright laws to the foundation of the Society of Authors in 1884.

Among the arts at the *fin de siècle* probably the most unstable and contested was the drama. Theatre had long been a highly remunerative business for managers and actors, but it was only at the end of the nineteenth century that it became a financially rewarding forum for writers. This was due to a combination of factors, including a change of theatrical fashion from mixed bills of numerous short entertainments to single long runs of individual plays, the passing of international copyright laws to protect dramatic texts, and negotiation by playwrights to receive a percentage of box-office takings rather than just a flat fee for their script. While the theatre became a more financially attractive forum for writers at the *fin de siècle*, it was still tightly constrained by censorship. Every play performed on the public stage had first to be submitted to the Lord Chamberlain's Office, where the playscript would be read and any requisite cuts or changes prescribed before a decision was taken to grant or refuse a performance licence.

As generations of playwrights complained, this system held the drama in an extended infancy compared to the other arts, rendering impossible any adult discussion of controversial issues. Melodrama, with its recognisable character-types, sensational events and strong emotions

---

2 Oscar Wilde, 'The Soul of Man under Socialism', *The Complete Works of Oscar Wilde*, Vol. 4: *Criticism*, ed. Josephine Guy, Oxford University Press, 2007, p. 251.

retained its popular cross-class appeal right to the end of the century, with new technology providing ever more spectacular effects. Sentimental comedies, farces and burlesques were also enduringly popular, as was Shakespeare. The French 'well-made' play, mechanical in form and concerned with complex plotting, copious letters and carefully timed revelations, was imported into England but carefully adapted and sanitised to remove any serious discussion of sexual or moral questions. The increasing social respectability of the theatre attracted higher proportions of middle- and upper-class playgoers, and the class profile of plays and audiences developed together; society dramas set in luxurious drawing rooms became the norm, and first nights at the most fashionable West End playhouses became events in the social calendar, where the social elite donned black tie and tiaras to offer a spectacle to rival that on stage.

The greatest challenge to this comfortable continuity came with the arrival of Ibsen's plays. Though their unglamorous petit-bourgeois naturalism and their questioning of traditional gender roles and notions of social duty prevented them becoming mainstream commercial successes, the radical impact of Ibsen's dramas made the English theatre's traditionally sentimental fare look hopelessly outmoded, while encouraging those who believed the theatre could be a medium for intellectual debate as well as escapist entertainment. For those seeking to push the drama into radical new territory the private theatre club became a vital means of performing plays refused a licence by the Lord Chamberlain's Office. Private clubs like J. T. Grein's Independent Theatre Society, founded in 1891, bypassed the censorship system by staging plays exclusively to subscribing members of the society rather than to the general public, thus evading the need for a public licence – a system which facilitated the performance of many of the most controversial plays of the period, from Ibsen's *Ghosts* to Shaw's *Widowers' Houses* and *Mrs Warren's Profession*.

For all his proud declarations of artistic autonomy and disdain for public opinion, Wilde's relation to popular Victorian theatre was a complex one. He was a confessed admirer of Ibsen's plays, praising *Hedda Gabler* as instilling pity and terror like a Greek tragedy, and requesting copies of *Little Eyolf* and *John Gabriel Borkman* to read in Reading gaol.[3] His admiration for French avant-garde symbolist theatre was clearly reflected in the style and concerns of his play *Salome*, whose depiction of perverse and explicit desire resulted in a ban on public performance from the Lord Chamberlain, leaving the play unperformed until 1896, when it was finally presented by the experimental Théâtre de l'Oeuvre in Paris. Despite the

---

3 Letter to the Earl of Lytton, ? May 1891, and letter to Robert Ross, 6 April 1897, *Complete Letters of Oscar Wilde*, pp. 480 and 792.

fact that *Lady Windermere's Fan* and *A Woman of No Importance* were produced at the St James's and the Haymarket theatres respectively, two of the most luxurious and elite venues in London, Wilde resisted characterisations of his plays as stylistically or morally conventional. Writing to the radical socialist George Bernard Shaw in 1893, Wilde coupled his own plays with Shaw's *Widowers' Houses*, describing them together as 'the Great Celtic School' whose mission was to clear away English intellectual fogs – a potentially surprising claim given that Shaw's play was a trenchant attack on capitalist profiteering and slum land-lordism, which only secured a private staging by the Independent Theatre Society.[4] Wilde was undoubtedly concerned to maximise the financial rewards from his playwriting, and negotiated lucrative contracts which accorded him a percentage share of each theatre's box-office takings.[5] An interest in commercial returns does not, however, necessarily imply loss of integrity, submission to the market or the abandonment of an opposi-tional voice; whilst Shaw was openly committed to writing confrontational and provocative propagandist plays, he also sought advice from Henry Arthur Jones on how to secure similar financial deals.[6]

Wilde's society dramas were unquestionably the product of a man steeped in the fashionable and essentially conservative theatre of his day. *Lady Windermere's Fan* (1892) and *A Woman of No Importance* (1893) both drew on character types, situations and plot devices from a wide range of plays by French playwrights such as Victorien Sardou, Alexandre Dumas *fils* and Jules Lemaître, and by English dramatists such as Arthur Wing Pinero, Henry Arthur Jones, Haddon Chambers and Sydney Grundy.[7] Contemporary reviewers were quick to spot Wilde's literary debts, and many dismissed his work as overly familiar and formulaic, but others were puzzled or provoked by his failure to conform to the genres from which he so copiously borrowed. *Lady Windermere's Fan* conformed to dramatic expectations with Lady Windermere's return to her husband and child and the maternal sacrifice of Mrs Erlynne to save the reputation of the daughter she once abandoned. Strikingly unconventional, however, was Mrs

---

4 Letter to Bernard Shaw, postmark 9 May 1893, *Complete Letters*, pp. 563–4.
5 For full details of Wilde's contracts and negotiations with theatre managers, see Josephine Guy and Ian Small, *Oscar Wilde's Profession: Writing and the Culture Industry in the Late Nineteenth Century*, Oxford University Press, 2000, chap. 4, and John Russell Stephens, *The Profession of the Playwright: British Theatre, 1800–1900*, Cambridge University Press, 2006, chap. 3.
6 See e.g. letter to Henry Arthur Jones, 24 April 1894, *Bernard Shaw Collected Letters, vol. 1: 1874–1897*, ed. Dan H. Laurence, Max Reinhart, 1965, pp. 429–30.
7 See Kerry Powell, *Oscar Wilde and the Theatre of the 1890s*, Cambridge University Press, 1990, and Sos Eltis, *Revising Wilde: Society and Subversion in the Plays of Oscar Wilde*, Oxford University Press, 1996.

Erlynne's rejection of a tearful reunion with her daughter, eschewing motherhood and repentance with an airy assertion that they suited neither her dress nor her lifestyle. Moreover, Mrs Erlynne ends the play in possession of a rich and adoring spouse, in stark contrast to the sexually fallen heroines in contemporary plays, who suffer painful and often self-inflicted deaths. Her insouciant exit raised the ire of morally conservative critics, who were similarly puzzled by the play's failure to supply conventionally neat closure, with all plot strands tied up, secrets revealed, misdemeanours punished and virtues rewarded. Instead, unsettlingly, both Lord and Lady Windermere end the play ignorant of each other's secrets, still too rigidly and naively judgemental to accept the complex truth of their lives. Where melodrama traditionally ended with the revelation of true moral character beneath all the disguises, deceits and false accusations, Wilde's drama destabilised the distinction between sincerity and performance, and questioned the definition and indeed validity of the term 'good'.

A Woman of No Importance similarly offered a familiar story-line in the form of Mrs Arbuthnot, an unmarried mother who was once seduced and abandoned by a wicked aristocrat, but Wilde again failed to play by the genre's rules, switching and combining idioms to disorienting effect. Fiercely possessive and disturbingly passionate, Mrs Arbuthnot is hardly the conventional shamed woman: she declares she did not care for the sick or the poor whom she tended – they were merely the accidental recipients of a love rightly meant for Gerald – nor has she ever repented, as she exclaims to her son: 'How could I repent of my sin when you, my love, were its fruit!'[8] The confrontation between the fallen woman and her former lover, Lord Ilingworth, in which he coolly deflates her high-flown rhetoric with his calm rationality, was judged by the critic William Archer to be 'the most virile and intelligent . . . piece of English dramatic writing of our day'.[9] The result was a morally ambiguous play which did not simply challenge the sexual double standard but defamiliarised and critiqued the rhetoric of sexual judgement, while anatomising the emotional distortions, power games and guilt which accompany a punitive morality. So Wilde commented of the theatregoing public, 'I have given them what they like, so that they may learn to like what I give to them.'[10]

---

8 Ian Small, ed., A Woman of No Importance, in Two Society Comedies, ed. Ian Small, New Mermaids, 1983, IV, 251–2.

9 William Archer, The Theatrical 'World' for 1893, Benjamin Blom, reissued edn, 1969, p. 107.

10 Quoted in Hesketh Pearson, Beerbohm Tree: His Life and Laughter, Methuen, 1956, p. 67.

The Play

Genre

Stylistically, *An Ideal Husband* draws upon and mixes together a number of dramatic genres: the central role played by mislaid and purloined letters and jewellery belongs to the French well-made play with its complex and precise plotting; the multiple exits, entries and confusions in Lord Goring's rooms in Act III seem to belong to farce; the unmasking and defeat of the blackmailing Mrs Cheveley are reminiscent of melodrama; and the debate over gender roles, idealism, and the difference between men's and women's love links *An Ideal Husband* to contemporary problem plays by writers such as Shaw, Ibsen and Pinero. All these various elements are tied together by the play's stylised, epigrammatic language, each character talking with a crystallised, non-naturalistic wit which complicates notions of sincerity, self-expression and truth.[11]

Wilde, while underlining his aestheticist disdain for public opinion, laid emphasis upon the play's intellectual engagement with ideas and issues. Interviewed before the premiere, Wilde provocatively denied any interest in his play's success with audiences – and when questioned by a journalist about the impression it would make on the public, Wilde replied, 'Which public? There are as many publics as there are personalities.'[12] Despite his declared indifference to critical reviews and his pleasure in the multifarious and various possible interpretations playgoers might arrive at, Wilde went on to reproach reviewers for having misjudged the play, for having missed

> 'Its entire psychology – the difference in the way in which a man loves a woman from that in which a woman loves a man, the passion that women have for making ideals (which is their weakness) and the weakness of a man who dare not show his imperfections to the thing he loves. The end of Act I, the end of Act II, and the scene in the last act, where Lord Goring points out the higher importance of a man's life over a woman's – to take three prominent instances – seem to have been quite missed by most of the critics. They failed to see their meaning: they really thought it was a play about a bracelet. We must educate our critics – we must really educate them,' said Mr Wilde, half to himself.[13]

11 For an excellent analysis of Wilde's style and the problem of interpretation, see Neil Sammells, *Wilde Style: The Plays and Prose of Oscar Wilde*, Pearson Education, 2000.
12 'A Talk with Mr Oscar Wilde', by Gilbert Burgess, *The Sketch*, 8 (9 Jan 1895), 495.
13 Ibid.

Wilde thus objected to the critics treating *An Ideal Husband* as a melodrama or well-made play, centring on the twists and turns of the blackmail plot which are finally resolved by the stolen bracelet, and instead he invited audiences to treat it as a problem play, a society drama engaging with contemporary issues.

An Ideal Husband diverges markedly, however, from the conventional structure and stance of problem plays and society dramas by other contemporary playwrights, including some of those from which Wilde borrowed plot elements and devices for his own play. Society dramas by French and English playwrights, from Sardou and Dumas to Pinero, Grundy and Jones, were marked by an essential conservatism: whatever the complexity of the issues raised, their plays conclude with a clear message, often delivered by the play's *raisonneur*, a character who stands outside the plot's confusions and draws out the moral of the preceding action, usually a few moments before the final curtain falls upon a clear and satisfying resolution. The message in such plays was almost invariably an assertion of the need for social conformity, and a validation of orthodox morality as both natural and inevitable. Pinero's *The Second Mrs Tanqueray* (1893), for example, hinged on the question of whether a sexually fallen woman could be reformed and re-integrated into society as a respectable wife, to which question the answer was a clear and resounding 'No'. Pinero's *The Cabinet Minister* (1890) is a drama of blackmail and intrigue surrounding the government's support for the Rajputana Canal, and ends with a foolish wife rescued by a wise and flawless husband, whose political probity is never in question – though his choice of a lower-class spouse is. In a host of such contemporary plays on topical issues, from Pinero's *The Weaker Sex* (1888) and *The Times* (1891), to Grundy's *The New Woman* (1894) and H. A. Jones's *The Case of Rebellious Susan* (1894), a clear and explicit message is delivered to the audience, whether about the foolishness of women, the dangers of social climbing, or the impossibility of allowing women the same sexual freedoms as men.

An Ideal Husband debates contemporary issues, as Wilde highlighted in his comments in interview, but it eschews the intellectual and dramatic closure associated with other contemporary society plays. The play does not establish a consistent viewpoint on the issues it raises; instead its characters offer a series of mutually contradictory statements and attitudes which do not finally resolve into a coherent conclusion. This is particularly noticeable in the case of the speeches and issues which Wilde highlighted in interview. In Sir Robert's speech at the end of Act II, for example, he declares that man's love is 'wider, larger, more human than a woman's' (II, 1092–3), being unconditional where women's idealising love depends upon the man's perfection. Yet it is Sir Robert who ends the play describing his wife as 'the white image of all good things' whom 'sin can never touch' (IV, 780–1), while it is Lady Chiltern who accepts not only her husband's feet of clay but also that his love is conditional on her continuing support for his political ambitions.

Goring's fourth-act speech in which he asserts the superior value of male intellect over female emotion is particularly problematic; it is positioned as the traditional *raisonneur*'s final verdict, but, like Kate's speech on wifely submission at the end of Shakespeare's *The Taming of the Shrew*, it is a speech which comes as something of a surprise from the character who delivers it and is hard to read as the logical conclusion of the preceding action. In his second-act conversation with Sir Robert, Lord Goring dismissed his friend's worship of wealth and power over others as 'a thoroughly shallow creed' (II, 151), and yet by the fourth act Goring now is persuading Lady Chiltern that is it precisely such ambition and desire for power which make men's lives more valuable than women's; it is hard to see how the intervening action could have given Goring a higher opinion of his friend's desire for greater political power. In his fourth-act speech Goring separates male intellect from female emotion and apparently consigns women to a purely domestic and supportive role. This division echoes the opening stage-direction description of Sir Robert as a man who has achieved '*an almost complete separation of passion and intellect, as though thought and emotion were each isolated in its own sphere through some violence of will-power*' (I, 182–5). Given the crisis which Sir Robert has suffered in his unsustainable attempt to hold apart the different aspects of his life and personality, it is surprising to hear Lord Goring making such divisions a basis for his guidance to Lady Chiltern. Furthermore, in performance Lady Chiltern's unlikely word-for-word parroting of Goring's advice tends not to validate his words but rather to teeter on the edge of absurdity – an inherent instability which leads most directors to cut her speech drastically.

Nor does the promotion into the Cabinet of a man who was ready to use criminal means to further his career not once but twice offer the conventional dramatic closure. It is crucially unclear whether Lady Chiltern ends the play cowed, politically sidelined, coldly pragmatic, or educated in a more humane and charitable understanding of others' frailty. It is left to the subtleties of staging and body language in performance to indicate whether Sir Robert's entry into the heart of government is to be unfettered by wifely oversight, or whether the ambitious politician is to be partnered by a forgiving but morally watchful wife, upon whose approval and judgement he will continue to rely.

The play has revealed English high society and government as in thrall to wealth and birth, hypocritically veiling its failings with a supposed adherence to high moral ideals. Far from humanising or educating the wider society of the play, *An Ideal Husband*'s conclusion ironically cements the public's self-congratulatory sense of moral superiority through the promotion to the Cabinet of a man who in the smugly patriotic words of the *Times*, 'Represents what is best in English public life', and who stands in 'Noble contrast to the lax morality so common among foreign politicians' (IV, 83–5).

Sir Robert does not beat the system but join it – a pessimistic conclusion similar to the ending of Shaw's radical critique of slum landlordism in *Widowers' Houses*, where the young Trench finally shrugs his shoulders and accepts his dirty income exacted from starving rent-payers. The Chilterns may each have learnt greater wisdom and self-knowledge in the course of the play's events, but there is no suggestion of any wider reform in a society which worships wealth while flattering itself with a reputation for high moral values. Whether the Chilterns are welcomed into the heart of government as a reforming force or as part of a corrupt system remains unclear – that depends upon the audience's reading of Sir Robert's inner character and whether his wife and her principles have been set aside or whether she remains a vital influence in his life, though one softened by a deeper understanding of human frailty. The uncertainty of the play's conclusion is in this sense markedly similar to that of Shaw's later play *Major Barbara* (1905), in which an idealistic heroine learns harsh lessons in pragmatic realism and finally accepts her husband's decision to run her father's armaments business – a partnership which could signify capitulation or reform from within. *An Ideal Husband* similarly complicates, develops and discusses issues, but does not reduce them to opinion or argument, and is thus perhaps closest to the Shavian 'Play of Ideas'. As Shaw observed in his wonderfully perceptive review of the play, 'Mr. Wilde is to me our only thorough playwright. He plays with everything: with wit, with philosophy, with drama, with actors and audience, with the whole theatre.'[14]

Character

The characters in *An Ideal Husband* relate clearly to certain familiar dramatic types: Mabel Chiltern the *ingénue*; Sir Robert the man with a dark secret; Mrs Cheveley the scheming adventuress; and Lady Chiltern

---

14 *Saturday Review* (12 January 1895), 44–5. For further discussion of the relation between Wilde and the Shavian play of ideas, see J. L. Wiesenthal, 'Wilde, Shaw, and the Play of Conversation', *Modern Drama* 37 (1994), 206–19.

the strict puritan wife. But Wilde took pains in the nine different successive drafts of his play to move its characters away from theatrical stereotypes in order to produce more complex and unpredictable protagonists. Mabel Chiltern starts out as a simpering *ingénue*, constantly sent out of the room to protect her from dangerous knowledge, a naive girl who is handed over as reward to a father-figure Lord Goring, who declares he has loved her 'ever since that bleak winters [*sic*] day when she came home from school'.[15] The pert, independent-minded and self-possessed young woman who can disconcert Lord Goring by adeptly matching his witticisms only emerges gradually through slow but consistent revisions. Similarly Lady Chiltern appears in early drafts as a harsh, cold woman, alternately icily judgemental and hysterical. Lord Goring deliberately entices her into abandoning her husband and seeking solace in his arms, and the dandy then uses her moment of moral weakness to teach her a vital and personal lesson about human frailty. Wilde revised Lady Chiltern's character and the play's plot to make her both more dignified and humane and personally free of error; she forgives her husband's crimes having committed none herself. Lord Goring in early drafts is a morally conventional figure, who talks of 'good' and 'bad' women, and insists that telling the truth 'keeps one in good condition'.[16] His idleness is consistent, but only in later drafts is it accompanied by a dandyesque critical detachment from his society's moral codes.

There is a deliberate opacity to the play's *dramatis personae*; their dialogue glitters with wit, or offers weighty moral pronouncements, but these do not serve to fix or reveal an essential and readable 'self' beneath. Theirs is a society of surface and reputation, where outward appearance is all that counts, as those at home in it are well aware: Lady Basildon and Mrs Marchmont perform bored insouciance with studied skill, and Mabel Chiltern complains about Tommy Trafford's confidential manner of proposing marriage and wishes that he would do so loudly enough to produce some effect on the public. The plot of *An Ideal Husband* openly hinges on the question of Sir Robert Chiltern's integrity, who he really is under the surface. Lady Chiltern confidently declares her belief that a dishonest past can never be escaped, unaware of its relevance to her own husband. Mrs Cheveley assumes the origin of Sir Robert's wealth reveals his 'real character' (III, 763), and Lord Goring responds that it is precisely because his friend's action was dishonourable, shameful and unworthy that it is 'not his true character' (III, 768–9). But the play never gives a definitive answer to the crucial question of which (if either) represents the 'real' man – if a notion of stable identity is to be believed in. Sir Robert

15 British Library Add. MS 37946, IV, p. 268.
16 Ibid, II, 141–3, III, 233.

varies his moral standpoint according to circumstances, alternating as the occasion demands between assertions of unshakeable English integrity, political pragmatism, defiant rebellion and resentful self-pity. Significantly, the scene in which he rescues his career by denouncing the Argentine Canal scheme as a fraud remains offstage, reported only in ironically idealising terms by the *Times*.

The difficulty (or indeed impossibility) of determining inner moral 'truth' is exacerbated by the deliberate parallels established between the play's supposed villain and heroes. There is a notable consonance between Mrs Cheveley's and Lord Goring's anatomising of society's love of scandal; both characters are sharp-eyed critics of moral hypocrisy but one is the play's ostensible villainess, the other a dandy whose inherited status and wealth allow him the luxuries of idleness and detachment. Mrs Cheveley is even more deliberately paralleled with her victim, both guilty of a crime which the other labels 'a swindle' (I, 675, 790) – a similarity which the adventuress gleefully embraces, declaring herself intimately bound to Sir Robert by their shared sin.

These indeterminacies are not incidental but crucial to the play's unsettling effect. The absence of clearly 'good' or 'bad' characters means that individual speeches cannot be identified as expressing the playwright's own views nor simply dismissed as the expression of corrupt or villainous values. The cynicism or optimism of the play's ending depends entirely upon each audience member's figuring of Sir Robert's 'inner' character and his future relation to his humanised, educated, or silenced wife.

Themes

Idealism

For all the complexity of the play's structure and the ambiguity of its ending, one theme that does emerge coherently from the play is its critique of the dangers of idealism, both on a personal and a national level. It is the demand for absolute moral probity from both his wife and the wider British public which lays Sir Robert Chiltern open to blackmail, rendering it impossible for him to confess his past crime without being ruined and disgraced. Both his marriage and the country's financial integrity are rendered vulnerable through an insistence upon unrealisable standards of morality. As Mrs Erlynne advised her daughter in *Lady Windermere's Fan*: 'Ideals are dangerous things. Realities are better. They wound but they are better.'[17] Idealism and the punitive, puritan morality which so often accompanies it are targets for criticism and ridicule in a plethora of Wilde's works, from the education of Lady Windermere and Hester Worsley in

17 Wilde, *Lady Windermere's Fan*, ed. Ian Small, New Mermaids, 1980, IV, 83, 304–5.

Wilde's other society dramas to the comic satirising of romantic duty in 'Lord Arthur Savile's Crime', and Gwendolen and Cecily's comic idealising of the name Ernest in *The Importance of Being Earnest*. Wilde's analysis of the socially destructive effects of rigidly maintained but unsustainable ideals, which crush individual freedom and self-expression, allied him closely to Ibsen's critique of idealism in plays such as *Ghosts* (1881) and *The Wild Duck* (1884) and to Shaw's radical attack on social hypocrisy and self-deception in polemical writings such as *The Quintessence of Ibsenism* (1891).

There was clear contemporary relevance in Wilde's portrait of a society flattering itself with an image of perfect probity, an image that society shores up by scapegoating all those caught out in error. Scandals regularly destroyed talented politicians, including Sir Charles Dilke, a radical reformist and Under-Secretary for Foreign Affairs, who was dropped from the Liberal government for being named as co-respondent in a divorce case, though never found guilty. Charles Stewart Parnell, leader of the Irish Nationalist parliamentary movement, was similarly thrown aside when he was named in a divorce case, though his relationship with the woman in question was longstanding and commonly acknowledged. Preparing the play for publication in 1899, Wilde wrote to his friend Reginald Turner that 'some of its passages seem prophetic of tragedy to come'.[18] Certainly Wilde's own trials and conviction and the orgy of journalistic outrage which accompanied them demonstrated the accuracy of the playwright's analysis.[19]

Women

An Ideal Husband's analysis of the dangers of idealism, and its engagement with questions of gender difference, and the division between public and private morality, were all central to late nineteenth-century debates about women's position in society: whether women were the natural guardians of society's higher ethical standards; whether women's moral qualities were best preserved by shielding them from public and political involvement or whether, on the contrary, British politics stood urgently in need of women's particular perspective. Women's campaigns for improved legal rights, access to the professions and higher education, and for the parliamentary vote, were gathering weight in the early 1890s, and the theatre largely responded by mocking their demands. The inherent absurdity of women aspiring to political activism or interfering in intellectual matters beyond

18 Letter to Reginald Turner (postmark 20 March) 1899, *Complete Letters*, p. 1132.
19 For analysis of the press reaction to Wilde's arrest and trials see Michael S. Foldy, *The Trials of Oscar Wilde: deviance, morality, and late-Victorian society*, Yale University Press, 1997, and Ed Cohen, *Talk on the Wilde Side: Towards a genealogy of a discourse on male sexualities*, Routledge, 1993.

their meagre abilities was a popular theme for a number of contemporary playwrights. In Pinero's *The Weaker Sex* and Grundy's *The New Woman*, for example, contemporary feminists were satirised as feeble-minded and ridiculous in their demands for further political and social rights, and both plays' plots end with the revelation that these self-deceiving women are really only in pursuit of a man, and will abandon their feminist crusade as soon as a prospective lover is in sight.

Gertrude Chiltern is a far cry from such parodies of feminist activism but, for all her dignity and poise, it remains uncertain whether the conclusion of Wilde's play confines her to a purely domestic role. Certainly Lord Goring's fourth-act advice, in which he divides male intellect and female emotion and relegates women to a purely supportive role, appears to recommend that women confine their activity to the private sphere – a view which was strongly conservative even in the 1890s. The audience has, however, previously been given a perfect demonstration of how the separate spheres argument can be used by a man to try and sideline a woman's perfectly valid and intelligent interest in political matters: in Act One, Sir Robert tried to fob off his wife's criticism of his newfound support for the Argentine Canal scheme by assuring her that 'public and private life are different things' (I,1107), implying that some political issues were beyond her female understanding. Wilde's own feminist sympathies were made clear by his editorship of the *Woman's World* magazine, for which he commissioned articles on, for example, professions for women, higher education for women, and women and economics. Gertrude Chiltern's active interest in politics and her membership of the Women's Liberal Association lead her to support 'Factory Acts, Female Inspectors, the Eight Hours Bill, the Parliamentary Franchise' (II, 399–400) – a set of humanitarian legislative reforms in line with Wilde's own political sympathies.[20] The question of how to interpret *An Ideal Husband*'s engagement with late-Victorian feminism is therefore a complex one.

An Ideal Husband's attack on idealism has been linked by a number of critics to the 'social purity' movement, a branch of late-Victorian feminism which challenged the notion that women should be held to a higher moral standard than men (especially as regards sexual behaviour), asserting instead that men ought to meet the same expectations of purity, self-control and virtue as they set for women.[21] Set against such writings as

---

20 See, e.g., Wilde's letters on prison reform, 'To the Editor of *Daily Chronicle*' (27 May 1897 and 23 March 1898), *Complete Letters*, pp. 847–55, 1045–9.

21 See e.g. Powell, *Oscar Wilde and the Theatre of the 1890s* and *Acting Wilde: Victorian sexuality, theatre, and Oscar Wilde*, Cambridge University Press, 2009, and Richard Dellamora, 'Oscar Wilde, Social Purity and *An Ideal Husband*', *Modern Drama*, 37 (1994), 120–38.

Sarah Grand's essay 'The New Aspect of the Woman Question', in which the American feminist called upon women to demand that men live up to their ideals of 'earnest purpose, plain living, high thinking and noble self-sacrifice', the re-education of Lady Chiltern and the assertion that her flawed husband's life is of 'more value' (IV, 686) than hers can be read as Wilde's rejection of contemporary feminist demands for male reform.[22] Conversely, if set against anti-feminist writings like 'An Appeal against Female Suffrage', which argued that women's sphere was naturally the private and domestic because only there could they preserve their superior moral status and idealism from the damaging pragmatism and competition of political life, then Wilde's play appears to reveal the damaging effects of excluding women from knowledge of social and political realities and making them the keepers of artificially preserved ideals.[23] In the light of feminist arguments that the impersonal male machinery of state stood in need of women's caring emotional qualities, a political partnership of Sir Robert and Lady Chiltern could optimistically be read as a uniting of heart and head, intellect and emotion.[24] Like the brooch which transforms into a bracelet, or Lady Chiltern's letter which takes on different meanings according to its addressee, so *An Ideal Husband* is a deceptive and indeterminate play, which can offer different meanings according to the assumptions of its audience members. Contemporary critics were accordingly divided; so, for example, the reviewer for the *Liverpool Mercury* described Sir Robert as 'rescued by his wife', noting that the play concluded with 'the success of the wife in preserving her ideal husband's honour', whereas the reviewer for the *Sheffield and Rotherham Independent* drew the opposite conclusion, remarking that, 'As usual when women interfere with affairs outside their proper sphere, . . . [Lady Chiltern] creates trouble beyond her power to allay'.[25] Wilde's drama plays with the issues surrounding women's political activism but leaves the individual audience member to negotiate the complexities of the arguments and draw their own conclusions.

22 Sarah Grand, 'The New Aspect of the Woman Question', *North American Review*, 158 (March 1894), 270–6, reprinted in Carolyn Christensen Nelson (ed.), *A New Woman Reader*, Broadview Press: Peterborough, Ontario, 2001, pp. 141–6.

23 See e.g. W. E. Gladstone, 'Female Suffrage: A Letter to Samuel Smith', and Mrs Humphrey Ward, et al., 'An Appeal against Female Suffrage', reprinted in Jane Lewis (ed.), *Before the Vote was Won: Arguments for and against Female Suffrage*, Routledge & Kegan Paul: London, 1987.

24 See e.g. Sos Eltis, *Revising Wilde*, pp. 152–69.

25 *Liverpool Mercury* (4 January 1895), 4; *Sheffield and Rotherham Independent* (5 January 1895), 5.

Money

One thing that is made clear throughout *An Ideal Husband* is that this is a society based on money. As Sir Robert declares, 'What this century worships is wealth. The God of this century is wealth. To succeed one must have wealth. At all costs one must have wealth.' (II, 90–1) Characterising his insider dealing not as fraud but as social rebellion, the politician claims to have fought the century with its own weapons, buying himself power over other people – his criminal act thus echoing the central dynamic of a society based on wealth, whose values are those of reputation, appearance and display. Beneath the extravagant spectacle, the ruling elite's money is founded in corruption or complacent privilege, as revealed in the comic snobbery of Lord Caversham and Lady Markby.

In the costly splendour of the tapestry representing Boucher's fleshly 'Triumph of Love' and the procession of bejewelled aristocrats, Wilde exploited to the full the high production values and costly sets which were part and parcel of fashionable society drama at theatres like the Haymarket and the St James's. Dramas set among the social elite entertained the lower ranks with a supposed glimpse into how the other half lived, while simultaneously acting as a shop-window for the luxury goods which formed an intrinsic part of the theatrical display. Haute-couture costumes on stage could set the fashion off stage, while the expensive trappings of society drama could reduce the theatre, in Bernard Shaw's despairing words, to a luxurious marketing opportunity in which 'a tailor's advertisement mak[es] sentimental remarks to a milliner's advertisement in the middle of an upholsterer's and decorator's advertisement'.[26] The high-class audiences taking up the Haymarket's most expensive seats were both consumers of its products, potential customers for the fashions it promoted, and a part of the spectacle itself, there both to see and be seen. Newspaper accounts of the Haymarket's opening nights commonly began by listing the notables in the audience, who in the case of *An Ideal Husband* included the Portugese Minister, Mr and Mrs Asquith, Lord and Lady Ribblesdale, Lord and Lady de Grey, and Sir Frederick Leighton.[27] It was left to individual audience members to decide how far the corruption beneath Wilde's gilded society reflected the reality in the theatre's stalls.

The elaborate stage directions that Wilde added to the 1899 published text of the play further emphasise the importance of appearance and display. By likening characters to works of art, the stage directions remind the reader of the visual richness of performance, while simultaneously emphasising the crucial role of surface image and reputation in this society.

26 *Saturday Review* (27 February 1897), 219.
27 *Belfast News-Letter* (4 January 1895), 7.

The ambitious outsider Mrs Cheveley, manoeuvring to secure a place in this centre of power, displays an image too obviously manufactured to fit in; she is '*A work of art, on the whole, but showing the influence of too many schools.* (I, 120–1). Equally revealingly, Lord Goring's 'Ideal Butler', Phipps, is described as '*a mask with a manner. Of his intellectual or emotional life history knows nothing. He represents the dominance of form*' (III, 9–11). The perfect servant is devoid of personality or individuality, an empty shell with an immaculate exterior. This comic detail also hints subtly at the reduction of domestic servant to furniture within the home, though Phipps's impassive but disconcerting responses to Lord Goring's witticisms suggest that he is as knowing and skilful in the game of appearances as his master.[28] The self effacement of the servant, the flippant pose of the master, and the convolutions and concealments of the ambitious politician all reveal the human cost involved in maintaining the apparently flawless and glittering surface of this society.

Set against the corrosive effects of wealth and power is the potentially redemptive force of love – not an idealising love but a humane and charitable love, accepting of human frailty and weakness. The zany courtship of Lord Goring and Mabel Chiltern serves as a charming sideshow to the strained relationship of the Chilterns. For all the flaws and tensions in his marriage, it is ultimately love that separates Sir Robert from his blackmailer; where Mrs Cheveley treats marriage as a financial transaction, seeking to buy Lord Goring's hand in return for his friend's letter, Sir Robert is finally ready to forgo his career rather than lose his wife's love.

The Play on Stage and Screen

Original Staging

An Ideal Husband opened at the Haymarket Theatre on 3 January 1895, under the direction of actor-manager Lewis Waller. The central role of Sir Robert Chiltern was taken by Waller himself, a popular romantic lead who did his best to convert the role into a more traditional portrait of the good, pure man trying to forget his one secret sin. The *Daily News* remarked approvingly that 'Mr Waller played Sir Robert with a force and earnestness which went far to atone for the inherent weakness of the character.'[29] H. G. Wells was less respectful of Waller's performance, ironically complimenting him on his repertoire of clichéd poses and effects:

28 For further analysis of the role of the perfect servant in relation to aestheticism, see Andrew Goldstone, 'Servants, Aestheticism, and "The Dominance of Form"', *English Literary History*, 77 (2010), 615–43.
29 *Daily News* (4 Jan 1895), 3.

His emotions are terrible, he clenches his fists – one may imagine the nails dug into his palms – he opens and shuts his voiceless lips, rolls his eyes and so lives through four terrible acts of mental torment ... If anything, we would object that he scarcely avails himself sufficiently of the hand clasped on the forehead – always a beautiful expression of a strong man's despair.[30]

Playing opposite Waller as Gertrude Chiltern was the dignified and statuesque Julia Neilson, who had previously played Wilde's Hester Worsley, another stern puritan forced to revise her moral absolutism in response to human frailty, though Neilson found the politician's wife a far less congenial part, describing her as 'an impossible prig'.[31] The comic actor, Charles Hawtrey, was cast against type as Lord Goring, and drew considerable critical praise for projecting the dual aspects of the 'careless, callous idler' and the 'sensible, shrewd man of the world'.[32] The blackmailing Mrs Cheveley was played by Florence West who, in Wells's opinion, was 'most human' in the first act and thereafter became 'an impossible wicked woman in equally impossible costumes'.[33] Shaw was struck by the innovation of making the villainess realistically 'second-rate', but agreed with Wells about the ugliness of her costumes.[34] In contrast to the stylish haute-couture gowns worn by the play's other leading women, the essential vulgarity of Mrs Cheveley's character was signalled in the first act by an evening dress trimmed with an entire flock of dead swallows – a decoration which was deemed offensively barbaric by a number of critics – and in the second act by what the *Sketch* described as a 'startling' dress made of yellow moiré, scarlet velvet and frilled lace, with a collar band of bright-green velvet and bunches of violets, and cream sleeves brocaded with roses and foliage, her red hair topped off with a hat of green straw bedecked with masses of orchids in various colours.[35] Mrs Cheveley was clearly not meant to blend into this aesthetically conscious society.

For all Waller's efforts to render *An Ideal Husband*'s central characters more reassuringly familiar, critics were largely disconcerted by the play's moral scheme. The *Era*'s critic dismissed Sir Robert as a 'sordid rogue', and William Archer, writing in the *Pall Mall Budget*, similarly noted that the politician 'proves himself one of those gentlemen who can be honest only

---

30 *Pall Mall Gazette* (4 January 1895), 3.
31 Julia Neilson, *This for Remembrance*, Hurst & Blackett, 1941, p. 139.
32 *Sporting Times* (5 January 1895), 6.
33 *Pall Mall Gazette* (4 January 1895), 3.
34 *Saturday Review* (12 January 1895), 45.
35 *Sketch* (9 January 1895), 541. For further details of the play's costumes see Joel Kaplan and Sheila Stowell, *Theatre and Fashion: Oscar Wilde to the Suffragettes*, Cambridge University Press, 1995, pp. 27–33.

so long as it is absolutely convenient'.[36] Those who expressed sympathy with Sir Robert frequently did so in unconventional moral terms; so, for example, the reviewer for *Pick-Me-Up* remarked that 'I'll always think kindly of a great man in future if found out to be a masterpiece of moral error. I shall put his drawbacks down to the fact that he must have an abnormally good wife.'[37] Critics were united in recognising Wilde's play as a criticism of high society and its values; 'cynical' was the most common term used to describe the play's plot and dialogue – a term which neatly acknowledged the play's satirical edge while remaining uncommitted as to its accuracy. A. B. Walkley, drama critic for the *Speaker*, sprang to society's defence, dismissing Wilde's portrait of political skulduggery as 'romantically absurd', but others greeted the play as an essentially realistic portrait of the ruling elite, however stylised the dialogue and extravagant the contrivances. The *Morning Post* noted Wilde's familiarity with the fashionable world of which his drama was 'a graphic and effective picture', while the *Freeman's Journal* remarked that Wilde's epigrams 'reflect in a manner the aims and ideals, or the lack of them, which inspire and animate "modern society", and will give the future historian a curious insight into the world-weary civilisation of this *fin de siècle* age'.[38] The play's combination of glamour, luxury, satire and wit proved popular at the box office, and it was only the eruption of the real-life scandal of Wilde's prosecution which prompted Waller to cut short its profitable run of 124 performances.

Recent Performance History

When it received its first major London revival at the St James's Theatre under George Alexander in 1914, *An Ideal Husband* was already viewed as 'from another age', a product of the theatre of Sardou and Scribe which had already been hopelessly out of date when it was first performed in 1895.[39] This remained the predominant view of Wilde's plays throughout the succeeding decades, treated as witty period pieces which called for glorious costumes and an artificial, self-conscious style of delivery. So Robert Donat's 1943 production at the Westminster Theatre, for example, was complimented on its 'wonderful escape value', and greeted as an artificial and frivolous work which was 'light as a feather' but offered 'exhilarating entertainment'.[40]

---

36 *Era* (5 January 1895), 13; *Pall Mall Budget* (10 Jan 1895).
37 *Pick-Me-Up* (19 January 1895), 246–7.
38 *Morning Post* (4 January 1895), 3; *Freeman's Journal* (5 January 1895), 6.
39 *Lady's Pictorial* (23 May 1914), 870.
40 *World Review* (February 1944); *New Statesman and Nation* (27 November 1943), 352.

The radical challenge to this performance tradition came in the 1980s with Philip Prowse's Glasgow Citizens Theatre productions of all three of Wilde's society plays, productions which re-envisioned them as uncomfortable, challenging and emotionally raw critiques of a moribund and corrupt society. Prowse's designs for his 1986 production of *An Ideal Husband* presented the Chilterns' home as a masterpiece of 'kitsch splendour' which mirrored the spiritual squalor of their society, one in which, as Michael Billington reported in the *Guardian,* 'elegant women pass out dead drunk on the sofa, evening-dressed men parade in front of them as in a sexual meat-market'.[41] With the exception of Lord Goring and his plea for charitable tolerance, the plays' characters were all depicted as merciless arrivistes and hypocritical vulgarians, dressing their greed in stylish epigrams. Nor did Prowse allow the play to end with any suggestion of the redemptive power of love: he cut the last line in which Lady Chiltern answers her husband's anxious question with the reassurance that what she feels for him is 'Love, and only love' (IV, 850). Instead the play ended with his question unanswered, the long silence resonating 'with anger and desolation as the Chilterns stare across the spattered gold apartments at one another into a chilling slow fade'.[42] In this context, as Sarah Hemming observed in *The Times,* the language of idealism and higher morality rang particularly false, underlining Wilde's 'subtle and serious' moral games in which he 'repeatedly prick[s] bubbles of empty rhetoric and moral sanctimoniousness'.[43]

The key to Prowse's directorial approach was a belief that Wilde's plays were not characterised by studied artificiality, but rather were products of a 'heightened realism', rooted in a 'rather terrifying vein of sentiment'.[44] A similar belief underpinned Peter Hall's influential and highly successful production of *An Ideal Husband* in 1992. Writing in the *Guardian,* Hall explained that he understood the play's dialogue as a very English expression of restrained feeling: 'Beneath the wit there is always an intense emotional reality'.[45] Carl Toms's set designs for Hall's production similarly highlighted the disjunction between appearance and substance: a huge golden medallion stamped with a head of Queen Victoria (which to some critics' eyes looked notably similar to Margaret Thatcher) rose to reveal a set built from perspex sheeting splattered with gold paint, which looked sumptuous at first glance but with subtle shifts of lighting could appear

---

41 *Guardian* (1 September 1986)

42 *Observer* (7 September 1986).

43 *Times* (2 September 1986).

44 Philip Prowse, quoted in Joel H. Kaplan, 'Staging Wilde's Society Plays: A Conversation with Philip Prowse (Glasgow Citizens Theatre)', *Modern Drama,* 37 (1994), 192–9.

45 *Guardian* (11 November 1992), Arts section, 4–5.

tawdry and cheap.[46] By placing the doors close together in Lord Goring's room in Act III, he also enhanced the underlying desperation in what was played as a blackly comic farce of manic entrances and exits. Compassion was, however, the keynote of the production, with Martin Shaw's Lord Goring made up and padded to resemble Wilde, his mask of flippancy concealing 'infinite reserves of charity and shrewdness'.[47] Characterized by an innate humaneness and wisdom, Shaw's Goring was the emotional centre of the play, delivering an ultimate message of forgiveness and charity. By underlining the biographical resonance of the play, which Hall saw as its particular significance, Goring's resemblance to Wilde also complicated its resolution, with a number of critics speculating as to whether Mabel Chiltern's married life was to echo that of Constance Wilde.[48] One thing that was not in question was the play's immediate political resonance; in the wake of scandals over the government's sales of arms to Iraq and the exposure of MPs' private lives, *Plays International's* critic noted that 'Over and over again in Wilde's barbed comments on politicians and the intrusions of the press into the private world of the rich and famous the play's appositeness to the here and now takes your breath away.'[49]

Peter Hall's production of *An Ideal Husband* has proved impressively enduring, but the play itself has also been kept fresh by an apparently ceaseless flow of political malfeasance in the present day. Where it was judged to be out of date at the beginning of the twentieth century, *An Ideal Husband* has been greeted as presciently relevant a hundred years later. Lindsay Posner's 2010 production opened amidst revelations about MPs' false claims for parliamentary expenses, and, as Michael Coveney commented, the intervening years had 'done nothing to blunt the play's cutting edge in discussion of power, morals and marriage'.[50] Modern audiences have proved readier to accept Wilde's analysis of the intimate and corrupting relation between power and wealth, and the moral complexity of the competing imperatives of public image, private integrity, political ambition and moral principle. The play's characters have been similarly reinvigorated; under Posner's direction Samantha Bond's Mrs Cheveley was not only 'handsome as hell' but an 'instrument of truth', her

---

46 *Plays International* (December 1992). For further details, see Richard Allen Cave, 'Wilde Designs: Some thoughts about recent British productions of his plays', *Modern Drama* 37 (1994), 175–91.

47 Michael Billington, *Guardian* (13 November 1992), Section 2, 11.

48 *Plays International* (December 1992), 17; *Time Out* (18 November 1992), 121.

49 *Plays International* (December 1992), 16.

50 *Whatsonstage* (11 November 2010). www.whatsonstage.com/reviews/theatre/london/E8831289469671/An+Ideal+Husband.html, accessed 20 August 2012.

resolute sureness reminding John Thaxter of a Shavian heroine.[51] As the similarities between Bond's Mrs Cheveley and Elliot Cowan's Lord Goring made clear, the choice Wilde offered was not between idealism and cynicism, but between exploitation or a compassionate acceptance of humanity's potential for error. As Paul Taylor observed in the *Independent*, 'Samantha Bond radiates a humbug puncturing wit that makes you realise that she and Lord Goring are, in a sense, exotic birds of a feather, the one as corrupted as the other is humanised by a talent for seeing through English hypocrisy.'[52]

Film Versions

Alexander Korda's 1947 film features extravagant sets and costumes by Cecil Beaton, then the favoured designer for all Wilde revivals. Apart from opening and closing credit sequences in Hyde Park and frequent establishing shots of the Houses of Parliament, Korda's film remains remarkably faithful to the settings, structure and dialogue of the play. Simplifying the play's ending, Lord Goring (Michael Wilding)'s speech on the lesser value of a woman's life is cut, and Lady Chiltern (Diana Wynyard) accedes simply to a plea to recognise the personal importance of her husband's political ambitions. The Chilterns' love for each other is never in doubt, despite their stiff formality, nor is Sir Robert's ultimate trustworthiness. Korda deliberately fills in the gap left by the politician's speech to the House of Commons, inserting a scene in which, under the eager gaze of Mrs Cheveley, Sir Robert (Hugh Williams) not only informs the House that the canal scheme is fraudulent but also announces, with clear personal relevance, that 'Now and in the future the law of conduct of British public life will be as a prime minister said when he was threatened with assassination, "I shall make my will, and I will do my duty".' It is left to the film's lighting to suggest the potentially darker side of Sir Robert; taking a cue from his Othello-like instruction to 'Put out the light' at the end of Act I, Sir Robert's private scenes, whether alone or with his wife, are cast in deep shadow, in sharp contrast to the brilliantly lit public scenes. Such ambiguities are cast aside at the film's end, when the Chilterns' political partnership is humanised by her newfound charity and under-pinned by his moral reform. The one subversive note is Paulette Goddard's Mrs Cheveley, a gleefully self-possessed strategist, who beams, purrs, sparkles, then strikes, her tone alternately seductive, mocking, factual,

---

51 Michael Billington, *Guardian* (11 Nov 2010); John Thaxter, TheStage.co.uk (11 Nov 2010). www.thestage.co.uk/reviews/review.php/30235/an-ideal-husband, accessed 20 August 2012.

52 *Independent* (12 November 2010).

precise and steely. So the closing credits mirror her first appearance in a carriage in Hyde Park, forever networking and furthering her dubious interests.

Oliver Parker's 1999 film takes greater liberties with Wilde's play but also treats it as inherently modern. Though chopped up and redistributed in multiple short scenes, scattered across a range of fashionable venues from clubs and hotels to a sauna and an art gallery, Parker's screenplay is predominantly constructed from the play's original dialogue. The Chilterns (Jeremy Northam and Cate Blanchett) are young and passionate – no question of their being past child-bearing age – so that Gertrude's idealism is born of naivety not self-righteousness, and Sir Robert's crime was committed when he was little more than a schoolboy – he appears ridiculously eager and fresh-faced in a flashback, listening to the suave seductions of Jeroen Krabbé's Baron Arnheim. This scene is part of the film's dextrous delivery of the homosexual implications of Sir Robert's secret sin and its relevance to Wilde's own life. Despite the casting of an openly gay actor, Rupert Everett, as Lord Goring, both male leads are played as unquestionably and enthusiastically heterosexual – the naked woman in Goring's bed is introduced before the man himself. In a witty and skilfully constructed scene, Parker then nimbly highlights the parallel between Sir Robert's crime and Wilde's own outlawed sexuality. In a packed theatre, as the final act of *The Importance of Being Earnest* is performed in the background, all the main characters eye each other through opera glasses, more interested in each other's performances than the play. When Wilde himself comes on stage to congratulate the audience on their intelligent appreciation of his delightful play, Gertrude Chiltern looks from the playwright to her husband, and asks him in suddenly tremulous tones whether there is 'any secret . . . any indiscretion' in his past of which she is unaware. As Robert reassures his wife, Wilde takes his final bows to thunderous applause and the score takes on a suddenly poignant tone – a whisper of the tragedy that followed. Krabbé's sensually intimate delivery of Baron Arnheim's gospel of gold helps underline the sexual undertones of Sir Robert's fall without interrupting the film's determinedly heterosexual emphasis.

There is no doubt about the politician's 'true' character, however. Dispensing altogether with the bracelet/brooch, Goring instead enters into a wager with Mrs Cheveley, so confident is he of his friend's ultimate probity: if Sir Robert condemns the Argentine Canal scheme, Goring wins and Mrs Cheveley hands over the letter; if he gives in to her blackmail and supports the scheme, Goring will become her husband. Equally sure of her brother's character, Mabel similarly advises Gertrude to attend the parliamentary debate. As all watch with bated breath, Sir Robert not only fulfils their high expectations, he also forswears Arnheim's philosophy; England, he declares, has fallen from commercial greatness into the pursuit of power and money for its own sake and at a cost to the nation's soul, the end of the century offers 'one honest chance to shed our sometimes imperfect past and to start again, to step unshackled into the next century, and to look our future squarely and proudly in the face'. Husband and wife are passionately reconciled, with no suggestion of the openly suffragist Lady Chiltern abandoning any of her political engagement. Her final confession of having lied about the letter to Lord Goring is greeted with laughing applause, apparently not so much for her having told the truth as for having learnt to lie in the first place. It is unquestionably love and charity which win out in Parker's film, Gertrude Chiltern having followed Goring's advice and found not only 'the great courage to see the world in all its tainted glory and still to love it', but the even greater courage 'to see it in the one you love'.

S.E.

THE AUTHOR

André Gide describes Oscar Wilde as he appeared in 1891, when 'his success was so certain that it seemed that it preceded [him] and that all he needed do was go forward and meet it':

> . . . He was rich; he was tall; he was handsome; laden with good fortune and honours. Some compared him to an Asiatic Bacchus; others to some Roman emperor; others to Apollo himself – and the fact is that he was radiant.[53]

The melodramatic contrast between this triumphant figure and the pathetic convict serving two years' hard labour was drawn by Wilde himself in *De Profundis*, the letter written from prison to his lover, Lord Alfred Douglas. He described his transfer in November 1895 from Wandsworth to Reading Gaol, little care being taken for his privacy:

> From two o'clock till half-past two on that day I had to stand on the centre platform at Clapham Junction in convict dress and handcuffed, for the world to look at. I had been taken out of the Hospital Ward without a moment's notice being given to me. Of all possible objects I was the most grotesque. When people saw me they laughed. Each train as it came up swelled the audience. Nothing could exceed their amusement. That was of course before they knew who I was. As soon as they had been informed, they laughed still more. For half an hour I stood there in the grey November rain surrounded by a jeering mob.[54]

Wilde insisted that his life was as much an artistic endeavour as his works – in *De Profundis* he claimed to have been 'a man who stood in symbolic relations to the art and culture of my age', and in conversation with Gide he remarked that the great drama of his life lay in his having put his talent

---

53 André Gide, 'In Memoriam' from *Oscar Wilde,* translated Bernard Frechtman (New York, 1949): quoted from the extract in Richard Ellmann, ed., *Oscar Wilde: A Collection of Critical Essays* (Englewood Cliffs, N.J., 1969), pp. 25–34. The principal sources for the present account of Wilde's career are H. Montgomery Hyde, *Oscar Wilde* (1975), Richard Ellmann, *Oscar Wilde* (1987) and Rupert Hart-Davis, ed., *The Letters of Oscar Wilde* (revised edn, 1963). Subsequent references to Wilde's *Letters* are to this edition.

54 Wilde, *Letters,* pp. 490–1. This long letter was written in Reading Gaol in January–March 1897. An abridged version was published by Robert Ross in 1905 as *De Profundis:* the most reliable edition is that contained in *Letters,* pp. 423–511.

into his works, and his genius into his life.[55] For an author who returned as often as Wilde to the proposition that art transforms and is the superior of Nature, such claims were more than boasting – they were an affirmation of faith.

Oscar Wilde was born in Dublin on 16 October 1854, second son of Sir William and Lady Wilde. The father was an eminent surgeon, the mother a poetess and fervent Irish nationalist who wrote as 'Speranza'. To medical distinction Sir William joined notoriety as a philanderer.[56] Both parents were enthusiasts for the study of Irish legend, folk-lore and history, an interest reflected in the first two of the names given to their son, Oscar Fingal O'Flahertie Wills Wilde. He was educated at Portora Royal School and Trinity College, Dublin, where he became a protégé of the classicist John Pentland Mahaffy. In 1875 he won a scholarship – a 'Classical Demyship' – to Magdalen College, Oxford, where he subsequently took first-class honours in the final school of *Literae Humaniores* (Greek and Roman literature, history and philosophy). He picked up a reputation for wit, charm and conversational prowess. Most important, he came under the influence of two eminent writers on art and its relation to life, John Ruskin and Walter Pater. Ruskin, the most distinguished contemporary art critic, championed the moral and social dimensions of art, and its ability to influence men's lives for the better. Under Ruskin's supervision, Wilde and a few other undergraduates had begun the construction of a road near Hinksey, as a practical demonstration of the aesthetic dignity of labour and the workmanlike qualities essential to the labours of the artist. From Pater, Wilde learned a conflicting interpretation of art as a means to the cultivation of the individual, an idea which received its most notorious statement in the 'Conclusion' to Pater's book *The Renaissance*. There the fully developed sensibility is claimed as the expression of a full existence: 'To burn always with this hard, gem-like flame, to maintain this ecstasy, is success in life'.[57] These two theories of the relation between art and life were to dominate Wilde's writing. The arguments of the painter James McNeill Whistler against the conservative critics' insistence on moral significance and pictorial verisimilitude in art also influenced Wilde deeply.[58] The close of his Oxford career was

---

55 Wilde, *Letters*, p. 466; Gide, 'In Memoriam', ed. cit., p. 34.

56 On Sir William and Lady Wilde see Terence de Vere White, *Parents of Oscar Wilde* (1967).

57 Walter Pater, *The Renaissance* (1873; Library ed., 1910), p. 236. This 'Conclusion' was omitted in the second edition (1877) and restored, in a modified form, in the third edition (1888).

58 Whistler later quarrelled with Wilde, accusing him of plagiarism. Some of their exchanges appeared in Whistler's *The Gentle Art of Making Enemies* (1890) and in *Wilde vs. Whistler* (1906).

marked by two triumphs – his first-class degree and the Newdigate Prize for his poem 'Ravenna' – and two failures. Wilde was not given the Chancellor's English Essay Prize for his essay 'The Rise of Historical Criticism' and he was not offered a fellowship at Magdalen.

Moving to London, Wilde set about making himself a name in the capital's fashionable artistic and literary worlds. He had enough poems to make a collected volume, published at his own expense in 1881, and he was seen at the right parties, first nights, and private views. Occasionally he wore the velvet coat and knee-breeches, soft-collared shirt and cravat, that became fixed in the popular imagination as 'aesthetic' dress (and which derived from a fancy-dress ball he had attended when an undergraduate). In December 1881 he embarked on a lecture tour of the United States organised by the impresario Richard D'Oyly Carte. This was a shrewd back-up to the tour of Gilbert and Sullivan's comic opera *Patience*, but it was also a simple exploitation of the American appetite for being lectured to. Although *Patience*, which satirised the Aesthetic Movement, featured rival poets dressed in a costume closely resembling that adopted by Wilde, the lecturer was taken seriously as a prophet of the 'new renaissance' of art. In his lectures he insisted on comparing the new preoccupation with life-styles with the aspirations of the Italian Renaissance and the Romantic Movement – this was 'a sort of new birth of the spirit of man', like the earlier rebirth 'in its desire for a more gracious and comely way of life, its passion for physical beauty, its exclusive attention to form, its seeking for new subjects for poetry, new forms of art, new intellectual and imaginative enjoyment ...' [59] The blend of aesthetic theory and enthusiasm for reform of design and colouring in dress and decorative art was derived from a variety of sources, not all successfully synthesized. In addition to Ruskin, Pater and Whistler, Wilde had absorbed the ideas of William Morris and the architect E. W. Godwin. The lectures were exercises in *haute vulgarisation* and not all the sources were acknowledged. Japanese and other oriental art, eighteenth-century furniture, distempered walls in pastel colours, stylised floral motifs – all had made their appearance in English art before Wilde became their advocate. But the influence of his popularising talents was, for all that, considerable. 'In fact,' wrote Max Beerbohm in 1895, looking back on 1880 as though it were a remote historical period, 'Beauty had existed long before 1880. It was Mr Oscar Wilde who managed her *début*.[60]

59 Wilde, 'The English Renaissance of Art', in Ross's edition of his *Essays and Lectures* (1909), pp. 111f. The text was edited by Ross from four drafts of a lecture first given in New York on 9 January 1882.

60 Max Beerbohm, *Works* (1922), p. 39.

As well as establishing him as a popular oracle on matters of art and taste, Wilde's lecture tour made him a great deal of badly needed money – he had no prospect of inheriting a family fortune, and would have to make his own way. On his return the velvet suits were discarded, and his hair, worn long and flowing in his 'Aesthetic' period, was cut short in a style resembling the young Nero. The figure described by Gide was beginning to emerge. After a holiday in Paris, Wilde moved into rooms at 9 Charles Street, Grosvenor Square. He returned briefly to New York for the first performance of his melodrama *Vera; or, the Nihilists* and then prepared for an autumn lecture tour of the United Kingdom. On 26 November he became engaged to Constance Lloyd, and they married on 29 May 1884. In January 1885 they moved into a house designed by Godwin at 16 Tite Street, Chelsea. Two sons, Cyril and Vyvyan, were born in 1885 and 1886 respectively. In the early years of his marriage Wilde was working hard as a journalist. He contributed reviews to magazines (including the *Pall Mall Gazette* and the *Dramatic Review*) and even for a while undertook the editorship of one, *Woman's World*, which he hoped to turn into 'the recognised organ through which women of culture and position will express their views, and to which they will contribute'.[61] By and by Constance came into a small inheritance, but money was never plentiful. The life of a professional journalist was laborious and demanded a high degree of craftsmanship, but it offered a training from which Wilde, like Shaw, Wells and many others, profited immensely. Wilde became a fastidious and tireless reviser of his own work, and his reviews show him as an acute critic of others'.

In 1891 four of Wilde's books appeared, all consisting of earlier work, some of it in a revised form: *Intentions*, a collection of critical essays; *Lord Arthur Savile's Crime and Other Stories*; *The Picture of Dorian Gray*, considerably altered from the version published in *Lippincott's Magazine* in 1890; and a collection of children's stories, *A House of Pomegranates*. In the same year a verse tragedy written in 1882, *The Duchess of Padua*, was produced in New York by Lawrence Barrett under the title *Guido Ferranti*. Like *Vera* it was poorly received, but Wilde was already turning away from the pseudo-Elizabethan dramatic form that had preoccupied so many nineteenth-century poets and contemplating a newer, more commercially acceptable mode. In the summer of 1891 he began work on the first of a series of successful plays for the fashionable theatres of the West End: *Lady Windermere's Fan* (St James's, 20 February 1892), *A Woman of No Importance* (Haymarket, 19 April 1893) and *An Ideal Husband*

---

61 Wilde, *Letters*, p. 202 (to Mrs Alfred Hunt, August 1887).

(Haymarket, 3 January 1895). The refusal of a performance licence to the exotic biblical tragedy *Salomé* (in 1892) proved a temporary setback: acclaim as a dramatic author confirmed Wilde's career in what seemed an irresistible upward curve.

The summer of 1891 was also remarkable for the beginning of an association that was to be the direct cause of his downfall: the poet Lionel Johnson introduced him to 'Bosie', Lord Alfred Douglas, third son of the Marquess of Queensberry. Wilde appears to have been already a practising homosexual, and his marriage was under some strain. The affair with Douglas estranged him further from Constance, and the drain it caused on Wilde's nervous and financial resources was formidable. Douglas was happy to let Wilde spend money on him after his father stopped his allowance; more seriously, he made ceaseless demands on the time set aside for writing. In *De Profundis* Wilde described his attempts to finish *An Ideal Husband* in an apartment in St James's Place:

> I arrived . . . every morning at 11.30, in order to have the opportunity of thinking and writing without the interruptions inseparable from my own household, quiet and peaceful as that household was. But the attempt was vain. At twelve o'clock you drove up, and stayed smoking cigarettes and chattering till 1.30, when I had to take you out to luncheon at the Café Royal or the Berkeley. Luncheon with its *liqueurs* lasted usually till 3.30. For an hour you retired to White's [Club]. At tea-time you appeared again, and stayed until it was time to dress for dinner. You dined with me either at the Savoy or at Tite Street. We did not separate as a rule till after midnight, as supper at Willis's had to wind up the entrancing day.[62]

This was in 1893. A year later Wilde was working on what was to prove his last play, *The Importance of Being Earnest*, the first draft of which had been composed during a family holiday (largely Douglas-free) at Worthing. In October, Constance had returned to London with the children. Wilde and Douglas stayed together in Brighton, first at the Metropole Hotel, then in private lodgings. Douglas developed influenza and Wilde nursed him through it. He in turn suffered an attack of the virus, and Douglas (by Wilde's account) more or less neglected him. The result was what seemed like an irrevocable quarrel, with Douglas living at Wilde's expense in a hotel but hardly bothering to visit him. In hindsight Wilde claimed that this cruelty afforded him a moment of clear understanding:

---

62 Wilde, *Letters*, p. 426.

Is it necessary for me to state that I saw clearly that it would be a dishonour to myself to continue even an acquaintance with such a one as you had showed [sic] yourself to be? That I recognised that ultimate moment had come, and recognised it as being really a great relief? And that I knew that for the future my Art and Life would be freer and better and more beautiful in every possible way? Ill as I was, I felt at ease.[63]

But reconciliation followed.

On 3 January 1895 *An Ideal Husband* was given its first performance. Meanwhile George Alexander, actor-manager of the St James's Theatre, had turned down the new comedy. It found a taker in Charles Wyndham, who intended to bring it out at the Criterion. Then Alexander found himself at a loss for a play to replace Henry James's *Guy Domville*, which had failed spectacularly. Wyndham agreed to release *The Importance of Being Earnest* on the condition that he had the option on Wilde's next play, and it was put into rehearsal at the St James's. At first Wilde attended rehearsals, but his continual interruptions made Alexander suggest that he might leave the manager and his company to their own resources. He agreed with good grace and left with Douglas for a holiday in Algeria. There they encountered André Gide, who was told by Wilde that he had a premonition of some disaster awaiting him on his return.[64] Although his artistic reputation was beyond question, and he was shortly to have two plays running simultaneously in the West End, Wilde was already worried by the activities of Douglas's father. Queensberry was a violent, irrational man, who hated his son's lover and was capable of hurting both parties. Bosie insisted on flaunting his relationship with Wilde to annoy his father and he was reckless of the effect of this public display of unconventional behaviour. Homosexuality was no less a fact of life in 1895 than it is now: moreover, the artistic and theatrical world accommodated it better than society at large. It had a flourishing and varied subculture and a number of sophisticated apologists. The double life that it entailed was by no means a simple matter of deceit and guilt for Wilde: it suited the cultivation of moral independence and detachment from society that he considered essential to art. None the less, if his affair with Douglas should ever come to be more public, and if the law were to be invoked, Wilde

---

63 Wilde, *Letters*, p. 438.

64 'I am not claiming that Wilde clearly saw prison rising up before him; but I do assert that the dramatic turn which surprised and astounded London, abruptly turning Wilde from accuser to accused, did not, strictly speaking, cause him any surprises' (Gide, 'In Memoriam', ed. cit., p. 34).

would be ruined. There had been scandals and trials involving homo-sexuals of the upper classes, which had to a degree closed their ranks to protect their own. But Wilde had made powerful enemies in a country whose leaders, institutions and press seemed devoted to Philistinism and where art itself was always suspect as constituting a threat to the moral fibre of the nation. *Dorian Gray* in particular had aroused violent mistrust, especially in its original form, and a satirical novel by Robert Hichens, *The Green Carnation* (1894), had hinted at a homosexual relationship between two characters obviously based on Wilde and Douglas. Queensberry had made his feelings about his son's private life well known in Clubland. On the first night of *The Importance of Being Earnest*, which opened on 14 February 1895, he tried to cause a disturb-ance at the theatre, but was thwarted by the management. The play was a great success – according to one of the actors, 'The audience rose in their seats and cheered and cheered again.'[65] As it settled down to what promised to be a long run, Wilde's career was at its height.

A fortnight later, on 28 February, Queensberry left a card at the Albe-marle Club 'For Oscar Wilde posing as a somdomite' [*sic*]. The club porter put the card in an envelope, noting on the back the time and date, and Wilde was given it when he arrived at the club later that evening. The events that followed ruined him within a few months. Urged on by Douglas, but against the advice of most of his friends, Wilde sued Queensberry for criminal libel. The case went against Wilde, who found himself answering charges under the 1885 Criminal Law Amendment Act, which made both private and public homosexual relations between men illegal. Significs-antly, the accusations against him did not include his affair with Douglas: he was alleged to have committed acts of gross indecency on a number of occasions and to have conspired to procure the committing of such acts. The men involved were 'renters', young, lower-class, male prostitutes, and there was a strong sense in the proceedings that Wilde was being tried for betraying his class's social as well as sexual ethics. Much was made of the alleged immorality of his works, especially *Dorian Gray*. The jury at what was effectively the second trial of Wilde (after the hearings in his charge against Queensberry) failed to agree, and a retrial was ordered. Finally, on 25 May 1895, Wilde was convicted and sentenced to two years' imprison-ment with hard labour. In the autumn he was declared bankrupt and all his effects were auctioned, including drafts and manuscripts of published and unpublished works. On 19 May 1897 he was released, and took up residence in France. During his imprisonment he had composed a long, bitter letter to Douglas, later published under the title *De Profundis*.

---

65   Allen Aynesworth, quoted by Hesketh Pearson, *The Life of Oscar Wilde* (1946), p. 257.

Shortly after his release he completed a narrative poem, *The Ballad of Reading Gaol.* These and a few letters to the press on prison reform apart, Wilde published nothing new after his imprisonment. He did manage to arrange for the publication of *The Importance of Being Earnest* and *An Ideal Husband*, which appeared in 1899. Projects for further plays came to nothing. The affair with Douglas was taken up again and continued sporadically. They led a nomadic life on the continent, Wilde often chronically in debt despite the good offices of his friends. His allowance from Constance was withdrawn when he resumed living with Bosie. His plays were not yet being revived in England and his published works brought in little by way of royalties.

Wilde died on 30 November 1900 in Paris, from cerebral meningitis which set in after an operation on his ear. The day before he had been received into the Roman Catholic Church. He was buried at Bagneux, but in 1909 his remains were moved to the Père Lachaise cemetery, where they now rest under a monument by Jacob Epstein.

R.J.

NOTE ON THE TEXT

The text printed in this volume follows that of the first edition, published by Leonard Smithers in 1899 and limited to 1,000 copies. Smithers' edition was printed from copy prepared by Wilde and from proofs revised by him (PR). In the absence of a promptbook it is not possible to positively establish a version of the play as performed in the first production, but the typescript supplied to Daniel Frohman (F) seems to derive directly from the acted text. Readings noted as making their first appearance in the proofs (PR) were the product of Wilde's revisions when he was working on copy for Smithers' printer in 1899: the typescript used for this purpose may be that now at Texas Christian University.

In the manuscript and in most of the subsequent typescript drafts Wilde made numerous alterations in pencil and a variety of inks. It is not possible to confidently identify successive stages of revision within each document: in the manuscripts, for example, Wilde began in ink, continued in pencil and revised in both mediums, often leaving gaps to be filled in later. In references to the manuscripts (MS) I have generally cited the *final* state of the draft. In the case of typescripts (BLTS, C, LC, F) I have distinguished where necessary between the typed version and its revised state.

The footnotes to the present edition give an account of Wilde's revisions to the play up to the first performance and in preparation for publication. Critical annotation of the text has generally been restricted to indicating Wilde's use of material from his other works and to explaining contemporary references or nuances of meaning which a contemporary audience would have readily caught. The punctuation and spelling of a few words (principally 'to-night', 'sha'n't', 'one's-self' and 'now-a-days') have been changed to accord with modern practice. Some minor errors in the 1899 edition have been corrected.[66]

R.J.

---

66 The following emendations have been made to the first edition: I, 18 'Hartlocks' for 'Hartlocks'; I, 24 'why I go.' for 'why I go'; I, 810 'ruined,' for 'ruined'; II, 45 ' ... ' for ' .... '; II, 78 'almost?' for 'almost'; II, 658 'remember' for 'remember,'; II, 886 'I think,' for 'I think'; II, 1074 'to me.' for 'to me'; III, 1 'Adam' for 'Adams' in s.d.; III, 98 'Berkshires" for 'Berkshires'; III, 376 addition to s.d.; IV, 64 *'Times'* for *'Times'*; IV, 95 'Parliament.' for 'Parliament?'; IV, 426 'mine?' for 'mine!'.

ABBREVIATIONS

References to *An Ideal Husband* (abbreviated to *Husband* in the annotation) are to the line numbering of this edition; *The Importance of Being Earnest* (*Earnest*) and *Lady Windermere's Fan* (*LWF*) are cited in the respective New Mermaid editions by Russell Jackson (1980; 4th impression, 1992) and Ian Small (1980). *A Woman of No Importance* is referred to by the line numbering common to the edition by Ian Small in *Two Society Comedies* (1983) and his revised edition (1993). Reference to *The Picture of Dorian Gray* (abbreviated to *Dorian Gray* or *DG*) is to the edition by Isobel Murray (Oxford, 1974), and Wilde's other fiction is cited from the same editor's *Complete Shorter Fiction of Oscar Wilde* (*CSF*) (Oxford, 1979). Other works are referred to by the title of the volume in which they appear in Robert Ross's edition of the *Works* (1908). For convenience of reference I have also given page numbers from the Collins *Complete Works* (1979), which is designated *CW*. *The Letters of Oscar Wilde*, edited by Sir Rupert Hart-Davis (1963), is abbreviated to *Letters*. The drafts and texts of the play are referred to as follows:

MS	Manuscript drafts of the four acts (including two versions of Act II): British Library, MS Add. 37946.
BLTS	Typescripts of the four acts, with manuscript revisions: British Library, MS Add. 37947.
C	Typescripts of the four acts, with manuscript revisions: William Andrews Clark Memorial Library.
HTC	Typescript of Act I, with manuscript revisions: Harvard Theatre Collection (uncatalogued).
LC	Typescript of the four acts, submitted to the Lord Chamberlain's Office: British Library, MS Add. 53566(A).
F	Typescripts of the four acts, the fourth with manuscript stage-directions (not in Wilde's hand), used by Daniel Frohman: New York Public Library at Lincoln Center, N.C.19-/NCOF.
Pbk	Typescript of Act I, apparently marked as a prompt book (some revisions in hand(s) other than author's): Harvard Theatre Collection (uncatalogued).
PR	Page-proofs of the first edition, with Wilde's manuscript revisions: William Andrews Clark Memorial Library, Finzi 2456.

1st Ed.   *An Ideal Husband, by the author of 'Lady Windermere's Fan'* (London: Leonard Smithers, 1899).

OTHER ABBREVIATIONS

OED   *Oxford English Dictionary.*
s.d.   stage direction(s).

In the notes the names of some characters are abbreviated to initials.

R.J.

FURTHER READING

Bibliography

Ian Fletcher and John Stokes, 'Oscar Wilde' in *Anglo-Irish Literature: A Review of Research*, ed. R. J. Finneran (New York, 1976)

'Stuart Mason' (C. S. Millard), *Bibliography of Oscar Wilde* (London, 1908; reissued 1967)

E. H. Mikhail *Oscar Wilde: An Annotated Bibliography of Criticism* (London, 1987)

Ian Small, *Oscar Wilde Revalued: An Essay on New Materials and Methods of Research* (Greensboro, N.C., 1993).

————— , *Oscar Wilde: Recent Research: a Supplement to 'Oscar Wilde Revalued'* (Greensboro, 2000)

John Stokes, *Oscar Wilde* (London, 1978)

Biography

Richard Ellmann, *Oscar Wilde* (London, 1987)

Merlin Holland, *Irish Peacock and Scarlet Marquess: the Real Trial of Oscar Wilde* (London, 2004)

H. Montgomery Hyde, *The Trials of Oscar Wilde* (rev. edn, London, 1973)

————— , *Oscar Wilde* (London, 1975)

E. H. Mikhail, ed., *Oscar Wilde: Interviews and Recollections* (London, 2 vols., 1979)

Richard Pine, *Oscar Wilde* (Dublin, 1983)

Collections of Criticism

Karl Beckson, ed., *Oscar Wilde: The Critical Heritage* (London, 1970)

Joseph Bristow, ed., *Oscar Wilde and Modern Culture: The Making of a Legend* (Athens, 2008)

————— , ed., *Wilde Writings: Contextual Conditions* (London, 2003)

Richard Ellmann, ed., *Oscar Wilde: A Collection of Critical Essays* (Englewood Cliffs, New Jersey, 1969)

Regenia Gagnier, ed., *Critical Essays on Oscar Wilde* (Upper Saddle River, N.J., 1996)

Jarlath Killeen, ed., *Oscar Wilde: Irish Writers in their Time* (Dublin, 2011)

Frederick S. Roden, ed., *Palgrave Advances in Oscar Wilde Studies* (New York, 2004)

George Sandulescu, ed., *Rediscovering Oscar Wilde* (Gerrards Cross, 1994)

William Tydeman, ed., *Wilde: Comedies: A Casebook* (London, 1982)

Criticism

Karl Beckson, *London in the 1890s: A Cultural History* (New York and London, 1992)

Alan Bird, *The Plays of Oscar Wilde* (London, 1977)

Richard Allen Cave, 'Wilde Designs: Some Thoughts about Recent British Productions of his Plays', *Modern Drama* 37 (1994), 175–91.

Ed Cohen, *Talk on the Wilde Side: Towards a Genealogy of a Discourse on Male Sexualities* (London, 1993)

Richard Dellamora, 'Oscar Wilde, Social Purity, and *An Ideal Husband*', *Modern Drama*, 37 (1994), 120–38

Jonathan Dollimore, 'Different Desires: Subjectivity and Transgression in Wilde and Gide', *Textual Practice*, I, 1 (1987), 48–67

Richard Ellmann, 'Romantic Pantomime in Oscar Wilde', *Partisan Review*, 30 (1963), 342–55

Sos Eltis, *Revising Wilde: Society and Subversion in the Plays of Oscar Wilde* (Oxford, 1996)

Michael S. Foldy, *The Trials of Oscar Wilde: Deviance, Morality, and Late-Victorian Society* (New Haven, 1997)

Regenia Gagnier, *Idylls of the Marketplace: Oscar Wilde and the Victorian Public* (London, 1987)

Arthur H. Ganz, 'The Divided Self in the Society Comedies of Oscar Wilde', *Modern Drama*, 3 (1960), 16–23

Ian Gregor, 'Comedy and Oscar Wilde', *Sewanee Review*, 74 (1966), 501–21

Josephine Guy and Ian Small, *Oscar Wilde's Profession* (Oxford, 2000)

Joel H. Kaplan, 'Staging Wilde's Society Plays: A Conversation with Philip Prowse (Glasgow Citizens Theatre)', *Modern Drama*, 37 (1994), 192-9

Joel Kaplan and Sheila Stowell, 'The Dandy and the Dowager: Oscar Wilde and Audience Resistance', *New Theatre Quarterly*, 15 (1999), 318–31

————— , *Theatre and Fashion: Oscar Wilde to the Suffragettes* (Cambridge, 1994)

Norbert Kohl, *Oscar Wilde: The Works of a Conformist Rebel* (Cambridge, 1988)

Jerusha McCormack, 'Masks Without Faces: The Personalities of Oscar Wilde', *English Literature in Transition*, 22 (1979), 253–69

Christopher M. Nassaar, *Into the Demon Universe: A Literary Exploration of Oscar Wilde* (New Haven, Conn., 1974)

Kerry Powell, *Oscar Wilde and the Theatre of the 1890s* (Cambridge, 1990)

————— , *Acting Wilde: Victorian Sexuality, Theatre and Oscar Wilde*, (Cambridge, 2009)

Peter Raby, *Oscar Wilde* (Cambridge, 1988)

————— , ed., *The Cambridge Companion to Oscar Wilde* (Cambridge, 1997)

Neil Sammells, *Wilde Style: the Plays and Prose of Oscar Wilde* (Harlow, 2000)

Gary Schmidgall, *The Stranger Wilde: Interpreting Oscar* (London, 1994)

Rodney Shewan, *Oscar Wilde: Art and Egotism* (London, 1977)

Alan Sinfield, *The Wilde Century: Effeminacy, Oscar Wilde and the Queer Movement* (London, 1994)

J. L. Wiesenthal, 'Wilde, Shaw, and the Play of Conversation', *Modern Drama*, 37 (1994), 206-19

Katharine Worth, *Oscar Wilde* (London, 1983)

AN IDEAL HUSBAND

OSCAR WILDE

TO

FRANK HARRIS

A SLIGHT TRIBUTE TO
HIS POWER AND DISTINCTION
AS AN ARTIST
HIS CHIVALRY AND NOBILITY
AS A FRIEND

Dedication
Frank Harris (1856–1931), journalist and man of letters; loyal friend and vivid biographer of
Wilde. His most notable publication is the sexually explicit and tantalisingly unreliable
autobiography, *My Life and Loves* (5 vols., 1923–7; one vol., 1963).

Persons of the Play
As in his other plays, Wilde employed place-names for some of the characters and ensured that titles did not correspond to those of any living person. Of particular interest here is *Goring*, where Wilde began work on *Husband*. E.H. Mikhail suggests that *de Nanjac* has been taken from the name of a character in Dumas *fils'* play *Le Demi-Monde* (1885). Other names in the present list appear elsewhere in Wilde, notably *Markby* (the firm of solicitors who represent Jack in *Earnest*), *Montford* (original name of Algernon Moncrieff in the same play) and *Mason* (used for a servant in drafts of *Woman*). In the first drafts of the play *Mabel* is referred to as Violet: the name *Mabel* also appears in the early drafts of *Woman*.

2

THE PERSONS OF THE PLAY

[Haymarket Theatre, 3 January 1895]

THE EARL OF CAVERSHAM K.G. . . . . *Mr Alfred Bishop*

VISCOUNT GORING, *his son* . . . . *Mr Charles H. Hawtrey*

SIR ROBERT CHILTERN, BART.,
   Under-Secretary for Foreign Affairs . . . . *Mr Lewis Waller*

VICOMTE DE NANJAC,   5
   Attaché at the French Embassy in London . . . . *Mr Cosmo Stuart*

MR MONTFORD . . . . *Mr Harry Stanford*

MASON, *Butler to Sir Robert Chiltern* . . . . *Mr H. Deane*

PHIPPS, *Lord Goring's Servant* . . . . *Mr C.H. Brookfield*

JAMES   ⎫ *footmen* . . . . ⎧ *Mr Charles Mayrick*   10
HAROLD ⎭   ⎨   *Mr Goodheart*

LADY CHILTERN . . . . *Miss Julia Neilson*

LADY MARKBY . . . . *Miss Fanny Brough*

THE COUNTESS OF BASILDON . . . . *Miss Vane Featherston*

MRS MARCHMONT . . . . *Miss Helen Forsyth*   15

MISS MABEL CHILTERN,
   Sir Robert Chiltern's sister . . . . *Miss Maude Millet*

MRS CHEVELEY . . . . *Miss Florence West*

---

2   Charles *Hawtrey* (1858–1923): a fine light comedian 'with a quiet humorous style of his own', he had a 'very pale face, accentuated by jet black hair' and a black moustache (*The Dramatic Peerage*, 1892).

4   Lewis *Waller* (1860–1915): a strikingly handsome actor, excelling in 'costume' plays of a romantic, heroic kind – less well suited to contemporary comedy, but appropriate to the serious role he played in *Husband*. According to *The Times* he played it 'in his manliest and most robust style'. This was his first step in management.

9   Charles *Brookfield* (1860–1912): a generous choice for the role, since he had written a satirical playlet against Wilde (*The Poet and the Puppets*, 1892) and made no secret of his antipathy. He collected evidence to support Queensberry's case in the libel action.

12   Julia *Neilson* (1868–1957): a statuesque, graceful actress whose first success had been as Cynisca in a production of Gilbert's *Pygmalion and Galatea*.

13   Fanny *Brough* (1854–1914): daughter of the dramatist Robert Brough and niece of the comic actor Lionel Brough. *The Dramatic Peerage* praises her 'quaint humour, intelligent brightness, and quickness of repartee' but notes that she suffers from first-night nerves. This may explain her poor reception in the part (*The Theatre* was surprised that a comedian of her reputation should give 'so ineffective a sketch')

3

The Scenes of the Play

Act I   *The Octagon Room in Sir Robert Chiltern's House in Grosvenor Square.*

Act II   *Morning-room in Sir Robert Chiltern's House.*

Act III   *The Library of Lord Goring's House in Curzon Street.*

Act IV   *Same as Act II.*

Time – The Present

Place – London

The Action of the Play is completed within twenty-four hours.

ACT I

Scene – The Octagon room at SIR ROBERT CHILTERN*'s house
in Grosvenor Square.*

*The room is brilliantly lighted and full of guests. At the top
of the staircase stands* LADY CHILTERN, *a woman of grave
Greek beauty, about twenty-seven years of age. She receives*   5
*the guests as they come up. Over the well of the staircase
hangs a great chandelier with wax lights, which illumine
a large eighteenth-century French tapestry – representing the
Triumph of Love, from a design by Boucher – that is stretched
on the staircase wall. On the right is the entrance to the*   10
*music-room. The sound of a string quartette is faintly heard.
The entrance on the left leads to other reception-rooms.*
MRS MARCHMONT *and* LADY BASILDON, *two very pretty
women, are seated together on a Louis Seize sofa. They are
types of exquisite fragility. Their affectation of manner has*   15
a delicate charm. Watteau would have loved to paint them.

MRS MARCHMONT
Going on to the Hartlocks' tonight, Margaret?
LADY BASILDON
I suppose so. Are you?   20
MRS MARCHMONT
Yes. Horribly tedious parties they give, don't they?
LADY BASILDON
Horribly tedious! Never know why I go. Never know why I go
anywhere.   25
MRS MARCHMONT
I come here to be educated.

---

1   s.d. first appears in full in PR. Earlier drafts indicate the setting as the Chilterns'
drawing-room, brilliantly lit and full of guests. F gives details of the movements of
the non-speaking actors (40 in all) and specifies '*Music in Music Room (classical quartette) to open*' and '*flowers in scene*'. *Grosvenor Square* had many titled residents in
1895, including Lord Randolph Churchill. The paintings by *Boucher* (1703–70) and
Watteau (1684–1721) reflect fashionable interest in these French painters of pastoral,
mythological and delicately erotic subjects. In Pater's *Imaginary Portraits* (1887) the
'exquisite fragility' and 'delicate charm' of Watteau's figures had been emphasized.
Wilde specified *Louis Seize* furniture in drafts of *LWF* and a discarded passage in
Husband credited Baron Arnheim with the tastes reflected here. Cf. Appendix I.

LADY BASILDON
Ah! I hate being educated!

MRS MARCHMONT   30
So do I. It puts one almost on a level with the commercial
classes, doesn't it? But dear Gertrude Chiltern is always telling
me that I should have some serious purpose in life. So I come
here to try to find one.

LADY BASILDON (*Looking round through her lorgnette*)   35
I don't see anybody here tonight whom one could possibly call
a serious purpose. The man who took me in to dinner talked to
me about his wife the whole time.

MRS MARCHMONT
How very trivial of him!   40

LADY BASILDON
Terribly trivial! What did your man talk about?

MRS MARCHMONT
About myself.

LADY BASILDON (*Languidly*)   45
And were you interested?

MRS MARCHMONT (*Shaking her head*)
Not in the smallest degree.

LADY BASILDON
What martyrs we are, dear Margaret!   50

MRS MARCHMONT (*Rising*)
And how well it becomes us, Olivia!

They rise and go towards the music-room. The VICOMTE DE
NANJAC, *a young attaché known for his neckties and his Anglo-
mania, approaches with a low bow, and enters into conversation*   55

31   *commercial* (lower LC, BLTS, C). The sentence does not appear in MS. Wilde added
     it to HTC, then added and deleted another line: 'I think education [?was] made for
     the lower classes. They appreciate it so much. We don't'. Cf. Lady Bracknell on
     education: 'Fortunately in England, at any rate, education produces no effect
     whatsoever. If it did, it would prove a serious danger to the upper classes, and
     probably lead to acts of violence in Grosvenor Square' (*Earnest*, I, 498–502).

40   *trivial* an important word for Wilde, who could not decide on the appropriate
     balance between this and the line following. In BLTS 'trivial' is substituted here for
     'rude' in the typescript (and HTC, MS), with a corresponding change in the next
     line. C has 'very trivial . . . , very rude'. In Pbk 'rude . . . trivial' has been changed to
     'trivial . . . rude'.

54, 58 s.d. descriptions of de Nanjac and Lord C first appear in PR. On neckties, cf. *Woman*,
     III, 61–6 ('A well-tied necktie is the first serious step in life'). Lord C recalls the
     character of Lord Fermor in *Dorian Gray*, Chapter III: 'In politics he was a Tory,

MASON (*Announcing guests from the top of the staircase*)
  Mr and Lady Jane Barford. Lord Caversham.

> *Enter* LORD CAVERSHAM, *an old gentleman of seventy,*
> *wearing the riband and star of the Garter. A fine Whig type.*
> *Rather like a portrait by Lawrence* 60

LORD CAVERSHAM
  Good evening, Lady Chiltern! Has my good-for-nothing young
  son been here?
LADY CHILTERN (*Smiling*)
  I don't think Lord Goring has arrived yet. 65
MABEL CHILTERN (*Coming up to* LORD CAVERSHAM)
  Why do you call Lord Goring good-for-nothing?

> MABEL CHILTERN *is a perfect example of the English type of*
> *prettiness, the apple-blossom type. She has all the fragrance*
> *and freedom of a flower. There is ripple after ripple of sunlight* 70
> *in her hair, and the little mouth, with its parted lips, is expectant,*
> *like the mouth of a child. She has the fascinating tyranny of youth,*
> *and the astonishing courage of innocence. To sane people she is not*
> *reminiscent of any work of art. But she is really like a Tanagra*
> *statuette, and would be rather annoyed if she were told so* 75

LORD CAVERSHAM
  Because he leads such an idle life.
MABEL CHILTERN
  How can you say such a thing? Why, he rides in the Row at ten

> except when the Tories were in office, during which period he roundly abused them
> for being a pack of Radicals . . . Only England could have produced him, and he
> always said that the country was going to the dogs. His principles were out of date,
> but there was a good deal to be said for his prejudices' (*DG* p. 31/*CW* p. 38). Wilde
> makes Lord C a *Whig* (the landed, aristocratic staple of early 19th-century
> Liberalism) so that his intimacy with the Liberal administration will be credible. Sir
> Thomas *Lawrence* (1769–1830) was the most notable British portraitist of his
> generation.
>
> 68 s.d. again, a descriptive s.d. that first appears in PR. Both Sybil Vane in *Dorian Gray*
> (*DG*, p. 75/*CW*, p. 67) and Sybil Merton in *Lord Arthur Savile's Crime* (*CSF*, p.
> 32/*CW*, pp. 177–8) are compared to the small statuettes of terracotta found in tombs
> in the late 4th and 3rd centuries BC at *Tanagra* in Greece. Miss Merton's lips are also
> 'slightly parted' and she emanates 'all the tender purity of girlhood'. The insistence
> on the *tyranny of youth* recalls Gwendolen's regret in *Earnest* that 'the old-fashioned
> respect for the young is fast dying out'(I, 703–4). Wilde's use of *sane* implies a casual
> taunt for critics who found his work 'unhealthy'.
>
> 79 *in the Row* i.e. Rotten Row, in Hyde Park. Details of the daily routine vary from draft
> to draft. F follows LC and earlier versions in reading 'twice a day' for *ten in the*

o'clock in the morning, goes to the Opera three times a week,   80
changes his clothes at least five times a day, and dines out every
night of the season. You don't call that leading an idle life, do
you?

LORD CAVERSHAM (*Looking at her with a kindly twinkle in his
eyes*)   85

You are a very charming young lady!

MABEL CHILTERN

How sweet of you to say that, Lord Caversham! Do come to us
more often. You know we are always at home on Wednesdays,
and you look so well with your star!   90

LORD CAVERSHAM

Never go anywhere now. Sick of London Society. Shouldn't
mind being introduced to my own tailor; he always votes on the
right side. But object strongly to being sent down to dinner with
my wife's milliner. Never could stand Lady Caversham's bonnets.   95

MABEL CHILTERN

Oh, I love London Society! I think it has immensely improved.
It is entirely composed now of beautiful idiots and brilliant
lunatics. Just what Society should be.

LORD CAVERSHAM   100

Hum! Which is Goring? Beautiful idiot, or the other thing?

MABEL CHILTERN (*Gravely*)

I have been obliged for the present to put Lord Goring into a
class quite by himself. But he is developing charmingly!

---

morning (1st ed, PR). In PR *changes . . . a day* first appears (with 'six' altered in
manuscript to *five*). Before PR we are informed that Lord Goring dines out every
night 'of his life' and F adds 'twice on Sundays'.

86–90   *You are . . . your star!* MS has a longer version of the conversation, in which Lord C
observes that his wife 'has grown rather short sighted in the last few years. I don't
think she quite sees my good qualities', to which Mabel retorts, 'How strange! for
they are all on the surface are they not?' She claims that to be considered 'dangerous'
is the dream of her life when Lord C suggests that she will be a danger to Goring.
After additions and revisions through HTC, Pbk and C, the passage was dropped,
and does not appear in LC.

90   *your star* i.e. the insignia of the Order of the Garter. In *Lord Arthur Savile's Crime* 'Six
Cabinet Ministers had come on [to the reception] from the Speaker's Levee in their
stars and ribands' (*CSF*, p. 19/*CW*, p. 168).

92–5   *Sick . . . bonnets* elaborated in the course of revision from a simple line in MS: 'Hate
London Society. The thing has gone to the dogs, a lot of demmed nobodies talking
about nothing' (cf. note ll. 54, 58. s.d. above). In F only Lord C remarks that 'all
tailors are volunteers'. HTC has an addition – 'It has got so mixed' – also found in
the Pbk typescript but deleted there. Cf. below, ll. 756–9).

97   *immensely improved* In MS and HTC it has 'become quite ideal'.

LORD CAVERSHAM 105
Into what?
MABEL CHILTERN (*With a little curtsey*)
I hope to let you know very soon, Lord Caversham!
MASON (*Announcing guests*)
Lady Markby. Mrs Cheveley. 110

Enter LADY MARKBY *and* MRS CHEVELEY. LADY MARKBY *is
a pleasant, kindly, popular woman, with gray hair à la marquise
and good lace.* MRS CHEVELEY, *who accompanies her, is tall and
rather slight. Lips very thin and highly-coloured, a line of scarlet
on a pallid face. Venetian red hair, aquiline nose, and long throat.* 115
*Rouge accentuates the natural paleness of her complexion.
Gray-green eyes that move restlessly. She is in heliotrope, with
diamonds. She looks rather like an orchid, and makes great
demands on one's curiosity. In all her movements she is
extremely graceful. A work of art, on the whole, but showing* 120
the influence of too many schools

LADY MARKBY
Good evening, dear Gertrude! So kind of you to let me bring
my friend, Mrs Cheveley. Two such charming women should
know each other! 125
LADY CHILTERN (*Advances towards* MRS CHEVELEY *with a sweet
smile. Then suddenly stops, and bows rather distantly*)
I think Mrs Cheveley and I have met before. I did not know she
had married a second time.
LADY MARKBY (*Genially*) 130
Ah, nowadays people marry as often as they can, don't they? It
is most fashionable. (*To* DUCHESS OF MARYBOROUGH) Dear
Duchess, and how is the Duke? Brain still weak, I suppose?
Well, that is only to be expected, is it not? His good father was
just the same. There is nothing like race, is there? 135

111–21 s.d. *Lady Markby is a pleasant . . . too many schools* first appears in PR. Lady M's hair
is dressed in a popular style derived from the period of Louis XV. The description
of Mrs C. is consistent with the later description by Lord G (II, 325–6) and with the
accounts of contemporary reviewers. William Archer described her as 'tawny-haired,
red-cheeked, white-shouldered'; to *The Times* she was 'an overdressed adventuress
of cosmopolitan experience.' For a description of her dress, see Appendix II.

131 *nowadays . . . as they can* a recurrent joke in Wilde, who enjoyed speaking flippantly
of such topics of solemn contemporary debate as divorce law reform. Cf. *Earnest*, I,
707: 'I may marry someone else, and marry often'.

134–5 *His good father . . . is there?* first appears in PR. It is difficult not to read this 1898–99

MRS CHEVELEY (*Playing with her fan*)

But have we really met before, Lady Chiltern? I can't remember where. I have been out of England for so long.

LADY CHILTERN

We were at school together, Mrs Cheveley.   140

MRS CHEVELEY (*Superciliously*)

Indeed? I have forgotten all about my schooldays. I have a vague impression that they were detestable.

LADY CHILTERN (*Coldly*)

I am not surprised!   145

MRS CHEVELEY (*In her sweetest manner*)

Do you know, I am quite looking forward to meeting your clever husband, Lady Chiltern. Since he has been at the Foreign Office, he has been so much talked of in Vienna. They actually succeed in spelling his name right in the newspapers. That in   150 itself is fame, on the continent.

LADY CHILTERN

I hardly think there will be much in common between you and my husband, Mrs Cheveley!   *Moves away*

VICOMTE DE NANJAC   155

Ah! chère Madame, quelle surprise! I have not seen you since Berlin!

addition in the light of Wilde's experience of the Douglas family. At this point F notes *'music off '* (i.e. off-stage) to motivate the departure of most of the guests to the music-room: later in the same script one extra is deputed to *'tell crowd to disperse'*.

143   *detestable* in MS and HTC this is followed by Lady M recalling that she had 'no schooldays' herself and that in her time 'it was not considered the thing for young people to know too much'. This material (originally from drafts of *Woman* – see note to *Woman*, II, 219–21) was later revised and transferred to Act II (810 etc.). It was deleted from the HTC typescript of Act I.

148–9   *Since . . . Vienna* in MS, HTC, Pbk Chiltern has 'had charge of the Foreign Office', which does not leave enough scope for promotion in the final act. In BLTS this is changed (in manuscript) to 'has been undersecretary for Foreign Affairs'. The present reading first appears in PR.

149–51   *They actually . . . continent* these two sentences first appear in PR, and the final three words were added in manuscript to the proof.

153– 4   *I hardly . . . Mrs Cheveley!* MS and HTC include a reference to Mrs C's schoolgirl misdemeanours in an exchange deleted from HTC:

MRS CHEVELEY

Oh! we can always talk of finance. I am deeply interested in finance.

LADY CHILTERN

So I remember.   (*Turns away*)

156–9   *Ah! chère . . . Vicomte* the passage first appears in this form in an addition to Pbk.

MRS CHEVELEY

Not since Berlin, Vicomte. Five years ago!

VICOMTE DE NANJAC   160

And you are younger and more beautiful than ever. How do
you manage it?

MRS CHEVELEY

By making it a rule only to talk to perfectly charming people
like yourself.   165

VICOMTE DE NANJAC

Ah! you flatter me. You butter me, as they say here.

MRS CHEVELEY

Do they say that here? How dreadful of them!

VICOMTE DE NANJAC   170

Yes, they have a wonderful language. It should be more widely
known.

*SIR ROBERT CHILTERN enters. A man of forty, but looking
somewhat younger. Clean-shaven, with finely-cut features,
dark-haired and dark-eyed. A personality of mark. Not popular –*   175
*few personalities are. But intensely admired by the few, and
deeply respected by the many. The note of his manner is that
of perfect distinction, with a slight touch of pride. One feels
that he is conscious of the success he has made in life. A nervous
temperament, with a tired look. The firmly-chiselled mouth*   180
*and chin contrast strikingly with the romantic expression
in the deep-set eyes. The variance is suggestive of an almost
complete separation of passion and intellect, as though thought
and emotion were each isolated in its own sphere through*

164–5   *By making . . . like yourself* further evidence of her un-British outlook is given in MS
        and HTC: 'And so are you, Baron. You know you have something that these
        Englishmen haven't got, a style, an air, something. You have, really. No one would
        ever mistake you for an Englishman.' This would scarcely be a compliment to an
        Anglophile, and may have been dropped for the sake of consistency.

167   *Ah! . . . here* in HTC and one of the revisions in MS this is followed by Lady M's
        speech on curates (transferred to II, 872 etc.).

171–2   *Yes . . . known* first appears in PR.

173   s.d. *A man . . . his head* first appears in PR. The idealised picture of Sir Robert owes
        more to Wilde's private imagery than to the actor's appearance (Waller, who first
        played the part, was famous for his more robust, conventional good looks). The
        hands recall the 'cool, white, flower-like hands' of Lord Henry Wotton (*DG* p. 21/*CW*
        p. 31) and the 'white lily hands' attributed to Willie Hughes in 'The Picture of Mr
        W.H.' (*CSF*, p. 159/*CW*, p. 1169). Sir Anthony *Vandyck*, a Flemish painter, (1599–
        1641) worked in London from 1631 and executed many portraits of Charles I's court.

> *some violence of will-power. There is nervousness in the nostrils,* 185
> *and in the pale, thin, pointed hands. It would be inaccurate*
> *to call him picturesque. Picturesqueness cannot survive*
> *the House of Commons. But Vandyck would have liked to have*
> *painted his head*

SIR ROBERT CHILTERN   190

Good evening, Lady Markby! I hope you have brought Sir John with you?

LADY MARKBY

Oh! I have brought a much more charming person than Sir John. Sir John's temper since he has taken seriously to politics 195 has become quite unbearable. Really, now that the House of Commons is trying to become useful, it does a great deal of harm.

SIR ROBERT CHILTERN

I hope not, Lady Markby. At any rate we do our best to waste 200 the public time, don't we? But who is this charming person you have been kind enough to bring to us?

LADY MARKBY

Her name is Mrs Cheveley! One of the Dorsetshire Cheveleys, I suppose. But I really don't know. Families are so mixed now- 205 adays. Indeed, as a rule, everybody turns out to be somebody else.

SIR ROBERT CHILTERN

Mrs Cheveley? I seem to know the name.

LADY MARKBY   210

She has just arrived from Vienna.

SIR ROBERT CHILTERN

Ah! yes. I think I know whom you mean.

---

191   *Good evening* F indicates that he shakes her hand, the customary greeting between close friends.

194–207 *Oh! . . . somebody else* at this point MS and HTC include Lady M's account of the effect of Parliament on her husband (transferred to II, 822 etc.). The first two speeches are added to Pbk and carried into C; the first two sentences of the third speech also appear in addition to Pbk, but the final sentence does not appear until PR.

209–21 *Mrs Cheveley? . . . see her* F, LC, BLTS, C and Pbk have a simpler form of this, omitting the reference to the chef. In MS and HTC Lady M observes: 'Oh yes, she is here in white satin and gold, but Markby, whose brutality of Language is notorious, tells me to my face that it does not suit me' (del. from HTC). Later the colour of Mrs C's gown became 'green', then, finally 'heliotrope' (i.e. a shade of purple).

LADY MARKBY

Oh! she goes everywhere there, and has such pleasant scandals   215
about all her friends. I really must go to Vienna next winter. I
hope there is a good chef at the Embassy.

SIR ROBERT CHILTERN

If there is not, the Ambassador will certainly have to be
recalled. Pray point out Mrs Cheveley to me. I should like to   220
see her.

LADY MARKBY

Let me introduce you. (*To* MRS CHEVELEY) My dear, Sir
Robert Chiltern is dying to know you!

SIR ROBERT CHILTERN (*Bowing*)   225

Everyone is dying to know the brilliant Mrs Cheveley. Our
attachés at Vienna write to us about nothing else.

MRS CHEVELEY

Thank you, Sir Robert. An acquaintance that begins with a
compliment is sure to develop into a real friendship. It starts in   230
the right manner. And I find that I know Lady Chiltern already.

SIR ROBERT CHILTERN

Really?

MRS CHEVELEY

Yes. She has just reminded me that we were at school together.   235
I remember it perfectly now. She always got the good conduct
prize. I have a distinct recollection of Lady Chiltern always
getting the good conduct prize!

SIR ROBERT CHILTERN (*Smiling*)

And what prizes did you get, Mrs Cheveley?   240

MRS CHEVELEY

My prizes came a little later on in life. I don't think any of them
were for good conduct. I forget!

SIR ROBERT CHILTERN

I am sure they were for something charming!   245

MRS CHEVELEY

I don't know that women are always rewarded for being
charming. I think they are usually punished for it! Certainly,
more women grow old nowadays through the faithfulness of
their admirers than through anything else! At least that is the   250
only way I can account for the terribly haggard look of most of
your pretty women in London!

SIR ROBERT CHILTERN

What an appalling philosophy that sounds! To attempt to classify you, Mrs Cheveley, would be an impertinence. But may 255 I ask, at heart, are you an optimist or a pessimist? Those seem to be the only two fashionable religions left to us nowadays.

MRS CHEVELEY

Oh, I'm neither. Optimism begins in a broad grin, and Pessimism ends with blue spectacles. Besides, they are both of 260 them merely poses.

SIR ROBERT CHILTERN

You prefer to be natural?

MRS CHEVELEY

Sometimes. But it is such a very difficult pose to keep up. 265

SIR ROBERT CHILTERN

What would those modern psychological novelists, of whom we hear so much, say to such a theory as that?

MRS CHEVELEY

Ah! the strength of women comes from the fact that psychology 270 cannot explain us. Men can be analyzed, women . . . merely adored.

SIR ROBERT CHILTERN

You think science cannot grapple with the problem of women?

MRS CHEVELEY 275

Science can never grapple with the irrational. That is why it has no future before it, in this world.

SIR ROBERT CHILTERN

And women represent the irrational.

254   *appalling* first appears in PR (terrible LC, C, BLTS; modern Pbk, HTC, MS). F omits the line and picks up again with l. 267 ('What would . . . '). After the first sentence ('What . . . sounds!') the MS cuts to l. 283 ('Do sit down . . . ').

254–6   *To attempt . . . I ask* first appears in PR.

256   *an optimist or a pessimist* Cf. Act II, 516–17. Pessimism, associated in particular with the German philosopher Schopenhauer, was considered part of the decadent sensibility. Cf. 'The Decay of Lying': 'Schopenhauer has analysed the pessimism that characterises modern thought, but Hamlet invented it. The world has become sad because a puppet was once melancholy' (*Intentions*, p. 35/*CW*, p. 983).

256–7   *Those . . . nowadays* first appears in PR.

260   *blue spectacles* worn to protect the eyes from strong light: perhaps, in this context, the pessimistic equivalent of rose-tinted spectacles.

265   *Sometimes* altered from 'Yes' in manuscript changes to PR. In Pbk Wilde deleted another sentence: 'Ah, being natural is the most artificial pose of all.'

267   *modern psychological novelists* The term was used loosely by critics hostile to the modern movements, but Wilde may be thinking of Paul Bourget, whose novels and psychological studies he knew and whom he had met in Paris.

MRS CHEVELEY   280
  Well-dressed women do.
SIR ROBERT CHILTERN (*With a polite bow*)
  I fear I could hardly agree with you there. But do sit down. And
  now tell me, what makes you leave your brilliant Vienna for our
  gloomy London – or perhaps the question is indiscreet?   285
MRS CHEVELEY
  Questions are never indiscreet. Answers sometimes are.
SIR ROBERT CHILTERN
  Well, at any rate, may I know if it is politics or pleasure?
MRS CHEVELEY   290
  Politics are my only pleasure. You see nowadays it is not
  fashionable to flirt till one is forty, or to be romantic till one is
  forty-five, so we poor women who are under thirty, or say we
  are, have nothing open to us but politics or philanthropy. And
  philanthropy seems to me to have become simply the refuge of   295
  people who wish to annoy their fellow-creatures. I prefer politics.
  I think they are more . . . becoming!
SIR ROBERT CHILTERN
  A political life is a noble career!
MRS CHEVELEY   300
  Sometimes. And sometimes it is a clever game, Sir Robert. And
  sometimes it is a great nuisance.
SIR ROBERT CHILTERN
  Which do you find it?

285–9   *or perhaps . . . if it is* first appears in this form in PR, and (in different phrasing) in F.
291–7   *Politics . . . becoming!* details in this speech were altered in succesive drafts. Including
        the change in ages from 40 and 45 to 50 and 65 respectively. In MS 'pessimism' is the
        alternative to politics (1. 294) and the sentence following ('And . . . creatures') is
        absent. In PR, C, BLTS 'wish to annoy' is 'absolutely detest' and in Pbk this reading
        has been inserted to replace 'hate' in the typescript. MS follows this speech with
        further evidence of dandyism in Mrs C:

> SIR ROBERT
> Everything becomes you, Mrs Cheveley.
> MRS CHEVELEY
> Oh! not this month's bonnets. You must not see me in this month's
> bonnets. I look a fright in them. But a political life gives one colour,
> I think.

        On philanthropy, cf. *Woman.* I, 257–62 and *Dorian Gray*: 'Philanthropic people lose
        all sense of humanity. It is their distinguishing characteristic' (*DG*, p. 35/*CW*, p. 40).

MRS CHEVELEY   305
    I? A combination of all three.   *Drops her fan*
SIR ROBERT CHILTERN (*Picks up fan*)
    Allow me!
MRS CHEVELEY
    Thanks.   310
SIR ROBERT CHILTERN
    But you have not told me yet what makes you honour London
    so suddenly. Our season is almost over.
MRS CHEVELEY
    Oh! I don't care about the London season! It is too   315
    matrimonial. People are either hunting for husbands, or hiding
    from them. I wanted to meet you. It is quite true. You know
    what a woman's curiosity is. Almost as great as a man's!
    I wanted immensely to meet you, and . . . to ask you to do
    something for me.   320
SIR ROBERT CHILTERN
    I hope it is not a little thing, Mrs Cheveley. I find that little
    things are so very difficult to do.
MRS CHEVELEY (*After a moment's reflection*)
    No, I don't think it is quite a little thing.   325
SIR ROBERT CHILTERN
    I am so glad. Do tell me what it is.

---

306   *I?' . . . three* in MS and HTC Mrs. C claims to love the 'gambling element in politics',
     and says that she 'would rather play with people than with cards'. The conversation
     also turns to her relationship with one Count Horwitz in Vienna:
        SIR ROBERT
        They say you are his Egeria.
        MRS CHEVELEY
        I assure you that it is only for five o'clock tea that he comes to my political
        cave!
     (The reference is to the nymph Egeria, who instructed the Roman king Numa
     Pompilius in the foundations of his city's laws.)
315–18 *Oh! . . . a man's* om. MS and F. In LC, BLTS, C and Pbk the second and third sentences
     are replaced by 'It is only meant for the overdressed and the undereducated', echoing
     an epigram in *Dorian Gray* (*DG*, p. 182/*CW*, p. 138), *Earnest* (II, 396) and 'Phrases
     and Philosophies for the Use of the Young' (*CW*, p. 1205). It does not appear to have
     been added to *Earnest* until after the licensing copy of that play was prepared
     (January 1895). Cf. Act II, 544–5 (and footnote) below.
325   *No I don't . . . thing* in C and one of the alterations to Pbk. Mrs C's reasons for not
     telling him her request include the fact that 'There are either too many people, or too
     few in the room' because ' . . . to be without an audience is like being without a
     looking-glass. One can't understand oneself.'

MRS CHEVELEY
    Later on. (*Rises*) And now may I walk through your beautiful
    house? I hear your pictures are charming. Poor Baron Arnheim   330
    – you remember the Baron? – used to tell me you had some
    wonderful Corots.
SIR ROBERT CHILTERN (*With an almost imperceptible start*)
    Did you know Baron Arnheim well?
MRS CHEVELEY (*Smiling*)   335
    Intimately. Did you?
SIR ROBERT CHILTERN
    At one time.
MRS CHEVELEY
    Wonderful man, wasn't he?   340
SIR ROBERT CHILTERN (*After a pause*)
    He was very remarkable, in many ways.
MRS CHEVELEY
    I often think it such a pity he never wrote his memoirs. They
    would have been most interesting.   345
SIR ROBERT CHILTERN
    Yes: he knew men and cities well, like the old Greek.
MRS CHEVELEY
    Without the dreadful disadvantage of having a Penelope waiting
    at home for him.   350
MASON
    Lord Goring.

331–2   *used to tell me you had some* (told me you have two. I think he gave them to you, did
      he not? HTC, MS; told me you have two LC, C, Pbk). The MS and HTC version
      makes Arnheim's artistic seduction of Sir Robert more specific.
332   *Corot* Jean-Baptiste Corot (1796–1815), French landscape painter, liked to paint in
      the open air, and was noted for his twilight scenes. Cf. 'The Critic as Artist': 'It is
      twilight always for the dancing nymphs whom Corot set free among the silver
      poplars of France . . .' (*Intentions*, p. 139/CW, p. 1026).
334–50   *Did you know . . . at home for him* in MS and HTC these speeches are different, and
      the mysterious suddenness of Arnheim's death is remarked on. In BLTS 'At one time'
      is replaced by 'For a few years of my life, when I was very young'. Wilde may have had
      in mind the suicide of Baron Jaques Reinach, the banker involved in the Panama
      Canal scandal. Cf. note to ll. 679–81 below.
344–50   *I often think . . . at home for him* first appears in PR. The *old Greek* is Odysseus,
      described in Book I of Homer's *Odyssey*: 'He saw the cities of many men, and knew
      their mind'. *Penelope*, his wife, waited for him patiently in Ithaca, never giving up
      hope that he would return from Troy and warding off the attentions of a host of
      suitors. Mrs C is making a not-so-veiled attack on marriage.

Enter LORD GORING. *Thirty-four, but always says he is younger.*
A well-bred, expressionless face. He is clever, but would not like
   to be thought so. A flawless dandy, he would be annoyed if he   355
were considered romantic. He plays with life, and is on perfectly
good terms with the world. He is fond of being misunderstood.
             It gives him a post of vantage

SIR ROBERT CHILTERN

   Good evening, my dear Arthur! Mrs Cheveley, allow me to   360
   introduce to you Lord Goring, the idlest man in London.

MRS CHEVELEY

   I have met Lord Goring before.

LORD GORING (*Bowing*)

   I did not think you would remember me, Mrs Cheveley.   365

MRS CHEVELEY

   My memory is under admirable control. And are you still a
   bachelor?

LORD GORING

   I . . . believe so.   370

MRS CHEVELEY

   How very romantic!

LORD GORING

   Oh! I am not at all romantic. I am not old enough. I leave
   romance to my seniors.   375

SIR ROBERT CHILTERN

   Lord Goring is the result of Boodle's Club, Mrs Cheveley.

MRS CHEVELEY

   He reflects every credit on the institution.

LORD GORING   380

   May I ask are you staying in London long?

353–8   s.d. *Thirty-four . . . vantage* added in manuscript to PR. On lying about one's age cf.
        Woman, I, 427–8 and *Earnest*, III, 249–51.

  361   *the idlest man in London* om. F, LC, BLTS. Wilde is restoring part of the line from MS:
        'one of my friends and the idlest man in London'. The typescript of Pbk added
        'which is saying a good deal for him, as there is so much competition'. A manuscript
        alteration prolongs the joke with 'for that at present, amongst elder sons'. The fullest
        version then appears in C. Cf. Lady Bracknell in *Earnest*, reassured by Jack's
        admission that he smokes: 'A man should have an occupation of some kind. There
        are far too many idle men in London as it is' (I, 487–9).

367–79   *And are you . . . institution* first appears in PR. *Boodle's*, in St James's Street, is one of
        the oldest clubs in London.

MRS CHEVELEY
>That depends partly on the weather, partly on the cooking, and
>partly on Sir Robert.

SIR ROBERT CHILTERN   385
>You are not going to plunge us into a European war, I hope?

MRS CHEVELEY
>There is no danger, at present!

>>*She nods to* LORD GORING, *with a look of amusement*
>>*in her eyes, and goes out with* SIR ROBERT CHILTERN.   390
>>LORD GORING *saunters over to* MABEL CHILTERN

MABEL CHILTERN
>You are very late!

LORD GORING
>Have you missed me?   395

MABEL CHILTERN
>Awfully!

LORD GORING
>Then I am sorry I did not stay away longer. I like being missed.

MABEL CHILTERN   400
>How very selfish of you!

LORD GORING
>I am very selfish.

MABEL CHILTERN
>You are always telling me of your bad qualities, Lord Goring.   405

LORD GORING
>I have only told you half of them as yet, Miss Mabel!

MABEL CHILTERN
>Are the others very bad?

LORD GORING   410
>Quite dreadful! When I think of them at night I go to sleep at
>once.

MABEL CHILTERN
>Well, I delight in your bad qualities. I wouldn't have you part
>with one of them.   415

---

383 *partly on the cooking* first appears in PR.
389 s.d. PR's elaboration of a simple *exeunt* in earlier versions. In F, Goring is watching
     Sir Robert and Mrs C. Mabel Chiltern touches him on the arm to get his attention.
414 *I delight in your bad qualities* Wilde may have recalled Benedick's question in *Much*
     Ado About Nothing V, ii: 'And I pray thee now tell me, for which of my bad parts
     didst thou first fall in love with me?'

LORD GORING

How very nice of you! But then you are always nice. By the way,
I want to ask you a question, Miss Mabel. Who brought Mrs
Cheveley here? That woman in heliotrope, who has just gone
out of the room with your brother?   420

MABEL CHILTERN

Oh, I think Lady Markby brought her. Why do you ask?

LORD GORING

I hadn't seen her for years, that is all.

MABEL CHILTERN   425

What an absurd reason!

LORD GORING

All reasons are absurd.

MABEL CHILTERN

What sort of woman is she?   430

LORD GORING

Oh! a genius in the daytime and a beauty at night!

MABEL CHILTERN

I dislike her already.

LORD GORING   435

That shows your admirable good taste.

VICOMTE DE NANJAC (*Approaching*)

Ah, the English young lady is the dragon of good taste, is she
not? Quite the dragon of good taste.

LORD GORING   440

So the newspapers are always telling us.

VICOMTE DE NANJAC

I read all your English newspapers. I find them so amusing.

LORD GORING

Then, my dear Nanjac, you must certainly read between the   445
lines.

426–8 *What . . . absurd* om. MS, added to HTC.
  432 *Oh!* MS and HTC add 'a very interesting type' and Pbk 'a very characteristic modern
      type'. The phrase was deleted from HTC.
438–9 *Ah, . . . taste* added to HTC typescript.
  441 *newspapers* F and an alteration to BLTS specify 'evening newspapers'. Cf. *Woman*, II,
      376–7 and *Lord Arthur Savile's Crime* (*CSV*, p. 34/*CW*, p. 179).
443–8 *I read all . . . I should like to* om. LC. In MS this reads 'Ah! your English newspapers
      how gay they always are! Their gaiety is quite a . . . a serious thing is it not?' (Wilde's
      ellipsis) to which Sir Robert replies: 'It is no laughing matter I assure you'. After this
      de Nanjac leaves with Miss C and the equivalent of l. 461 follows ('Well, Goring,
      dissipating as usual!').

VICOMTE DE NANJAC

I should like to, but my professor objects. (*To* MABEL
CHILTERN) May I have the pleasure of escorting you to the
music-room, Mademoiselle? 450

MABEL CHILTERN (*Looking very disappointed*)

Delighted, Vicomte, quite delighted! (*Turning to* LORD
GORING) Aren't you coming to the music-room?

LORD GORING

Not if there is any music going on, Miss Mabel. 455

MABEL CHILTERN (*Severely*)

The music is in German. You would not understand it.

Goes out with the VICOMTE DE NANJAC

LORD CAVERSHAM *comes up to his son*

LORD CAVERSHAM 460

Well, sir! what are you doing here? Wasting your life as usual!
You should be in bed, sir. You keep too late hours! I heard of
you the other night at Lady Rufford's dancing till four o'clock
in the morning!

LORD GORING 465

Only a quarter to four, father.

LORD CAVERSHAM

Can't make out how you stand London Society. The thing has
gone to the dogs, a lot of damned nobodies talking about
nothing. 470

LORD GORING

I love talking about nothing, father. It is the only thing I know
anything about.

LORD CAVERSHAM

You seem to me to be living entirely for pleasure. 475

---

448 *but my professor objects* added in manuscript to PR.
457 *The music is in German* cf. 'The Critic as Artist' where one Baroness Bernstein is said
to have talked about music 'as if it were actually written in the German language.
Now whatever music sounds like, I am glad to say that it does not sound in the
smallest degree like German' (*Intentions*, p. 103/*CW*, p. 1610–11).
463 *Lady Rufford's* (Lady Radley's MS). The name is also used in *LWF*.
468–82 *Can't make out . . . Lady Basildon* this is omitted in MS and HTC, which use the first
speech earlier, at the equivalent of l. 92.
475–8 *You seem . . . happiness* first appears in additions to HTC typescript: taken up by
BLTS and F but absent in Pbk and LC. In F it is followed by the following exchange:
LORD CAVERSHAM
As far as I can make out you seem to care for no one but yourself.

21

LORD GORING
What else is there to live for, father? Nothing ages like
happiness.
LORD CAVERSHAM
You are heartless, sir, very heartless!   480
LORD GORING
I hope not, father. Good evening, Lady Basildon!
LADY BASILDON (*Arching two pretty eyebrows*)
Are you here? I had no idea you ever came to political parties!
LORD GORING   485
I adore political parties. They are the only place left to us where
people don't talk politics.
LADY BASILDON
I delight in talking politics. I talk them all day long. But I can't
bear listening to them. I don't know how the unfortunate men   490
in the House stand these long debates.
LORD GORING
By never listening.
LADY BASILDON
Really?   495
LORD GORING (*In his most serious manner*)
Of course. You see, it is a very dangerous thing to listen. If one
listens one may be convinced; and a man who allows himself to
be convinced by an argument is a thoroughly unreasonable
person.   500
LADY BASILDON
Ah! that accounts for so much in men that I have never
understood, and so much in women that their husbands never
appreciate in them!
MRS MARCHMONT (*With a sigh*)   505
Our husbands never appreciate anything in us. We have to go
to others for that!
LADY BASILDON (*Emphatically*)
Yes, always to others, have we not?

LORD GORING
    To be very fond of oneself is the beginning of a life-long romance.
The second speech appears, slightly altered, in 'Phrases and Philosophies for the Use
of the Young' (*CW*, p. 1206). Cf. references to living for pleasure in *Earnest*, including
Lady Bracknell's description of the widowed Lady Harbury 'who seems . . . to be
living entirely for pleasure now' (I, 319–20).
497–500 *If one listens . . . person* Cf. *Earnest*, III, 383–4: 'I dislike arguments of any kind. They
are always vulgar, and often convincing'.

LORD GORING (*Smiling*)   510

And those are the views of the two ladies who are known to have the most admirable husbands in London.

MRS MARCHMONT

That is exactly what we can't stand. My Reginald is quite hopelessly faultless. He is really unendurably so, at times!   515
There is not the smallest element of excitement in knowing him.

LORD GORING

How terrible! Really, the thing should be more widely known!

LADY BASILDON   520

Basildon is quite as bad; he is as domestic as if he was a bachelor.

MRS MARCHMONT (*Pressing* LADY BASILDON *'s hand*)

My poor Olivia! We have married perfect husbands, and we are well punished for it.   525

LORD GORING

I should have thought it was the husbands who were punished.

MRS MARCHMONT (*Drawing herself up*)

Oh, dear no! They are as happy as possible! And as for trusting us, it is tragic how much they trust us.   530

LADY BASILDON

Perfectly tragic!

LORD GORING

Or comic, Lady Basildon?

LADY BASILDON   535

Certainly not comic, Lord Goring. How unkind of you to suggest such a thing!

MRS MARCHMONT

I am afraid Lord Goring is in the camp of the enemy, as usual.
I saw him talking to that Mrs Cheveley when he came in.   540

516–7 *There . . . knowing him* this version of the speech first appears in PR. F, LC and BLTS read 'He has got all the seven deadly virtues in their most exaggerated British form,' an elaboration on earlier texts. HTC contains an additional line (subsequently deleted) in manuscript: 'If I allowed him he would have tea with me at five every afternoon'. There is a reference to the seven deadly sins in *Woman* (I, 302–4).

521–2 *a bachelor* in MS and HTC she continues: 'He hasn't a single weakness. He won't even quarrel. I do nothing but yawn when I am with him' (carried into Pbk, where the second sentence is deleted). Cf. *Earnest*, II, 584–7: 'The home seems to me to be the proper sphere for the man'.

532–4 *tragic . . . comic* Wilde's work abounds in pseudo-definitions of tragedy and comedy (e.g. *Woman*, I, 474–9, III, 159–63 and IV, 454–5) and deliberate misapplications of the terms.

LORD GORING

Handsome woman, Mrs Cheveley!

LADY BASILDON (*Stiffly*)

Please don't praise other women in our presence. You might
wait for us to do that! 545

LORD GORING

I did wait.

MRS MARCHMONT

Well, we are not going to praise her. I hear she went to the
Opera on Monday night, and told Tommy Rufford at supper 550
that, as far as she could see, London Society was entirely made
up of dowdies and dandies.

LORD GORING

She is quite right, too. The men are all dowdies and the women
are all dandies, aren't they? 555

MRS MARCHMONT (*After a pause*)

Oh! do you really think that is what Mrs Cheveley meant?

LORD GORING

Of course. And a very sensible remark for Mrs Cheveley to
make, too. 560

Enter MABEL CHILTERN. *She joins the group*

MABEL CHILTERN

Why are you talking about Mrs Cheveley? Everybody is talking
about Mrs Cheveley! Lord Goring says – what did you say, Lord
Goring, about Mrs Cheveley? Oh! I remember, that she was a 565
genius in the daytime and a beauty at night.

LADY BASILDON

What a horrid combination! So very unnatural!

MRS MARCHMONT (*In her most dreamy manner*)

I like looking at geniuses, and listening to beautiful people. 570

LORD GORING

Ah! that is morbid of you, Mrs Marchmont!

551–2   *as far as she could see . . . dandies* Cf. *Woman*, III, 275–6. MS, HTC, Pbk and C have
a different comparison, of which Pbk gives the fullest version: 'she had never seen
so many dowdies and dandies in the whole course of her life! said that it reminded
her of a badly-arranged conservatory full of nothing but wallflowers and orchids!'.

554–60   *She is . . . to make, too* see Appendix I.

561   s.d. F and LC place this entrance earlier, after l. 555 ('dowdies and dandies').

568   *What . . . unnatural!* first appears in Pbk.

MRS MARCHMONT (*Brightening to a look of real pleasure*)
> I am so glad to hear you say that. Marchmont and I have been
> married for seven years, and he has never once told me that   575
> I was morbid. Men are so painfully unobservant!

LADY BASILDON (*Turning to her*)
> I have always said, dear Margaret, that you were the most
> morbid person in London.

MRS MARCHMONT   580
> Ah! but you are always sympathetic, Olivia!

MABEL CHILTERN
> Is it morbid to have a desire for food? I have a great desire for
> food. Lord Goring, will you give me some supper?

LORD GORING   585
> With pleasure, Miss Mabel. (*Moves away with her*)

MABEL CHILTERN
> How horrid you have been! You have never talked to me the
> whole evening!

LORD GORING   590
> How could I? You went away with the child-diplomatist.

MABEL CHILTERN
> You might have followed us. Pursuit would have been only polite.
> I don't think I like you at all this evening!

LORD GORING   595
> I like you immensely.

MABEL CHILTERN
> Well, I wish you'd show it in a more marked way!
>>   *They go downstairs*

MRS MARCHMONT   600
> Olivia, I have a curious feeling of absolute faintness. I think I
> should like some supper very much. I know I should like some
> supper.

LADY BASILDON
> I am positively dying for supper, Margaret!   605

MRS MARCHMONT
> Men are so horribly selfish, they never think of these things.

583–4   *I have a great desire for food* MS adds 'I am positively starving'.
591   *The child-diplomatist* first appears in PR, replacing the cruder phrase of earlier
        versions: 'that dreadful little Frenchman'.
593–4   *Pursuit would have been only polite* added in manuscript to HTC typescript.
598   *Well . . . way!* F has the s.d. 'stop music' to motivate an influx of guests from the
        music-room.

LADY BASILDON
Men are grossly material, grossly material!

The VICOMTE DE NANJAC *enters from the music-room*   610
with some other guests. After having carefully examined all
the people present, he approaches LADY BASILDON

VICOMTE DE NANJAC
May I have the honour of taking you down to supper,
Comtesse?   615

LADY BASILDON (*Coldly*)
I never take supper, thank you, Vicomte. (*The* VICOMTE *is*
about to retire. LADY BASILDON, *seeing this, rises at once and*
takes his arm) But I will come down with you with pleasure.

VICOMTE DE NANJAC   620
I am so fond of eating! I am very English in all my tastes.

LADY BASILDON
You look quite English, Vicomte, quite English.

They pass out. MR MONTFORD, *a perfectly groomed*
young dandy, approaches MRS MARCHMONT   625

MR MONTFORD
Like some supper, Mrs Marchmont?

614   *supper* 'At an evening party or a ball the supper ... forms an important element ...
which closely resembles a wedding breakfast' (*Etiquette of Good Society*, ed. Lady
Colin Campbell, 1895). The appropriate form for taking a lady in to supper after
dancing with her also applied (with modifications) to the equivalent situation at an
evening party: 'The gentleman asks his partner whether she will take any refresh-
ment, and if she replies in the affirmative he escorts her to the room and procures
her an ice, offers to hold a cup for her, and when the music for the next dance begins,
he conducts her to her chaperon, when she disengages herself from his arm, they
bow to one another, and he leaves her'.

617   s.d. like others at ll. 629–30 and 640–1, this s.d. first appears in PR.

621   *I am so fond ... tastes* MS and HTC read: 'I always eat a great deal in England. I do
it on purpose. It is an occupation. In eating, as you say, I always take the cake.' Lady
Basildon replies: 'Oh! but I don't say that, Vicomte!' The lines are deleted from Pbk
and do not appear in C, which locates l. 168 ('Ah! you butter me ...') at this point.
Cf. the earlier references to the chef at Vienna and 'cooking' in London (ll. 217, 383).
In the drafts of *Earnest* Algernon's debt of £762 14s 2d is for meals at the Savoy, and
Miss Prism observes that 'There can be little good in any young man who eats so
much, and so often' (*Earnest*, Appendix I, p. 108). Although the eating of cucumber
sandwiches and muffins plays a significant comic role in *Earnest* Wilde was (he later
claimed) fighting a serious, losing battle against the extravagant tastes of Lord Alfred
Douglas, for which he was usually expected to pay the bill.

MRS MARCHMONT (*Languidly*)

Thank you, Mr Montford, I never touch supper. (*Rises hastily and takes his arm*) But I will sit beside you, and watch you.   630

MR MONTFORD

I don't know that I like being watched when I am eating!

MRS MARCHMONT

Then I will watch someone else.

MR MONTFORD   635

I don't know that I should like that either.

MRS MARCHMONT (*Severely*)

Pray, Mr Montford, do not make these painful scenes of jealousy in public!

> *They go downstairs with the other guests, passing*   640
> SIR ROBERT CHILTERN *and* MRS CHEVELEY, *who now enter*

SIR ROBERT CHILTERN

And are you going to any of our country houses before you leave England, Mrs Cheveley?

MRS CHEVELEY   645

Oh, no! I can't stand your English house-parties. In England people actually try to be brilliant at breakfast. That is so dreadful of them! Only dull people are brilliant at breakfast. And then the family skeleton is always reading family prayers. My stay in England really depends on you, Sir Robert. (*Sits*   650
down on the sofa)

SIR ROBERT CHILTERN (*Taking a seat beside her*)

Seriously?

MRS CHEVELEY

Quite seriously. I want to talk to you about a great political and   655

---

634   *Then ... else* F has the s.d. 'check sunlight', indicating that the lights are to be lowered ('check' being the equivalent of the verb 'dim'). The 'sunlight' was usually the large chandelier that served as principal source of light in the auditorium: it is possible that until this point the house lights have not been dimmed. Although Henry Irving at the Lyceum had adopted the practice of darkening the auditorium during performances, it was not yet a matter of course in every theatre.

641   s.d. F and LC locate the entrance earlier, after l. 627.

643–51 *And are you going ...* (Sits down on sofa) this passage first appears thus in PR and, in slightly different form, in F. In MS Sir Robert is anxious to reach the House of Commons before an important division. This is deleted in HTC, where Wilde has added a version of the lines about country house-parties, which is absent from Pbk, the typescript of BLTS and LC. It reappears in manuscript alterations to BLTS, and is taken up in F.

647   *actually* manuscript substitution for 'always' in PR.

financial scheme, about this Argentine Canal Company, in fact.

SIR ROBERT CHILTERN

What a tedious, practical subject for you to talk about, Mrs Cheveley!

MRS CHEVELEY 660

Oh, I like tedious, practical subjects. What I don't like are tedious, practical people. There is a wide difference. Besides, you are interested, I know, in International Canal schemes. You were Lord Radley's secretary, weren't you, when the Government bought the Suez Canal shares? 665

SIR ROBERT CHILTERN

Yes. But the Suez Canal was a very great and splendid undertaking. It gave us our direct route to India. It had imperial value. It was necessary that we should have control. This Argentine scheme is a commonplace Stock Exchange 670 swindle.

MRS CHEVELEY

A speculation, Sir Robert! A brilliant, daring speculation.

SIR ROBERT CHILTERN

Believe me, Mrs Cheveley, it is a swindle. Let us call things by 675 their proper names. It makes matters simpler. We have all the information about it at the Foreign Office. In fact, I sent out a special Commission to inquire into the matter privately, and they report that the works are hardly begun, and as for the money already subscribed, no one seems to know what has 680

658–62   *What . . . Besides* added to BLTS typescript and adopted in F; om. LC, Pbk, C, MS.
    664   *Lord Radley's* the name had been used as that of Dorian Gray's guardian: in MS and HTC we are told that Sir Robert had been Lord C's secretary at the time.
    667   *Yes* F precedes this with the s.d. *'look'.* The purchase of Suez shares took place in 1875, on Disraeli's initiative.
667–71   *Yes . . . swindle* a number of details were added in the course of revision. *It gave . . . India* first appears in C, *It had. . . control* in PR. The swindle is *commonplace* in Pbk and *Stock Exchange* appears in C.
679–81   *and as for . . . The whole thing* first appears in PR ('It' LC, etc.). After the *Panama Canal* project foundered in 1889, with massive debts and unaccounted-for expenditures, a national scandal in France resulted in legal action against the speculators, who were revealed to have involved senators and deputies in the corruption. A series of trials took place in Paris in 1892–3 but one of the principal backers of the scheme, Baron Jaques Keinach, took his life on the day he was to face the court. The Canal was later completed after a new directorate had been set up. In MS and HTC there are additional details of Mrs C's scheme, including the fact that it is in the hands (as Sir Robert tells her) 'of three rather shady bankers, one in Paris, one in Berlin and one . . . one in Vienna' (Wilde's ellipsis). The passage was deleted from HTC.

become of it. The whole thing is a second Panama, and with
not a quarter of the chance of success that miserable affair ever
had. I hope you have not invested in it. I am sure you are far too
clever to have done that.

MRS CHEVELEY   685

I have invested very largely in it.

SIR ROBERT CHILTERN

Who could have advised you to do such a foolish thing?

MRS CHEVELEY

Your old friend – and mine.   690

SIR ROBERT CHILTERN

Who?

MRS CHEVELEY

Baron Arnheim.

SIR ROBERT CHILTERN (*Frowning*)   695

Ah! yes. I remember hearing, at the time of his death, that he
had been mixed up in the whole affair.

MRS CHEVELEY

It was his last romance. His last but one, to do him justice.

SIR ROBERT CHILTERN (*Rising*)   700

But you have not seen my Corots yet. They are in the music-
room. Corots seem to go with music, don't they? May I show
them to you?

MRS CHEVELEY (*Shaking her head*)

I am not in a mood tonight for silver twilights, or rose-pink   705
dawns. I want to talk business. (*Motions to him with her fan to
sit down again beside her*)

SIR ROBERT CHILTERN

I fear I have no advice to give you, Mrs Cheveley, except to
interest yourself in something less dangerous. The success of   710
the Canal depends, of course, on the attitude of England, and

---

686   *I have . . . in it* in versions before PR she adds 'and I hope to invest still more!'.
688–711 *Who could have . . . England, and* om. F and LC, where Sir Robert replies 'I am sorry
       to hear it Lady [sic] Cheveley, as I am going . . . ' and continues with l. 712. In F he
       brings a chair over from the fireplace and sits down.
699   *His last but one, to do him justice* added in MS to PR, perhaps implying that Mrs C
       had been his final romance.
705–6 *or rose-pink dawns* added to PR. *Rose-pink* has connotations of both deceit and
       theatrical make-up (cf. the examples from Carlyle, Meredith and Dickens in *OED*).
709–13 *I fear . . . tomorrow night* in MS and HTC Sir Robert declares his intention to warn
       the Argentine Republic of the Syndicate's machinations.
709–10 *except . . . dangerous* added to PR.

I am going to lay the report of the Commissioners before the House tomorrow night.

MRS CHEVELEY

That you must not do. In your own interests, Sir Robert, to say   715
nothing of mine, you must not do that.

SIR ROBERT CHILTERN (*Looking at her in wonder*)

In my own interests? My dear Mrs Cheveley, what do you mean? (*Sits down beside her*)

MRS CHEVELEY   720

Sir Robert, I will be quite frank with you. I want you to withdraw the report that you had intended to lay before the House, on the ground that you have reasons to believe that the Commissioners have been prejudiced or misinformed, or something. Then I want you to say a few words to the effect that   725
the Government is going to reconsider the question, and that you have reason to believe that the Canal, if completed, will be of great international value. You know the sort of things ministers say in cases of this kind. A few ordinary platitudes will do. In modern life nothing produces such an effect as a   730
good platitude. It makes the whole world kin. Will you do that for me?

SIR ROBERT CHILTERN

Mrs Cheveley, you cannot be serious in making me such a proposition!   735

MRS CHEVELEY

I am quite serious.

SIR ROBERT CHILTERN (*Coldly*)

Pray allow me to believe that you are not!

MRS CHEVELEY (*Speaking with great deliberation and emphasis*)   740
Ah! but I am. And, if you do what I ask you, I . . . will pay you very handsomely!

715–16   *to say nothing of mine* first appears in PR.
   713   *House* LC and earlier versions read 'Cabinet' (cf. note to ll. 148–9, above). In MS and HTC more details of the plan are given: Mrs C reminds Sir Robert that news of the government's support will send up the value of the stock, enabling the Syndicate to sell at a profit 'and leave the wretched poor investors in the lurch'. This was deleted from HTC. BLTS has two versions of similar material, with 'Cut???' beside them.
729–32   *A few ordinary platitudes . . . for me?* first appears in alterations to Pbk. The allusion is to Shakespeare's *Troilus and Cressida* (III, iii, 171 etc.): 'One touch of nature makes the whole world kin' – the 'touch' being a disposition to praise 'newborn gauds/Though they are made and moulded of things past/And give to dust that is a little gilt/More laud than gilt o'e'r-dusted.' Wilde may be thinking of the phrase's own status as an 'ordinary platitude' rather than the irony of its original context.

SIR ROBERT CHILTERN
    Pay me!
MRS CHEVELEY   745
    Yes.
SIR ROBERT CHILTERN
    I am afraid I don't quite understand what you mean.
MRS CHEVELEY (*Leaning back on the sofa and looking at him*)
    How very disappointing! And I have come all the way from   750
    Vienna in order that you should thoroughly understand me.
SIR ROBERT CHILTERN
    I fear I don't.
MRS CHEVELEY (*In her most nonchalant manner*)
    My dear Sir Robert, you are a man of the world, and you have   755
    your price, I suppose. Everybody has nowadays. The draw-
    back is that most people are so dreadfully expensive. I know I
    am. I hope you will be more reasonable in your terms.
SIR ROBERT CHILTERN (*Rises indignantly*)
    If you will allow me, I will call your carriage for you. You have   760
    lived so long abroad, Mrs Cheveley, that you seem to be unable
    to realize that you are talking to an English gentleman.
MRS CHEVELEY (*Detains him by touching his arm with her fan,
    and keeping it there while she is talking*)
    I realize that I am talking to a man who laid the foundation of   765
    his fortune by selling to a Stock Exchange speculator a Cabinet
    secret.
SIR ROBERT CHILTERN (*Biting his lip*)
    What do you mean?
MRS CHEVELEY (*Rising and facing him*)   770
    I mean that I know the real origin of your wealth and your
    career, and I have got your letter, too.
SIR ROBERT CHILTERN
    What letter?
MRS CHEVELEY (*Contemptuously*)   775
    The letter you wrote to Baron Arnheim, when you were Lord
    Radley's secretary, telling the Baron to buy Suez Canal shares –
    a letter written three days before the Government announced
    its own purchase.
SIR ROBERT CHILTERN (*Hoarsely*)   780
    It is not true.

748–55   *I am afraid . . . of the world, and* added to HTC. The s.d. in this sequence first appear
    in PR, although F indicates *'fan business'* at l. 763.

31

MRS CHEVELEY

You thought that letter had been destroyed. How foolish of
you! It is in my possession.

SIR ROBERT CHILTERN   785

The affair to which you allude was no more than a speculation.
The House of Commons had not yet passed the bill; it might
have been rejected.

MRS CHEVELEY

It was a swindle, Sir Robert. Let us call things by their proper   790
names. It makes everything simpler. And now I am going to sell
you that letter, and the price I ask for it is your public support
of the Argentine scheme. You made your own fortune out of
one canal. You must help me and my friends to make our
fortunes out of another!   795

SIR ROBERT CHILTERN

It is infamous, what you propose – infamous!

MRS CHEVELEY

Oh, no! This is the game of life as we all have to play it, Sir
Robert, sooner or later!   800

SIR ROBERT CHILTERN

I cannot do what you ask me.

MRS CHEVELEY

You mean you cannot help doing it. You know you are standing
on the edge of a precipice. And it is not for you to make terms.   805
It is for you to accept them. Supposing you refuse –

SIR ROBERT CHILTERN

What then?

MRS CHEVELEY

My dear Sir Robert, what then? You are ruined, that is all!   810
Remember to what a point your Puritanism in England has

783–4   *You thought . . . possession* in successive drafts of the lines leading up to this speech,
        Wilde tidied up the business of introducing the letter into the play: the earliest
        versions of ll. 776–9 include interesting details of Mrs C's relationship with Arnheim,
        and the means by which she obtained the incriminating evidence. Cf. Appendix I.

810–39 *My dear . . . this scheme* the principal alterations to this speech consisted in the
        removal of two passages from MS and HTC which served to amplify Sir Robert C's
        'splendid position' and the ironies of his prospective degradation. Both passages
        reached the Pbk typescript but were deleted there. In BLTS a variation on the
        material dealing with scandal was marked for cutting: on the page opposite Wilde
        noted 'Tartuffe and Caliban hounding you down together'. For the text of these
        omissions. see Appendix I In F there is considerable rearrangement: the speech is
        slightly shorter and less rhetorically mannered. Among the *scandals* of which the

brought you. In old days nobody pretended to be a bit better
than his neighbours. In fact, to be a bit better than one's
neighbour was considered excessively vulgar and middle-class.
Nowadays, with our modern mania for morality, everyone has   815
to pose as a paragon of purity, incorruptibility, and all the other
seven deadly virtues – and what is the result? You all go over
like ninepins – one after the other. Not a year passes in England
without somebody disappearing. Scandals used to lend charm,
or at least interest, to a man – now they crush him. And yours   820
is a very nasty scandal. You couldn't survive it. If it were known
that as a young man, secretary to a great and important
minister, you sold a Cabinet secret for a large sum of money,
and that that was the origin of your wealth and career, you
would be hounded out of public life, you would disappear   825
completely. And after all, Sir Robert, why should you sacrifice
your entire future rather than deal diplomatically with your
enemy? For the moment I am your enemy. I admit it! And I am
much stronger than you are. The big battalions are on my side.
You have a splendid position, but it is your splendid position   830
that makes you so vulnerable. You can't defend it! And I am in
attack. Of course I have not talked morality to you. You must
admit in fairness that I have spared you that. Years ago you did
a clever, unscrupulous thing; it turned out a great success. You
owe to it your fortune and position. And now you have got to   835
pay for it. Sooner or later we all have to pay for what we do. You
have to pay now. Before I leave you tonight, you have got to
promise me to suppress your report, and to speak in the House
in favour of this scheme.

SIR ROBERT CHILTERN   840
What you ask is impossible.

MRS CHEVELEY
You must make it possible. You are going to make it possible.
Sir Robert, you know what your English newspapers are like.
Suppose that when I leave this house I drive down to some   845
newspaper office, and give them this scandal and the proofs of
it! Think of their loathsome joy, of the delight they would have
in dragging you down, of the mud and mire they would plunge

---

speech may have reminded its first audience would have been the divorce
proceedings which in 1885 precipitated the fall of Sir Charles Dilke (1843–1911), a
brilliant statesman, once thought a potential leader of the Liberal Party.
847   *loathsome* (terrible F).

you in. Think of the hypocrite with his greasy smile penning his
leading article, and arranging the foulness of the public   850
placard.

SIR ROBERT CHILTERN

Stop! You want me to withdraw the report and to make a short
speech stating that I believe there are possibilities in the scheme?

MRS CHEVELEY (*Sitting down on the sofa*)   855

Those are my terms.

SIR ROBERT CHILTERN (*In a low voice*)

I will give you any sum of money you want.

MRS CHEVELEY

Even you are not rich enough, Sir Robert, to buy back your past.   860
No man is.

SIR ROBERT CHILTERN

I will not do what you ask me. I will not.

MRS CHEVELEY

You have to. If you don't . . .   *Rises from the sofa*   865

SIR ROBERT CHILTERN (*Bewildered and unnerved*)

Wait a moment! What did you propose? You said that you
would give me back my letter, didn't you?

MRS CHEVELEY

Yes. That is agreed. I will be in the Ladies' Gallery tomorrow   870
night at half-past eleven. If by that time – and you will have
had heaps of opportunity – you have made an announcement
to the House in the terms I wish, I shall hand you back your
letter with the prettiest thanks, and the best, or at any rate the
most suitable, compliment I can think of. I intend to play quite   875
fairly with you. One should always play fairly . . . when one has
the winning cards. The Baron taught me that . . . amongst other
things.

SIR ROBERT CHILTERN

You must let me have time to consider your proposal.   880

MRS CHEVELEY

No; you must settle now!

---

849   *greasy* (oily F). In BLTS Wilde tried 'cunning' but did not adopt it subsequently.

856   *Those are my terms* MS and HTC have a shorter version of the sequence following,
       in which ll. 858–93 are omitted ('*I will give you . . . on the subject*'). These lines were
       added to Pbk and adopted in the C typescript.

870–8 *I will be . . . amongst other things* first appears in PR. A separate *Ladies' Gallery*, with
       a grille in front of it, was provided above the Press Gallery in the House of
       Commons.

SIR ROBERT CHILTERN

Give me a week – three days!

MRS CHEVELEY 885

Impossible! I have got to telegraph to Vienna tonight.

SIR ROBERT CHILTERN

My God! what brought you into my life?

MRS CHEVELEY

Circumstances. *Moves towards the door* 890

SIR ROBERT CHILTERN

Don't go. I consent. The report shall be withdrawn. I will arrange
for a question to be put to me on the subject.

MRS CHEVELEY

Thank you. I knew we should come to an amicable agreement. 895
I understood your nature from the first. I analyzed you, though
you did not adore me. And now you can get my carriage for
me, Sir Robert. I see the people coming up from supper, and
Englishmen always get romantic after a meal, and that bores me
dreadfully. 900

Exit SIR ROBERT CHILTERN

Enter GUESTS, LADY CHILTERN, LADY MARKBY,
LORD CAVERSHAM, LADY BASILDON, MRS MARCHMONT,
VICOMTE DE NANJAC, MR MONTFORD

LADY MARKBY 905

Well, dear Mrs Cheveley, I hope you have enjoyed yourself. Sir
Robert is very entertaining, is he not?

MRS CHEVELEY

Most entertaining! I have enjoyed my talk with him immensely.

LADY MARKBY 910

He has had a very interesting and brilliant career. And he has

---

888–90 *My God! . . . Circumstances* first appears in PR.

892–3   *I will . . . subject* first appears in PR. Wilde is specifying the appropriate parliamentary
procedure: a question from his own side of the house will be set up to facilitate his
making a statement.

896–7   *I understood . . . adore me* first appears in additions to Pbk. The second sentence is
omitted in F. The opposition *analyse/adore* is a characteristic Wildean contrast of
pseudo-scientific detachment (as in Lord G's 'psychological experiments') and its
most extreme contrary: cf. ll. 254–5, above ('To attempt to classify you, Mrs Cheveley
would be an impertinence').

898–900 *I see . . . dreadfully* first appears in PR, where 'Englishmen' has been altered in
manuscript from 'English people' and 'dreadfully' has been added.

911   *He has had . . . career* in MS and HTC Lady Markby gives further details of his

married a most admirable wife. Lady Chiltern is a woman
of the very highest principles, I am glad to say. I am a little too
old now, myself, to trouble about setting a good example, but I
always admire people who do. And Lady Chiltern has a very   915
ennobling effect on life, though her dinner-parties are rather
dull sometimes. But one can't have everything, can one? And
now I must go, dear. Shall I call for you tomorrow?

MRS CHEVELEY

Thanks.   920

LADY MARKBY

We might drive in the Park at five. Everything looks so fresh in
the Park now!

MRS CHEVELEY

Except the people!   925

LADY MARKBY

Perhaps the people are a little jaded. I have often observed that
the Season as it goes on produces a kind of softening of the
brain. However, I think anything is better than high intellectual
pressure. That is the most unbecoming thing there is. It makes   930
the noses of the young girls so particularly large. And there
is nothing so difficult to marry as a large nose, men don't
like them. Good-night dear! (*To* LADY CHILTERN) Good-night,
Gertrude!

                                       Goes out on LORD CAVERSHAM's *arm*   935

MRS CHEVELEY

What a charming house you have, Lady Chiltern! I have spent
a delightful evening. It has been so interesting getting to know
your husband.

> background: see Appendix I. The passage is deleted from HTC and does not
> reappear. In alterations to Pbk (and in C) *career* is followed by 'And his philanthropy,
> of course, is very well known'. F provides s.d. for Lady C to be busy upstage, shaking
> hands with departing guests during this conversation.
>
> 917–18 *And now . . . dear* MS and HTC include here the passage concerning Blue Books
> subsequently transferred to II, 846, etc. The lines are deleted in HTC.
>
> 922 *the Park* i.e. Hyde Park (cf. note to l. 79).
>
> 932 *so difficult to many* i.e. dispose of in marriage, the preoccupation of mothers during
> the Season. The claim that intellectual development made women ugly was
> commonplace in anti-feminist propaganda and humour. An idiosyncratic specimen
> occurs in the MS of *Earnest*: 'She is one of those dull, intellectual girls one meets all
> over the place. Girls who have got large minds and large feet' (I, 667–8, note). Cf. ll.
> 1000–3, where Mabel complains that pearls make one look 'so plain, so good and so
> intellectual'. The play on physical plainness and moral worth occurs a number of
> times in *LWF*.

LADY CHILTERN   940
 Why did you wish to meet my husband, Mrs Cheveley?
MRS CHEVELEY
 Oh, I will tell you. I wanted to interest him in this Argentine
 Canal scheme, of which I dare say you have heard. And I found
 him most susceptible, – susceptible to reason, I mean. A rare   945
 thing in a man. I converted him in ten minutes. He is going to
 make a speech in the House tomorrow night in favour of the
 idea. We must go to the Ladies' Gallery and hear him! It will be
 a great occasion!
LADY CHILTERN   950
 There must be some mistake. That scheme could never have my
 husband's support.
MRS CHEVELEY
 Oh, I assure you it's all settled. I don't regret my tedious journey
 from Vienna now. It has been a great success. But, of course, for 955
 the next twenty-four hours the whole thing is a dead secret.
LADY CHILTERN (*Gently*)
 A secret? Between whom?
MRS CHEVELEY (*With a flash of amusement in her eyes*)
 Between your husband and myself.   960
SIR ROBERT CHILTERN (*Entering*)
 Your carriage is here, Mrs Cheveley!
MRS CHEVELEY
 Thanks! Good evening, Lady Chiltern! Good-night, Lord
 Goring! I am at Claridge's. Don't you think you might leave a   965
 card?
LORD GORING
 If you wish it, Mrs Cheveley!
MRS CHEVELEY
 Oh, don't be so solemn about it, or I shall be obliged to leave 970
 a card on you. In England I suppose that would be hardly
 considered *en règle*. Abroad, we are more civilized. Will you see

941–52   *Why did you wish . . . support* MS and HTC have a longer version of this dialogue,
          marked for deletion in the Pbk typescript.
954–60   *I don't regret . . . myself* the full version, with the insulting reference to a secret held
          in common with Sir Robert, does not appear until PR.
   965   *Claridge's* fashionable hotel in Brook Street, Mayfair.
971–2   *In England . . . civilized* first appears in alterations to BLTS, in a slightly different
          form: 'I suppose in England that would be considered most improper. In Vienna we
          are more civilized'. As printed, the line does not appear until PR. Mrs C is, of course,
          correct in assuming that it is contrary to etiquette for a lady to leave her card on a
          gentleman without first having received the courtesy from him.

me down, Sir Robert? Now that we have both the same interests at heart we shall be great friends, I hope!

Sails out on SIR ROBERT CHILTERN'*s arm*   975

LADY CHILTERN *goes to the top of the staircase and looks down at them as they descend. Her expression is troubled. After a little time she is joined by some of the guests, and passes with them into another reception-room*

MABEL CHILTERN   980
What a horrid woman!
LORD GORING
You should go to bed, Miss Mabel.
MABEL CHILTERN
Lord Goring!   985
LORD GORING
My father told me to go to bed an hour ago. I don't see why I shouldn't give you the same advice. I always pass on good advice. It is the only thing to do with it. It is never of any use to oneself.   990
MABEL CHILTERN
Lord Goring, you are always ordering me out of the room. I think it most courageous of you. Especially as I am not going to bed for hours. (*Goes over to the sofa*) You can come and sit down if you like, and talk about anything in the world, except   995
the Royal Academy, Mrs Cheveley, or novels in Scotch dialect. They are not improving subjects. (*Catches sight of something that is lying on the sofa half-hidden by the cushion*) What is this? Someone has dropped a diamond brooch! Quite beautiful, isn't it? (*Shows it to him*) I wish it was mine, but Gertrude won't   1000
let me wear anything but pearls, and I am thoroughly sick of

---

975   s.d. *Sails* altered in manuscript from 'Goes' in PR. In LC, etc., the s.d. is simply *'Exit'* without any of the detail supplied for the first time in PR.

989–90 *It is never . . . oneself* first appears in PR. F (following manuscript alterations to BLTS) reads 'I am not a bit selfish about it'.

993   *courageous* (rude LC, BLTS, C; foolish F and alterations to BLTS).

993–1036 *Especially . . . goodnight* this sequence, including the discovery of the brooch, does not appear in LC or earlier versions, except for some additions to BLTS. P gives a version slightly different to that printed in PR and 1st Ed.

996   *The Royal Academy* the Royal Academy of Arts, with its annual exhibitions of work by members, had come to represent the 'establishment'.
       Novels in Scotch dialect: in the MS draft of the dictation scene in *Earnest* (II, 439 etc.), Cecily tells Algernon not to cough because she, does not know how to spell a cough, although it is done 'by realistic novelists who write in horrid dialect'.

pearls. They make one look so plain, so good and so intellectual. I wonder whom the brooch belongs to.

LORD GORING

I wonder who dropped it.   1005

MABEL CHILTERN

It is a beautiful brooch.

LORD GORING

It is a handsome bracelet.

MABEL CHILTERN   1010

It isn't a bracelet. It's a brooch.

LORD GORING

It can be used as a bracelet.

> *Takes it from her, and pulling out a green letter-case, puts*
> *the ornament carefully in it, and replaces the whole thing*   1015
> *in his breast-pocket with the most perfect sangfroid*

MABEL CHILTERN

What are you doing?

LORD GORING

Miss Mabel, I am going to make a rather strange request to you.   1020

MABEL CHILTERN (*Eagerly*)

Oh, pray do! I have been waiting for it all the evening.

LORD GORING (*Is a little taken aback, but recovers himself*)

Don't mention to anybody that I have taken charge of this
brooch. Should anyone write and claim it, let me know at once.   1025

MABEL CHILTERN

That is a strange request.

LORD GORING

Well, you see I gave this brooch to somebody once, years ago.

MABEL CHILTERN   1030

You did?

LORD GORING

Yes.

> LADY CHILTERN *enters alone. The other guests have gone*

MABEL CHILTERN   1035

Then I shall certainly bid you good-night. Good-night,
Gertrude!   *Exit*

1016   s.d. *with . . . sangfroid* added to PR. The s.d. at ll. 1021, 1023, 1033 were added in the
same way: Wilde evidently did not feel the necessity of guiding the reader's
visualization of the scene until he saw it in print.

LADY CHILTERN

    Good-night, dear! (*To* LORD GORING) You saw whom Lady
Markby brought here tonight. 1040

LORD GORING

    Yes. It was an unpleasant surprise. What did she come here for?

LADY CHILTERN

    Apparently to try and lure Robert to uphold some fraudulent
scheme in which she is interested. The Argentine Canal, in fact. 1045

LORD GORING

    She has mistaken her man, hasn't she?

LADY CHILTERN

    She is incapable of understanding an upright nature like my
husband's! 1050

LORD GORING

    Yes. I should fancy she came to grief if she tried to get Robert
into her toils. It is extraordinary what astounding mistakes
clever women make.

LADY CHILTERN 1055

    I don't call women of that kind clever. I call them stupid!

LORD GORING

    Same thing often. Good-night, Lady Chiltern!

LADY CHILTERN

    Good-night! 1060

              Enter SIR ROBERT CHILTERN

SIR ROBERT CHILTERN

    My dear Arthur, you are not going? Do stop a little!

LORD GORING

    Afraid I can't, thanks. I have promised to look in at the 1065
Hartlocks'. I believe they have got a mauve Hungarian band
that plays mauve Hungarian music. See you soon. Good-bye!
                              Exit

SIR ROBERT CHILTERN

    How beautiful you look tonight, Gertrude! 1070

1066–7 *I believe . . . music* first appears in PR. *Hungarian* (usually, gypsy) bands enjoyed a
vogue at the time. The notion of *mauve* music is a comic application of the
contention that the terms of one sense should be used to describe the sensations of
another. For a serious use of it, cf. 'The Critic as Artist', Part I: 'Let me play to you
some mad scarlet thing by Dvorak' (*Intentions*, p. 115/*CW*, p. 1015).

   1070 *How beautiful you look* in LC and earlier versions the opening gambit is weaker:
'Perfectly lovely the flowers . . . ' (F and alterations to BLTS have a variant on the
line as printed).

LADY CHILTERN

    Robert, it is not true, is it? You are not going to lend your support to this Argentine speculation? You couldn't!

SIR ROBERT CHILTERN (*Starting*)

    Who told you I intended to do so? 1075

LADY CHILTERN

    That woman who has just gone out, Mrs Cheveley, as she calls herself now. She seemed to taunt me with it. Robert, I know this woman. You don't. We were at school together. She was untruthful, dishonest, an evil influence on everyone whose 1080 trust or friendship she could win. I hated, I despised her. She stole things, she was a thief. She was sent away for being a thief. Why do you let her influence you?

SIR ROBERT CHILTERN

    Gertrude, what you tell me may be true, but it happened many 1085 years ago. It is best forgotten! Mrs Cheveley may have changed since then. No one should be entirely judged by their past.

LADY CHILTERN (*Sadly*)

    One's past is what one is. It is the only way by which people should be judged. 1090

SIR ROBERT CHILTERN

    That is a hard saying, Gertrude!

LADY CHILTERN

    It is a true saying, Robert. And what did she mean by boasting that she had got you to lend your support, your name to a thing 1095 I have heard you describe as the most dishonest and fraudulent scheme there has ever been in political life?

SIR ROBERT CHILTERN (*Biting his lip*)

    I was mistaken in the view I took. We all may make mistakes.

LADY CHILTERN 1100

    But you told me yesterday that you had received the report from the Commission, and that it entirely condemned the whole thing.

SIR ROBERT CHILTERN (*Walking up and down*)

    I have reasons now to believe that the Commission was 1105

1081–2   *She stole things* MS and HTC include more details of the crime. Mrs C, when a young girl, was present at a house party when money and jewels were stolen from Lady C's room. A servant was blamed and dismissed on account of it, but Lady C later extracted a confession (in writing) from Mrs C. In early versions of the play Wilde used this 'confession' as the means by which Lord G defeated Mrs C's blackmail of Sir Robert. The passage was deleted from HTC typescript.

1089–90 *One's past . . . judged* first appears in PR.

prejudiced, or, at any rate, misinformed. Besides, Gertrude, public and private life are different things. They have different laws, and move on different lines.

LADY CHILTERN

They should both represent man at his highest. I see no dif-   1110
ference between them.

SIR ROBERT CHILTERN (*Stopping*)

In the present case, on a matter of practical politics, I have changed my mind. That is all.

LADY CHILTERN   1115

All!

SIR ROBERT CHILTERN (*Sternly*)

Yes!

LADY CHILTERN

Robert! Oh! it is horrible that I should have to ask you such a   1120
question – Robert, are you telling me the whole truth?

SIR ROBERT CHILTERN

Why do you ask me such a question?

LADY CHILTERN (*After a pause*)

Why do you not answer it?   1125

SIR ROBERT CHILTERN (*Sitting down*)

Gertrude, truth is a very complex thing, and politics is a very complex business. There are wheels within wheels. One may be under certain obligations to people that one must pay. Sooner or later in political life one has to compromise. Everyone does.   1130

LADY CHILTERN

Compromise? Robert, why do you talk so differently tonight from the way I have always heard you talk? Why are you changed?

SIR ROBERT CHILTERN   1135

I am not changed. But circumstances alter things.

LADY CHILTERN

Circumstances should never alter principles!

SIR ROBERT CHILTERN

But if I told you –   1140

LADY CHILTERN

What?

1106–18 *Besides . . . Yes!* this sequence, with its important distinctions between public and
private life, ideals and 'practical politics', does not appear until C.
1127–8 *a very complex business* the phrase was established after some difficulty. MS and HTC
read 'a very difficult complex business' changed in alterations to HTC to 'a very
vague complex business.'

SIR ROBERT CHILTERN
That it was necessary, vitally necessary.

LADY CHILTERN   1145
It can never be necessary to do what is not honourable. Or if it
be necessary, then what is it that I have loved! But it is not,
Robert; tell me it is not. Why should it be? What gain would
you get? Money? We have no need of that! And money that
comes from a tainted source is a degradation. Power? But   1150
power is nothing in itself. It is power to do good that is fine –
that, and that only. What is it, then? Robert, tell me why
you are going to do this dishonourable thing!

SIR ROBERT CHILTERN
Gertrude, you have no right to use that word. I told you it was   1155
a question of rational compromise. It is no more than that.

LADY CHILTERN
Robert, that is all very well for other men, for men who treat life
simply as a sordid speculation; but not for you, Robert, not for
you. You are different. All your life you have stood apart from   1160
others. You have never let the world soil you. To the world, as to
myself, you have been an ideal always. Oh! be that ideal still.
That great inheritance throw not away – that tower of ivory
do not destroy. Robert, men can love what is beneath them –
things unworthy, stained, dishonoured. We women worship   1165
when we love; and when we lose our worship, we lose everything. Oh! don't kill my love for you, don't kill that!

SIR ROBERT CHILTERN
Gertrude!

LADY CHILTERN   1170
I know that there are men with horrible secrets in their lives –
men who have done some shameful thing, and who in some
critical moment have to pay for it, by doing some other act

1147   *what is it that I have loved!* LC and earlier versions have 'What a thing have I loved!',
        recalling perhaps the exclamation of the painter Hallward when he learns the secret
        of Dorian Gray's double life (*DG*, p. 157/*CW*, p. 122): 'Christ! what a thing I must
        have worshipped!'
1150   *degradation* MS, HTC and Pbk add 'I know you too well to think that one can't love
        a man for ten years as I have loved you, without knowing him well' (del. from Pbk).
1152   *What is it then?* F indicates a pause after this.
1163–4 *That great . . . destroy* like Mrs Arbuthnot and Hester Worsley, Lady C falls at
        moments of crisis into a 'scriptural' mode of speech. F om. this sentence, perhaps
        reflecting stage practice. The final speeches of the scene underwent only minor
        revisions between MS and publication.

of shame – oh! don't tell me you are such as they are! Robert,
is there in your life any secret dishonour or disgrace? Tell me, 1175
tell me at once, that –

SIR ROBERT CHILTERN

That what?

LADY CHILTERN (*Speaking very slowly*)

That our lives may drift apart. 1180

SIR ROBERT CHILTERN

Drift apart?

LADY CHILTERN

That they may be entirely separate. It would be better for us
both. 1185

SIR ROBERT CHILTERN

Gertrude, there is nothing in my past life that you might not
know.

LADY CHILTERN

I was sure of it, Robert, I was sure of it. But why did you say 1190
those dreadful things, things so unlike your real self? Don't let
us ever talk about the subject again. You will write, won't you,
to Mrs Cheveley, and tell her that you cannot support this scan-
dalous scheme of hers? If you have given her any promise you
must take it back, that is all! 1195

SIR ROBERT CHILTERN

Must I write and tell her that?

LADY CHILTERN

Surely, Robert! What else is there to do?

SIR ROBERT CHILTERN 1200

I might see her personally. It would be better.

LADY CHILTERN

You must never see her again, Robert. She is not a woman you
should ever speak to. She is not worthy to talk to a man like
you. No; you must write to her at once, now, this moment, and 1205
let your letter show her that your decision is quite irrevocable!

SIR ROBERT CHILTERN

Write this moment!

1180   *drift apart* in MS, HTC and Pbk she speaks more frankly of 'leaving' him. The
       alterations to Pbk that result in this vaguer threat may be designed to protect Lady
       C from the imputation of a reprehensible public breach with her husband. F, which
       om. ll. 1175–85 ('that – . . . us both'), is even less specific.
1206   *irrevocable* F cuts to l. 1214 ('She must know'), removing the additional
       prevarication.

44

LADY CHILTERN

Yes.   1210

SIR ROBERT CHILTERN

But it is so late. It is close on twelve.

LADY CHILTERN

That makes no matter. She must know at once that she has been
mistaken in you – and that you are not a man to do anything   1215
base or underhand or dishonourable. Write here, Robert. Write
that you decline to support this scheme of hers, as you hold it
to be a dishonest scheme. Yes – write the word dishonest. She
knows what that word means. (SIR ROBERT CHILTERN *sits
down and writes a letter. His wife takes it up and reads it*) Yes;   1220
that will do. (*Rings bell*) And now the envelope. (*He writes the
envelope slowly. Enter* MASON) Have this letter sent at once to
Claridge's Hotel. There is no answer. (*Exit* MASON. LADY
CHILTERN *kneels down beside her husband and puts her arms
round him*) Robert, love gives one a sort of instinct to things. I   1225
feel tonight that I have saved you from something that might
have been a danger to you, from something that might have
made men honour you less than they do. I don't think you realize
sufficiently, Robert, that you have brought into the political life
of our time a nobler atmosphere, a finer attitude towards life, a   1230
freer air of purer aims and higher ideals – I know it, and for that
I love you, Robert.

SIR ROBERT CHILTERN

Oh, love me always, Gertrude, love me always!

LADY CHILTERN   1235

I will love you always, because you will always be worthy of
love. We needs must love the highest when we see it!

1216–19 *Write that you decline . . . means* first appears in C.
1230–1 *a freer . . . ideals* om. F.
  1237 *We needs . . . when we see it!* om. F. Cf. the lament of the guilty Queen in Tennyson's
        'Guinevere' (*Idylls of the King*, 1854):
              It was my duty to have loved the highest:
              It surely was my profit had I known:
              It would have been my pleasure had I seen.
              We needs must love the highest when we see it.
              Not Lancelot, nor another.
        In these lines 'the highest' is King Arthur, described earlier in terms not inappro-
        priate to Sir Robert Chiltern: he is 'cold, / High, self-contain'd, and passionless' and
        has the 'pure severity of perfect light'.

Kisses him and rises and goes out. SIR ROBERT CHILTERN
*walks up and down for a moment; then sits down and
buries his face in his hands. The* SERVANT *enters and begins*   1240
putting out the lights. SIR ROBERT CHILTERN *looks up*

SIR ROBERT CHILTERN
Put out the lights, Mason, put out the lights!

The SERVANT *puts out the lights. The room becomes
almost dark. The only light there is comes from the*   1245
*great chandelier that hangs over the staircase
and illumines the tapestry of the Triumph of Love*

ACT-DROP

1243   *Put out . . . the lights!* perhaps reminiscent of Othello's 'Put out the light, and then
          put out the light' as he prepares to kill Desdemona (*Othello*, V.ii).
1245–7 s.d. *The only . . . 'Triumph of Love'* first appears in PR. F indicates 'lights down at
          back'.

ACT II

Scene – Morning-room at SIR ROBERT CHILTERN's *house*

LORD GORING, *dressed in the height of fashion, is lounging
in an armchair.* SIR ROBERT CHILTERN *is standing in front
of the fireplace. He is evidently in a state of great mental
excitement and distress. As the scene progresses he paces
nervously up and down the room*

LORD GORING

My dear Robert, it's a very awkward business, very awkward
indeed. You should have told your wife the whole thing. Secrets
from other people's wives are a necessary luxury in modern life.
So, at least, I am always told at the club by people who are bald
enough to know better. But no man should have a secret from
his own wife. She invariably finds it out. Women have a wonderful instinct about things. They can discover everything except
the obvious.

SIR ROBERT CHILTERN

Arthur, I couldn't tell my wife. When could I have told her? Not
last night. It would have made a life-long separation between
us, and I would have lost the love of the one woman in the
world I worship, of the only woman who has ever stirred love
within me. Last night it would have been quite impossible.

---

1   s.d. the full version of the s.d. first appears in PR: earlier texts simply indicate the
location and the discovery of the characters.
11–12   *So . . . know better* first appears in PR. Another play on the notion of 'the tyrany of
youth'. In BLTS the preceding sentence is deleted.
13–15   *Women . . . obvious* first appears in MS2.
18–21   *It would have made . . . quite impossible* om. MS1, which has 'She would have left
me' and the following exchange:

> LORD GORING
> Left you?
> SIR ROBERT
> Yes.
> LORD GORING
> Are you serious?

In MS2 the last line is 'Are you serious when you talk of a lifelong separation?' The
passage was given an approximation of its present form in the typescript of C. Cf.
the similar changes noted at the end of Act I (ll. 1180 etc.).

She would have turned from me in horror . . . in horror and in contempt.

LORD GORING
Is Lady Chiltern as perfect as all that?   25

SIR ROBERT CHILTERN
Yes; my wife is as perfect as all that.

LORD GORING (*Taking off his left-hand glove*)
What a pity! I beg your pardon, my dear fellow, I didn't quite mean that. But if what you tell me is true, I should like to have   30
a serious talk about life with Lady Chiltern.

SIR ROBERT CHILTERN
It would be quite useless.

LORD GORING
May I try?   35

SIR ROBERT CHILTERN
Yes; but nothing could make her alter her views.

LORD GORING
Well, at the worst it would simply be a psychological experiment.   40

SIR ROBERT CHILTERN
All such experiments are terribly dangerous.

LORD GORING
Everything is dangerous, my dear fellow. If it wasn't so, life wouldn't be worth living . . . Well, I am bound to say that I think   45
you should have told her years ago.

SIR ROBERT CHILTERN
When? When we were engaged? Do you think she would have married me if she had known that the origin of my fortune is such as it is, the basis of my career such as it is, and that I had   50
done a thing that I suppose most men would call shameful and dishonourable?

LORD GORING (*Slowly*)
Yes; most men would call it ugly names. There is no doubt of that.   55

22–23   *She . . . contempt* the first part of the sentence first appears in F, following an alteration to BLTS; the second in PR.

25–46   *Is Lady Chiltern . . . years ago* om. MS 1, MS2. A version of these lines first appears in C.

39–42   *Well, . . . dangerous* Wilde added to C a version of the exchange found in F, LC and BLTS: 'It would be quite a psychological experiment – Those experiments don't succeed with women'.

44–45   *Everything . . . living* first appears in PR.

SIR ROBERT CHILTERN (*Bitterly*)

Men who every day do something of the same kind themselves.
Men who, each one of them, have worse secrets in their own
lives.

LORD GORING   60

That is the reason they are so pleased to find out other people's
secrets. It distracts public attention from their own.

SIR ROBERT CHILTERN

And, after all, whom did I wrong by what I did? No one.

LORD GORING (*Looking at him steadily*)   65

Except yourself, Robert.

SIR ROBERT CHILTERN (*After a pause*)

Of course I had private information about a certain transaction
contemplated by the Government of the day, and I acted on it.
Private information is practically the source of every large   70
modern fortune.

LORD GORING (*Tapping his boot with his cane*)

And public scandal invariably the result.

SIR ROBERT CHILTERN (*Pacing up and down the room*)

Arthur, do you think that what I did nearly eighteen years ago   75
should be brought up against me now? Do you think it fair that
a man's whole career should be ruined for a fault done in one's
boyhood almost? I was twenty-two at the time, and I had the
double misfortune of being well-born and poor, two unforgiv-
able things nowadays. Is it fair that the folly, the sin of one's   80
youth, if men choose to call it a sin, should wreck a life like
mine, should place me in the pillory, should shatter all that I
have worked for, all that I have built up? Is it fair, Arthur?

LORD GORING

Life is never fair, Robert. And perhaps it is a good thing for   85
most of us that it is not.

---

57   *of the same kind* (infinitely worse C, MS2, MS1). The published phrase is added to C.
     themselves after this all versions before PR add an interjection by Lord G: 'That is why
     they know about it so well'. Lines 61–2 ('That is . . . their own') were added in MS2.

67   s.d. this and most of the other s.d. in this scene first appear in PR. In F there are
     notes for the placing of the characters on stage.

75   *nearly eighteen* (om. F). This fixes the time of the action as early 1893 (the Suez
     transaction took place in November 1875).

76–8   *Do you . . . almost* (om. F).

78–83   *I was twenty-two . . . Arthur?* first appears in MS2. The omission of Lady M's speech
        (in MS1 of Act I) on Chiltern's background makes this addition useful.

85–6   *And perhaps . . . not* first appears in MS2.

SIR ROBERT CHILTERN

Every man of ambition has to fight his century with its own weapons. What this century worships is wealth. The God of this century is wealth. To succeed one must have wealth. At all costs one must have wealth. 90

LORD GORING

You underrate yourself, Robert. Believe me, without wealth you could have succeeded just as well.

SIR ROBERT CHILTERN 95

When I was old, perhaps. When I had lost my passion for power, or could not use it. When I was tired, worn out, disappointed. I wanted my success when I was young. Youth is the time for success. I couldn't wait.

LORD GORING 100

Well, you certainly have had your success while you are still young. No one in our day has had such a brilliant success. Under-Secretary for Foreign Affairs at the age of forty – that's good enough for anyone, I should think.

SIR ROBERT CHILTERN 105

And if it is all taken away from me now? If I lose everything over a horrible scandal? If I am hounded from public life?

LORD GORING

Robert, how could you have sold yourself for money?

SIR ROBERT CHILTERN (*Excitedly*) 110

I did not sell myself for money. I bought success at a great price. That is all.

LORD GORING (*Gravely*)

Yes; you certainly paid a great price for it. But what first made you think of doing such a thing? 115

SIR ROBERT CHILTERN

Baron Arnheim.

LORD GORING

Damned scoundrel!

89–91   *The God . . . wealth* first appears in MS2.
96–128   *When I was old . . . the whole thing* first appears in MS2.
103–4   *Under-Secretary . . . I should think* first appears in PR. MS2, BLTS add 'My father is always holding you up to me as a model' (del. in C).
106–7   *over a horrible scandal* (om. LC, C, MS1, MS2). Added to BLTS typescript.

SIR ROBERT CHILTERN   120
  No; he was a man of a most subtle and refined intellect. A man
  of culture, charm, and distinction. One of the most intellectual
  men I ever met.
LORD GORING
  Ah! I prefer a gentlemanly fool any day. There is more to be   125
  said for stupidity than people imagine. Personally I have a great
  admiration for stupidity. It is a sort of fellow-feeling, I suppose.
  But how did he do it? Tell me the whole thing.
SIR ROBERT CHILTERN (*Throws himself into an armchair by the*
  writing-table)   130
  One night after dinner at Lord Radley's the Baron began talking
  about success in modern life as something that one could
  reduce to an absolutely definite science. With that wonderfully
  fascinating quiet voice of his he expounded to us the most
  terrible of all philosophies, the philosophy of power, preached 135
  to us the most marvellous of all gospels, the gospel of gold.
  I think he saw the effect he had produced on me, for some days
  afterwards he wrote and asked me to come and see him. He was
  living then in Park Lane, in the house Lord Woolcomb has now.
  I remember so well how, with a strange smile on his pale curved 140
  lips, he led me through his wonderful picture gallery, showed
  me his tapestries, his enamels, his jewels, his carved ivories,
  made me wonder at the strange loveliness of the luxury in
  which he lived; and then told me that luxury was nothing but a
  background, a painted scene in a play, and that power, power   145
  over other men, power over the world was the one thing worth
  having, the one supreme pleasure worth knowing, the one joy
  one never tired of, and that in our century only the rich
  possessed it.
LORD GORING (*With great deliberation*)   150
  A thoroughly shallow creed.
SIR ROBERT CHILTERN (*Rising*)
  I didn't think so then. I don't think so now. Wealth has given me
  enormous power. It gave me at the very outset of my life
  freedom, and freedom is everything. You have never been poor,   155

121–2   *A man of culture, charm and distinction* first appears in PR.
125–7   *a gentlemanly* first appears in PR (an honest LC etc.). *There . . . I suppose* first appears
        in PR: in C and MS2 the first sentence of the speech is followed by 'I am a little out
        of date' (del. from C, om. BLTS). F om. the first four sentences of the speech
        altogether.
131–49 *One night after dinner . . . possessed it.* See Appendix I.

and never known what ambition is. You cannot understand what a wonderful chance the Baron gave me. Such a chance as few men get.

LORD GORING

Fortunately for them, if one is to judge by results. But tell me 160
definitely, how did the Baron finally persuade you to – well, to do what you did?

SIR ROBERT CHILTERN

When I was going away he said to me that if I ever could give him any private information of real value he would make 165
me a very rich man. I was dazed at the prospect he held out to me, and my ambition and my desire for power were at that time boundless. Six weeks later certain private documents passed through my hands.

LORD GORING (*Keeping his eyes steadily fixed on the carpet*) 170
State documents?

SIR ROBERT CHILTERN

Yes.

LORD GORING *sighs, then passes his hand across his forehead*
and looks up 175

LORD GORING

I had no idea that you, of all men in the world, could have been so weak, Robert, as to yield to such a temptation as Baron Arnheim held out to you.

SIR ROBERT CHILTERN 180

Weak? Oh, I am sick of hearing that phrase. Sick of using it about others. Weak? Do you really think, Arthur, that it is weakness that yields to temptation? I tell you that there are terrible temptations that it requires strength, strength and courage, to yield to. To stake all one's life on a single moment, 185
to risk everything on one throw, whether the stake be power or pleasure, I care not – there is no weakness in that. There is a horrible, a terrible courage. I had that courage. I sat down the same afternoon and wrote Baron Arnheim the letter this

171–83   *State . . . I tell you* LC om. this and the two speeches following, and leads into l. 183
with 'I know that people always say that to yield to temptation is weak and shows
weakness. I don't think so. I think . . . '. The same arrangement is found in C and
BLTS. In F Chiltern's speech at 164–9 ('When . . . hands') is followed by 'I sat down
the same afternoon . . .' and ll. 176–88 ('I had no idea . . . terrible courage') are trans-
posed to follow l. 207 ('our prayers'). The final version does not emerge until PR.

woman now holds. He made three-quarters of a million over   190
the transaction.

LORD GORING
And you?

SIR ROBERT CHILTERN
I received from the Baron £110,000.   195

LORD GORING
You were worth more, Robert.

SIR ROBERT CHILTERN
No; that money gave me exactly what I wanted, power over
others. I went into the House immediately. The Baron advised   200
me in finance from time to time. Before five years I had almost
trebled my fortune. Since then everything that I have touched
has turned out a success. In all things connected with money
I have had a luck so extraordinary that sometimes it has made
me almost afraid. I remember having read somewhere, in some   205
strange book, that when the gods wish to punish us they answer
our prayers.

LORD GORING
But tell me, Robert, did you never suffer any regret for what you
had done?   210

SIR ROBERT CHILTERN
No. I felt that I had fought the century with its own weapons,
and won.

190   *three-quarters of a million* 1st ed., PR (a quarter of a million LC etc.).
195   *£110,000* 1st ed., PR (£85,000 LC, BLTS, C; £35,000 MS2; £50,000 MS1). Reviews of
      the first production specify C's profit as £85,000: the omission of the line in F
      suggests that it does not constitute a faithful transcript of the play as performed in
      London.
199–200   *power over others* 1st ed., PR (om. F; freedom of action LC; freedom of action,
      security of position and power over others BLTS, C, MS2). The first two reasons are
      deleted from BLTS.
200   *I went into . . . immediately* in LC, BLTS, C and MS2 Chiltern claims 'I went into
      Parliament at once. I made a name there. I held the position I was entitled to'. The
      final four words were deleted from BLTS. In F the amended BLTS version is followed
      ('a' for 'the' in the final sentence) and in PR only the first sentence appears, with
      'Parliament' changed in manuscript to 'the House'. Here, as in ll. 199–200, Chiltern's
      character is made slightly less unsympathetic and self-assertive by the alterations.
201–7   *Before . . . prayers* first appears in MS2 (with 'good fortune' for 'luck'). MS1 reads: 'In
      two years I had doubled the £50,000. I have security at my bank now for a quarter
      of a million.' The notion of a 'strange book' and its influence turns up frequently in
      Wilde, notably in *Dorian Gray*. Yeats records in *The Trembling of the Veil* that Wilde
      spoke of Pater's *Studies in the History of the Renaissance* as 'My golden book, I never
      travel anywhere without it' (*Autobiographies*, 1955, p. 130).

LORD GORING (*Sadly*)
　　You thought you had won?　　　　　　　　　　　　　　215
SIR ROBERT CHILTERN
　　I thought so. (*After a long pause*) Arthur, do you despise me for
　　what I have told you?
LORD GORING (*With deep feeling in his voice*)
　　I am very sorry for you, Robert, very sorry indeed.　　　　220
SIR ROBERT CHILTERN
　　I don't say that I suffered any remorse. I didn't. Not remorse in
　　the ordinary, rather silly sense of the word. But I have paid con-
　　science money many times. I had a wild hope that I might disarm
　　destiny. The sum Baron Arnheim gave me I have distributed　　225
　　twice over in public charities since then.
LORD GORING (*Looking up*)
　　In public charities? Dear me! what a lot of harm you must have
　　done, Robert!
SIR ROBERT CHILTERN　　　　　　　　　　　　　　　　230
　　Oh, don't say that, Arthur; don't talk like that.
LORD GORING
　　Never mind what I say, Robert. I am always saying what I
　　shouldn't say. In fact, I usually say what I really think. A great
　　mistake nowadays. It makes one so liable to be misunderstood.　　235
　　As regards this dreadful business, I will help you in whatever
　　way I can. Of course you know that.
SIR ROBERT CHILTERN
　　Thank you, Arthur, thank you. But what is to be done? What
　　can be done?　　　　　　　　　　　　　　　　　　　240
LORD GORING (*Leaning back with his hands in his pockets*)
　　Well, the English can't stand a man who is always saying he is
　　in the right, but they are very fond of a man who admits that
　　he has been in the wrong. It is one of the best things in them.
　　However, in your case, Robert, a confession would not do.　　245
　　The money, if you will allow me to say so, is . . . awkward.
　　Besides, if you did make a clean breast of the whole affair, you
　　would never be able to talk morality again. And in England

222–37　*I don't say . . . you know that* first appears in MS2. *Not remorse* first appears in PR.
　　　　The repetition emphasizes a characteristically Wildean refusal to accept an 'ordinary,
　　　　rather silly sense' of a word.
242　　*Well . . .* in MS2 and C this word is followed by a passage marked for deletion in C
　　　　and not subsequently relocated. Cf. Appendix I.
244　　*It is . . . in them* first appears in PR.

a man who can't talk morality twice a week to a large, popular, immoral audience is quite over as a serious politician. There   250
would be nothing left for him as a profession except Botany or the Church. A confession would be of no use. It would ruin you.

SIR ROBERT CHILTERN

It would ruin me. Arthur, the only thing for me to do now is to   255
fight the thing out.

LORD GORING (*Rising from his chair*)

I was waiting for you to say that, Robert. It is the only thing to do now. And you must begin by telling your wife the whole story.   260

SIR ROBERT CHILTERN

That I will not do.

LORD GORING

Robert, believe me, you are wrong.

SIR ROBERT CHILTERN   265

I couldn't do it. It would kill her love for me. And now about this woman, this Mrs Cheveley. How can I defend myself against her? You knew her before, Arthur, apparently.

LORD GORING

Yes.   270

SIR ROBERT CHILTERN

Did you know her well?

LORD GORING (*Arranging his necktie*)

So little that I got engaged to be married to her once, when I was staying at the Tenbys'. The affair lasted for three days . . .   275
nearly.

SIR ROBERT CHILTERN

Why was it broken off?

LORD GORING (*Airily*)

Oh, I forget. At least, it makes no matter. By the way, have you   280

249–50   *a large, popular, immoral audience* the third adjective first appears in F, where the second is omitted.

250–2   *There . . . Church* the sentence first appears in MS2, with 'bimetallism' for 'botany', which first appears in an alteration to C and is adopted in LC. On *bimetallism*, cf. *Woman*, III, 206.

252–3   *It would ruin you* first appears in MS2.

255   *It would ruin me* first appears in MS2, which omits a line from MS1: 'It would be of no use and it would rob me of my wife's love. If she thought I was guilty of something like that she would never forgive me'.

262   *That I will not do.* See Appendix I.

tried her with money? She used to be confoundedly fond of
money.

SIR ROBERT CHILTERN

I offered her any sum she wanted. She refused.

LORD GORING   285

Then the marvellous gospel of gold breaks down sometimes.
The rich can't do everything, after all.

SIR ROBERT CHILTERN

Not everything. I suppose you are right. Arthur, I feel that
public disgrace is in store for me. I feel certain of it. I never   290
knew what terror was before. I know it now. It is as if a hand of
ice were laid upon one's heart. It is as if one's heart were beating
itself to death in some empty hollow.

LORD GORING (*Striking the table*)

Robert, you must fight her. You must fight her.   295

SIR ROBERT CHILTERN

But how?

LORD GORING

I can't tell you how, at present. I have not the smallest idea. But
everyone has some weak point. There is some flaw in each one   300
of us. (*Strolls over to the fireplace and looks at himself in the
glass*) My father tells me that even I have faults. Perhaps I have.
I don't know.

SIR ROBERT CHILTERN

In defending myself against Mrs Cheveley, I have a right to use   305
any weapon I can find, have I not?

LORD GORING (*Still looking in the glass*)

In your place I don't think I should have the smallest scruple in
doing so. She is thoroughly well able to take care of herself.

· 289–91   *I feel . . . I know it now* first appears in alterations to C. The 10 lines following, from
       'It is as if . . .' to 'Perhaps I have' were added to BLTS and appear in F but are absent
       in LC. In LC and BLTS Mason arrives with a letter and announces that Lord
       Berkshire is waiting for an answer. In MS2 Chiltern has already received the 'curious
       letter' intimating that Lord Berkshire wishes to tell him about 'a certain person
       whom he saw here last night of whose character he feels sure that my wife and I
       know nothing.'

    302   *Perhaps I have* added in manuscript to PR.

    308   *In your place* F reads: 'In the case of a woman who dyes her hair, sex is a challenge,
       not a defence. Personally I admire women who dye their hair. They look so well at
       a distance'. This is followed by 'I don't think she should have . . .' (l. 308).

  308–9   *in doing so* MS2, C add 'she is a bad lot, and clever as they make them, too' (del.
       in C).

SIR ROBERT CHILTERN (*Sits down at the table and takes a pen in* 310
his hand)
Well, I shall send a cipher telegram to the Embassy at Vienna,
to inquire if there is anything known against her. There may be
some secret scandal she might be afraid of.

LORD GORING (*Settling his buttonhole*) 315
Oh, I should fancy Mrs Cheveley is one of those very modern
women of our time who find a new scandal as becoming as a
new bonnet, and air them both in the Park every afternoon at
five-thirty. I am sure she adores scandals, and that the sorrow
of her life at present is that she can't manage to have enough of 320
them.

SIR ROBERT CHILTERN (*Writing*)
Why do you say that?

LORD GORING (*Turning round*)
Well, she wore far too much rouge last night, and not quite 325
enough clothes. That is always a sign of despair in a woman.

SIR ROBERT CHILTERN (*Striking a bell*)
But it is worth while my wiring to Vienna, is it not?

LORD GORING
It is always worth while asking a question, though it is not 330
always worth while answering one.

Enter MASON

SIR ROBERT CHILTERN
Is Mr Trafford in his room?

312–14 *Well . . . afraid of* first appears, in substance, in F: see note to ll. 289–91, above.
   316 *very modern* (astounding C, MS2) changed in revision of C.
   325 *Well, she wore . . .* (She is not as handsome as she used to be, but she wore . . . C, MS2).
         The beginning of the speech was changed in a manuscript alteration to C.
   328 *wiring to Vienna* LC and earlier versions have 'seeing Lord Berkshire'.
 330–1 *It is always . . . answering one* first appears in a slightly different form in F, following
         MS revision to BLTS. At this point LC, BLTS and revised state of C have the
         following:
            LORD GORING
               Certainly, show me his letter.
            SIR ROBERT
               Here! (*Hands letter.*)
            LORD GORING
               It certainly is a very curious communication. (*Hands back letter.*)
         They then proceed with l. 353 ('I will fight her to the death'). In F l. 331 is followed
         by l. 377 ('Good afternoon, Lord Goring') and then l. 436 ('You are not going,
         Robert?'). The sequence as printed first appears in PR.

MASON   335
  Yes, Sir Robert.
SIR ROBERT CHILTERN (*Puts what he has written into an envelope,
  which he then carefully closes*)
  Tell him to have this sent off in cipher at once. There must not
  be a moment's delay.   340
MASON
  Yes, Sir Robert.
SIR ROBERT CHILTERN
  Oh! just give that back to me again.
                                        Writes something on the envelope.   345
                                 MASON *then goes out with the letter*

SIR ROBERT CHILTERN
  She must have had some curious hold over Baron Arnheim.
  I wonder what it was.
LORD GORING (*Smiling*)   350
  I wonder.
SIR ROBERT CHILTERN
  I will fight her to the death, as long as my wife knows nothing.
LORD GORING (*Strongly*)
  Oh, fight in any case – in any case.   355
SIR ROBERT CHILTERN (*With a gesture of despair*)
  If my wife found out, there would be little left to fight for. Well,
  as soon as I hear from Vienna, I shall let you know the result. It
  is a chance, just a chance, but I believe in it. And as I fought the
  age with its own weapons, I will fight her with her weapons. It   360
  is only fair, and she looks like a woman with a past, doesn't she?
LORD GORING
  Most pretty women do. But there is a fashion in pasts just as
  there is a fashion in frocks. Perhaps Mrs Cheveley's past is
  merely a slightly *décolleté* one, and they are excessively popular   365
  nowadays. Besides, my dear Robert, I should not build too high
  hopes on frightening Mrs Cheveley. I should not fancy Mrs
  Cheveley is a woman who would be easily frightened. She has

---

357–74   *Well, as soon as . . . my wife's voice* om. MS1. These lines first appear in MS2. In PR
         the references to telegraphing Vienna replace allusions to Lord Berkshire's
         communication; ll. 366–70 ('I should not fancy . . . presence of mind') first appear
         in PR. In LC and earlier versions 'a slightly décolleté one' reads 'one from Paris': the
         notion of a low-cut reputation seems to have come to Wilde as he prepared copy for
         Smithers' printer.

survived all her creditors, and she shows wonderful presence
of mind.   370

SIR ROBERT CHILTERN

Oh! I live on hopes now. I clutch at every chance. I feel like a
man on a ship that is sinking. The water is round my feet, and
the very air is bitter with storm. Hush! I hear my wife's voice.

Enter LADY CHILTERN *in walking dress*   375

LADY CHILTERN

Good afternoon, Lord Goring!

LORD GORING

Good afternoon, Lady Chiltern! Have you been in the Park?

LADY CHILTERN   380

No: I have just come from the Woman's Liberal Association,
where, by the way, Robert, your name was received with loud
applause, and now I have come in to have my tea. (*To* LORD
GORING) You will wait and have some tea, won't you?

LORD GORING   385

I'll wait for a short time, thanks.

LADY CHILTERN

I will be back in a moment. I am only going to take my hat off.

LORD GORING (*In his most earnest manner*)

Oh! please don't. It is so pretty. One of the prettiest hats I ever   390
saw. I hope the Woman's Liberal Association received it with
loud applause.

LADY CHILTERN (*With a smile*)

We have much more important work to do than to look at each
other's bonnets, Lord Goring.   395

LORD GORING

Really? What sort of work?

373–4   *The water. . . Hush!* (Stop! LC, BLTS, C, MS2). The elaboration first appears in PR.
381–3   *No . . . and now* (Yes, and LC etc.). The *Woman's Liberal Association* (now Women's
        Liberal Federation) founded in 1886; opposed Gladstone in 1892 by supporting the
        campaign for women's suffrage.
  388   *I am only going . . . off* LC and earlier versions omit this and the following six
        speeches. MS1 continues with l. 436 ('Are you going, Robert?'); MS2 with ll. 436–8
        ('Thanks . . . Robert'), 409–10 ('You . . . me') and a version of 419–21 ('Ah! I get rid
        of it as soon as possible. Bad habit, by the way. Makes one very unpopular. But it
        keeps one in good condition'). A number of other transpositions and alterations are
        made in C and BLTS.

LADY CHILTERN

Oh! dull, useful, delightful things, Factory Acts, Female Inspectors, the Eight Hours' Bill, the Parliamentary Franchise . . . Everything, in fact, that you would find thoroughly uninteresting.   400

LORD GORING

And never bonnets?

LADY CHILTERN (*With mock indignation*)

Never bonnets, never!   405

> LADY CHILTERN *goes out through the door*
> *leading to her boudoir*

SIR ROBERT CHILTERN (*Takes* LORD GORING'*s hand*)

You have been a good friend to me, Arthur, a thoroughly good friend.   410

LORD GORING

I don't know that I have been able to do much for you, Robert, as yet. In fact, I have not been able to do anything for you, as far as I can see. I am thoroughly disappointed with myself.

SIR ROBERT CHILTERN   415

You have enabled me to tell you the truth. That is something. The truth has always stifled me.

LORD GORING

Ah! the truth is a thing I get rid of as soon as possible! Bad habit, by the way. Makes one very unpopular at the club . . . with   420
the older members. They call it being conceited. Perhaps it is.

SIR ROBERT CHILTERN

I would to God that I had been able to tell the truth . . . to live the truth. Ah! that is the great thing in life, to live the truth. (*Sighs, and goes towards the door*) I'll see you soon again,   425
Arthur, shan't I?

LORD GORING

Certainly. Whenever you like. I'm going to look in at the Bachelors' Ball tonight, unless I find something better to do.

---

399   *dull, useful, delightful things* the list includes matters on which the Liberal Party had pledged itself to introduce legislation in its 1892 election manifesto (the 'Newcastle Programme'): the limiting of working hours, the introduction of female inspectors to monitor the application of the Factory Acts, and the reform of the franchise.

409–10   *a thoroughly good friend* first appears in PR, together with the s.d. at the beginning of the speech.

412–31   *I don't know . . . Curzon Street* much expanded in PR from the shorter versions of the scene in F, LC etc. The most notable addition is in ll. 423–5: 'to live the truth. Ah! that is the great thing in life, to live the truth'. *Curzon Street*, a respectable Mayfair address, is also Mrs Erlynne's home in *LWF*.

But I'll come round tomorrow morning. If you should want me 430
tonight by any chance, send round a note to Curzon Street.

SIR ROBERT CHILTERN

Thank you.

As he reaches the door, LADY CHILTERN *enters from her boudoir*

LADY CHILTERN 435

You are not going, Robert?

SIR ROBERT CHILTERN

I have some letters to write, dear.

LADY CHILTERN (*Going to him*)

You work too hard, Robert. You seem never to think of yourself, 440
and you are looking so tired.

SIR ROBERT CHILTERN

It is nothing, dear, nothing.

He kisses her and goes out

LADY CHILTERN (*To* LORD GORING) 445

Do sit down. I am so glad you have called. I want to talk to you
about . . . well, not about bonnets, or the Woman's Liberal
Association. You take far too much interest in the first subject,
and not nearly enough in the second.

LORD GORING 450

You want to talk to me about Mrs Cheveley?

LADY CHILTERN

Yes. You have guessed it. After you left last night I found out
that what she had said was really true. Of course I made Robert
write her a letter at once, withdrawing his promise. 455

LORD GORING

So he gave me to understand.

LADY CHILTERN

To have kept it would have been the first stain on a career that
has been stainless always. Robert must be above reproach. He is 460
not like other men. He cannot afford to do what other men do.
(*She looks at* LORD GORING, *who remains silent*) Don't you

---

429   *the Bachelors' Ball* the London 'season' included 'private' dances, given by the parents
      of marriageable girls, and 'public' festivities, organized by associations of like-
      minded acquaintances: the Bachelors' Ball was among the latter.

436   *You . . . Robert?* F and MS1 resume at this point (see note to l. 388).

446–9 *I want . . . second* first appears in PR. In F, C, MS2 and MS1 the introduction is
      different: 'Do sit down. I am so glad to have an opportunity of a moment's talk in
      private'. This is deleted from C and does not appear in BLTS or LC. The revisions to
      BLTS include the addition of s.d., which may reflect its being used during rehearsals.

453   *You have guessed it* first appears in PR.

agree with me? You are Robert's greatest friend. You are our
greatest friend, Lord Goring. No one, except myself, knows
Robert better than you do. He has no secrets from me, and I   465
don't think he has any from you.

LORD GORING
He certainly has no secrets from me. At least I don't think so.

LADY CHILTERN
Then am I not right in my estimate of him? I know I am right.   470
But speak to me frankly.

LORD GORING (*Looking straight at her*)
Quite frankly?

LADY CHILTERN
Surely. You have nothing to conceal, have you?   475

LORD GORING
Nothing. But, my dear Lady Chiltern, I think, if you will allow
me to say so, that in practical life –

LADY CHILTERN (*Smiling*)
Of which you know so little, Lord Goring –   480

LORD GORING
Of which I know nothing by experience, though I know something by observation. I think that in practical life there is
something about success, actual success, that is a little unscrupulous, something about ambition that is unscrupulous always.   485
Once a man has set his heart and soul on getting to a certain
point, if he has to climb the crag, he climbs the crag; if he has
to walk in the mire –

LADY CHILTERN
Well?   490

LORD GORING
He walks in the mire. Of course I am only talking generally
about life.

LADY CHILTERN (*Gravely*)
I hope so. Why do you look at me so strangely, Lord Goring?   495

LORD GORING
Lady Chiltern, I have sometimes thought that . . . perhaps you
are a little hard in some of your views on life. I think that . . .
often you don't make sufficient allowances. In every nature there

---

497–503 *Lady Chiltern . . . to some one* in MS1 this is blunter: 'Lady Chiltern, supposing that
Robert had, years ago . . .'. Later revisions make it less downright, and the full array of
qualifying phrases ('sometimes . . . perhaps . . . a little . . . some') does not appear until
PR.

are elements of weakness, or worse than weakness. Supposing,   500
for instance, that – that any public man, my father, or Lord
Merton, or Robert, say, had, years ago, written some foolish
letter to some one . . .

LADY CHILTERN

What do you mean by a foolish letter?   505

LORD GORING

A letter gravely compromising one's position. I am only putting
an imaginary case.

LADY CHILTERN

Robert is as incapable of doing a foolish thing as he is of doing   510
a wrong thing.

LORD GORING (*After a long pause*)

Nobody is incapable of doing a foolish thing. Nobody is incapable of doing a wrong thing.

LADY CHILTERN   515

Are you a Pessimist? What will the other dandies say? They
will all have to go into mourning.

LORD GORING (*Rising*)

No, Lady Chiltern, I am not a Pessimist. Indeed I am not sure
that I quite know what Pessimism really means. All I do know   520
is that life cannot be understood without much charity, cannot
be lived without much charity. It is love, and not German
philosophy, that is the true explanation of this world, whatever
may be the explanation of the next. And if you are ever in
trouble, Lady Chiltern, trust me absolutely, and I will help you   525
in every way I can. If you ever want me, come to me for my
assistance, and you shall have it. Come at once to me.

516–7   *Are you a Pessimist? . . . mourning* in F this line and the reply are as follows:
    LADY CHILTERN
        Surely you are not going to join the Pessimists?
    LORD GORING
        Oh, no. I can't stand the Pessimists. I don't like the way they wear
        their hair.
    This joke (which develops an idea in MS revisions to BLTS) was reported in *The
    Times'* review of the first performance. In MS1 the speech is 'You teach as a pessimist
    today; that is not like you' which was carried (with 'talk' for 'teach') into MS2, C,
    BLTS and LC. In MS1 this is followed by two blank leaves and a note indicating an
    entrance for Mabel (the manuscript picks up again at l. 678). A number of details
    in Lord G's reply first appear in PR: 'I am not sure . . . means' (519–20); 'Cannot be
    lived . . . charity' (521–2) and 'German' (522). LC and BLTS read 'as well as the next'
    at l. 523–4. On *Pessimism*, cf. l. 256, above.

LADY CHILTERN (*Looking at him in surprise*)

    Lord Goring, you are talking quite seriously. I don't think I ever
heard you talk seriously. before.   530

LORD GORING (*Laughing*)

    You must excuse me, Lady Chiltern. It won't occur again, if I
can help it.

LADY CHILTERN

    But I like you to be serious.   535

    Enter MABEL CHILTERN, *in the most ravishing frock*

MABEL CHILTERN

    Dear Gertrude, don't say such a dreadful thing to Lord Goring.
Seriousness would be very unbecoming to him. Good afternoon, Lord Goring! Pray be as trivial as you can.   540

LORD GORING

    I should like to, Miss Mabel, but I am afraid I am . . . a little out
of practice this morning; and besides, I have to be going now.

MABEL CHILTERN

    Just when I have come in! What dreadful manners you have!   545
I am sure you were very badly brought up.

LORD GORING

    I was.

MABEL CHILTERN

    I wish I had brought you up!   550

LORD GORING

    I am so sorry you didn't.

MABEL CHILTERN

    It is too late now, I suppose?

LORD GORING (*Smiling*)   555

    I am not so sure.

MABEL CHILTERN

    Will you ride tomorrow morning?

LORD GORING

    Yes, at ten.   560

MABEL CHILTERN

    Don't forget.

LORD GORING

    Of course I shan't. By the way, Lady Chiltern, there is no list

536   s.d. *Enter . . . frock* first appears in PR, developing the simple s.d. in earlier texts. For
        a description of the 'frock' see Appedix II.

564–80   *By the way . . . to guess it* the sequence does not appear before F, and the sentence

of your guests in *The Morning Post* of today. It has apparently 565
been crowded out by the County Council, or the Lambeth
Conference, or something equally boring. Could you let me
have a list? I have a particular reason for asking you.

LADY CHILTERN

I am sure Mr Trafford will be able to give you one. 570

LORD GORING

Thanks, so much.

MABEL CHILTERN

Tommy is the most useful person in London.

LORD GORING (*Turning to her*) 575

And who is the most ornamental?

MABEL CHILTERN (*Triumphantly*)

I am.

LORD GORING

How clever of you to guess it! (*Takes up his hat and cane*) 580
Good-bye, Lady Chiltern! You will remember what I said to
you, won't you?

LADY CHILTERN

Yes; but I don't know why you said it to me.

LORD GORING 585

I hardly know myself. Good-bye, Miss Mabel!

MABEL CHILTERN (*With a little moue of disappointment*)

I wish you were not going. I have had four wonderful adven-
tures this morning; four and a half, in fact. You might stop and
listen to some of them. 590

LORD GORING

How very selfish of you to have four and a half. There won't be
any left for me.

referring to the County Council and the Lambeth Conference first appears in PR.
The Morning Post was a leading society newspaper, especially noted for its
'fashionable intelligence': 'It was not only serviceable in the way of extending the
circulation . . . in aristocratic and fashionable circles, but "during the season" it
brought in a large amount of money in the shape of payments for the paragraphs
sent to its columns giving a list of the names of those that were present at dinner
parties, evening parties, or by whatever other name these gatherings of the West End
society were brought together' (James Grant, *The Newspaper Press: Its Origin, Progress
– and Present Position*, 1871). The *London County Council* was formed in 1889 to
gather together the functions of local government in the capital previously
discharged by parish 'vestries'. The *Lambeth Conference* of Anglican bishops is held
annually at Lambeth Palace, London residence of the Archbishop of Canterbury.

588   *four* F and earlier versions read 'seven' and om. 'four-and-a-half' in the line
following; *wonderful* is added in manuscript to C.

MABEL CHILTERN

I don't want you to have any. They would not be good for you.   595

LORD GORING

That is the first unkind thing you have ever said to me. How charmingly you said it! Ten tomorrow.

MABEL CHILTERN

Sharp.   600

LORD GORING

Quite sharp. But don't bring Mr Trafford.

MABEL CHILTERN (*With a little toss of the head*)

Of course I shan't bring Tommy Trafford. Tommy Trafford is in great disgrace.   605

LORD GORING

I am delighted to hear it.

Bows and goes out

MABEL CHILTERN

Gertrude, I wish you would speak to Tommy Trafford.   610

LADY CHILTERN

What has poor Mr Trafford done this time? Robert says he is the best secretary he has ever had.

MABEL CHILTERN

Well, Tommy has proposed to me again. Tommy really does   615

---

595   *They would not be good for you* F indicates '*bus. with hand*', but does not specify its nature. As Lord G is taking his leave of her, it would be natural for him to shake hands with Mabel: she may detain him by not releasing his hand.

598   *Ten* versions before PR read 'half-past ten'.

612–13   *Robert . . . had* first appears in BLTS: om. in LC. In view of the comic light in which he appears in the next speech, Wilde may have wished to establish Trafford's suitability for the trust placed in him by Sir Robert C.

615–40   *Well, Tommy . . . some attention* this speech (which might be compared with the 'proposal' in Act I of *Earnest*) was revised considerably after its introduction in MS2. The 'elaborate trio' is a duet in MS2; 'bimetallist' and 'bimetallism' are revised from 'socialist' and 'socialism' in manuscript alterations to C, where 'public' is substituted for 'people who heard him'. In LC and earlier versions 'quite out of date' is replaced by 'disgraceful'. In F (only) Mabel had checked Tommy by assuring him that she thought 'the first duty of woman was to look pretty, and that what the second duty was, no-one had yet discovered' (cf. 'Phrases and Philosophies for the Use of the Young': 'The first duty in life is to be as artificial as possible. What the second duty is no one has yet discovered' – *CW*, p. 1205). At this he 'looked so pleased' that she 'felt sure he must be shocked'. The naked, heroic statue of *Achilles* in Hyde Park was erected in 1822, inscribed by 'the women of England' to the Duke of Wellington 'and his brave companions in Arms'. On *bimetallism*, cf. *Woman*, III, 206. F has an s.d. '(*on arm of sofa*)' after the last word of the speech: in BLTS '(*sits on arm of Lady C's chair*)' is added to 'I know, dear' at l. 651.

nothing but propose to me. He proposed to me last night in the music-room, when I was quite unprotected, as there was an elaborate trio going on. I didn't dare to make the smallest repartee, I need hardly tell you. If I had, it would have stopped the music at once. Musical people are so absurdly unreason- 620 able. They always want one to be perfectly dumb at the very moment when one is longing to be absolutely deaf. Then he proposed to me in broad daylight this morning, in front of that dreadful statue of Achilles. Really, the things that go on in front of that work of art are quite appalling. The police should inter- 625 fere. At luncheon I saw by the glare in his eye that he was going to propose again, and I just managed to check him in time by assuring him that I was a bimetallist. Fortunately I don't know what bimetallism means. And I don't believe anybody else does either. But the observation crushed Tommy for ten minutes. He 630 looked quite shocked. And then Tommy is so annoying in the way he proposes. If he proposed at the top of his voice, I should not mind so much. That might produce some effect on the public. But he does it in a horrid confidential way. When Tommy wants to be romantic he talks to one just like a doctor. 635 I am very fond of Tommy, but his methods of proposing are quite out of date. I wish, Gertrude, you would speak to him, and tell him that once a week is quite often enough to propose to anyone, and that it should always be done in a manner that attracts some attention. 640

LADY CHILTERN

Dear Mabel, don't talk like that. Besides, Robert thinks very highly of Mr Trafford. He believes he has a brilliant future before him.

MABEL CHILTERN 645

Oh! I wouldn't marry a man with a future before him for any-thing under the sun.

LADY CHILTERN

Mabel!

MABEL CHILTERN 650

I know, dear. You married a man with a future, didn't you? But then Robert was a genius, and you have a noble, self-sacrificing

---

652   *self-sacrificing* first appears in PR.
       geniuses a favourite term with Wilde, especially when applied to himself. Chiltern is,
       like his creator, a brilliant man whose qualities isolate him and make him prey to
       envious scandal, likely to be idolised and destroyed by the public.

character. You can stand geniuses. I have no character at all, and
Robert is the only genius I could ever bear. As a rule, I think
they are quite impossible. Geniuses talk so much, don't they?   655
Such a bad habit! And they are always thinking about themselves, when I want them to be thinking about me. I must go
round now and rehearse at Lady Basildon's. You remember we
are having *tableaux*, don't you? The Triumph of something,
I don't know what! I hope it will be triumph of me. Only   660
triumph I am really interested in at present. (*Kisses* LADY
CHILTERN *and goes out; then comes running back*) Oh, Gertrude,
do you know who is coming to see you? That dreadful Mrs
Cheveley, in a most lovely gown. Did you ask her?

LADY CHILTERN (*Rising*)   665

Mrs Cheveley! Coming to see me? Impossible!

MABEL CHILTERN

I assure you she is coming upstairs, as large as life and not
nearly so natural.

LADY CHILTERN   670

You need not wait, Mabel. Remember, Lady Basildon is expect-
ing you.

MABEL CHILTERN

Oh! I must shake hands with Lady Markby. She is delightful. I
love being scolded by her.   675

Enter MASON

659   tableaux *tableaux vivants*, in which performers (usually amateur) gave a costumed
       representation of some familiar painting or historical scene, were a popular pastime
       and were often staged for charitable fund-raising events. Mabel's interest in self-
       display is comically indecorous. Cf. Mrs Eliza Lynn Linton's denunciation of the
       'Wild Women' whose 'advanced' behaviour seemed to threaten society. According to
       her, the 'Wild Woman' appears on the public stage 'and executes dances which one
       would not like one's daughter to see, still less perform. She herself knows no shame
       in showing her skill – and her legs' (*Nineteenth Century*, October 1891).

663–4 *That dreadful . . . gown* the last five words first appear in PR; *dreadful* is omitted in
       LC, and the whole sentence in F.

666   *Coming? . . . me* in LC and earlier versions her reaction is 'Impossible! No! I am glad
       she has come. I shall be able to tell her what I think of her, and prevent her ever
       entering my house again.' (C adds 'now' after 'tell her'.) Before PR the entry of the
       new guests is followed by a shorter exchange between Mabel and Lady M:

       LADY MARKBY
           Good afternoon, Mabel.
       MABEL
           Good afternoon, Lady Markby. I am just off . . .
       MS1 moves from the entrance to l. 732.

MASON

    Lady Markby. Mrs Cheveley.

        Enter LADY MARKBY *and* MRS CHEVELEY

LADY CHILTERN (*Advancing to meet them*)   680

    Dear Lady Markby, how nice of you to come and see me!
    (*Shakes hands with her, and bows somewhat distantly to* MRS
    CHEVELEY) Won't you sit down, Mrs Cheveley?

MRS CHEVELEY

    Thanks. Isn't that Miss Chiltern? I should like so much to know   685
    her.

LADY CHILTERN

    Mabel, Mrs Cheveley wishes to know you.

                MABEL CHILTERN *gives a little nod*

MRS CHEVELEY (*Sitting down*)   690

    I thought your frock so charming last night, Miss Chiltern. So
    simple and . . . suitable.

MABEL CHILTERN

    Really? I must tell my dressmaker. It will be such a surprise to
    her. Good-bye, Lady Markby!   695

LADY MARKBY

    Going already?

MABEL CHILTERN

    I am so sorry but I am obliged to. I am just off to rehearsal. I
    have got to stand on my head in some *tableaux*.   700

LADY MARKBY

    On your head, child? Oh! I hope not. I believe it is most
    unhealthy.

           Takes a seat on the sofa next LADY CHILTERN

MABEL CHILTERN   705

    But it is for an excellent charity: in aid of the Undeserving, the
    only people I am really interested in. I am the secretary, and
    Tommy Trafford is treasurer.

MRS CHEVELEY

    And what is Lord Goring?   710

---

706   *the Undeserving* in F the charity is 'the Grosvenor Square Mission' and its object 'to
       try and bring a little happiness into the homes of the Upper Classes'. Cf. Canon
       Chasuble's sermon on the Manna in the Wilderness, preached as a charity sermon
       for 'the Society for the Prevention of Discontent among the Upper Orders' (*Earnest*,
       II, 249–50). The distinction between the 'deserving' and 'undeserving' poor was
       important in Victorian philanthropy.

707–15 *I am the secretary . . . first* first appears in PR.

MABEL CHILTERN

Oh! Lord Goring is president.

MRS CHEVELEY

The post should suit him admirably, unless he has deteriorated
since I knew him first.   715

LADY MARKBY (*Reflecting*)

You are remarkably modern, Mabel. A little too modern, perhaps. Nothing is so dangerous as being too modern. One is
apt to grow old-fashioned quite suddenly. I have known many
instances of it.   720

MABEL CHILTERN

What a dreadful prospect!

LADY MARKBY

Ah! my dear, you need not be nervous. You will always be as
pretty as possible. That is the best fashion there is, and the only   725
fashion that England succeeds in setting.

MABEL CHILTERN (*With a curtsey*)

Thank you so much, Lady Markby, for England . . . and
myself.   *Goes out*

LADY MARKBY (*Turning to* LADY CHILTERN)   730

Dear Gertrude, we just called to know if Mrs Cheveley's
diamond brooch has been found.

LADY CHILTERN

Here?

MRS CHEVELEY   735

Yes. I missed it when I got back to Claridge's, and I thought I
might possibly have dropped it here.

LADY CHILTERN

I have heard nothing about it. But I will send for the butler
and ask.   *Touches the bell*   740

MRS CHEVELEY

Oh, pray don't trouble, Lady Chiltern. I daresay I lost it at the
Opera, before we came on here.

LADY MARKBY

Ah yes, I suppose it must have been at the Opera. The fact is, we   745
all scramble and jostle so much nowadays that I wonder we

718–20 *Nothing . . . instances of it* (Nothing ages one so rapidly as being too modern F, LC,
BLTS, C, MS2).

722–9 *What a dreadful prospect . . . and myself* first appears in PR.

732 *brooch* first appears in F: LC and earlier texts read 'star' throughout.

have anything at all left on us at the end of an evening. I know
myself that, when I am coming back from the Drawing Room,
I always feel as if I hadn't a shred on me, except a small shred
of decent reputation, just enough to prevent the lower classes   750
making painful observations through the windows of the
carriage. The fact is that our Society is terribly overpopulated.
Really, some one should arrange a proper scheme of assisted
emigration. It would do a great deal of good.

MRS CHEVELEY   755

I quite agree with you, Lady Markby. It is nearly six years since
I have been in London for the season, and I must say Society
has become dreadfully mixed. One sees the oddest people
everywhere.

LADY MARKBY   760

That is quite true, dear. But one needn't know them. I'm sure I
don't know half the people who come to my house. Indeed,
from all I hear, I shouldn't like to.

Enter MASON

LADY CHILTERN   765
What sort of a brooch was it that you lost, Mrs Cheveley?

747–54   *I know myself... of good* om. MS1, which follows 'evening' with ll. 739–43 ('But I will
      send ... came on here') and l. 766 ('What sort of a star ... '). The passage first appears
      in MS2, where Lady M's shred of reputation is, she says, 'just enough to cover me and
      prevent the lower classes making painful observations'. In manuscript revisions to
      C 'cover me and' is deleted and 'through the windows of the carriage' added.

748   *the Drawing Room* the formal presentation of ladies to the Queen and her court
      took place at a 'Drawing-Room'; 'Her Majesty is graciously accessible to all persons
      of rank and title, provided they bear a good character in society ... ' (*Etiquette of
      Good Society*, p. 204). Lady M would have been 'presenting' *débutantes* to the court.

753–4   *assisted emigration* frequently advocated as a radical means of reforming the
      'criminal classes' and practised by a number of charitable organizations as an aid to
      the respectable as well as the 'fallen'. (Cf. *Woman*, III, 245.) Such schemes were not
      usually proposed as a way of improving fashionable society in Lady M's sense of the
      word. F follows l. 754 with a variation on the *overdressed/educated* joke (cf. note to
      I, 315) and Mrs C observes: 'The overdressed should certainly be sent to the colonies,
      there is great demand for them there. The over-educated should certainly be kept in
      London, they are very much wanted.' Wilde is taking up material deleted from
      Woman, where the contrast between clothing (and nakedness) and civilization is
      used. It should be noted that dress for a 'Drawing Room' was especially elaborate,
      including a long, broad train attached to the costume and a head-dress of feathers,
      lace or tulle.

MRS CHEVELEY
A diamond snake-brooch with a ruby, a rather large ruby.

LADY MARKBY
I thought you said there was a sapphire on the head, dear?   770

MRS CHEVELEY (*Smiling*)
No, Lady Markby – a ruby.

LADY MARKBY (*Nodding her head*)
And very becoming, I am quite sure.

LADY CHILTERN   775
Has a ruby and diamond brooch been found in any of the rooms this morning, Mason?

MASON
No, my lady.

MRS CHEVELEY   780
It really is of no consequence, Lady Chiltern. I am so sorry to have put you to any inconvenience.

LADY CHILTERN (*Coldly*)
Oh, it has been no inconvenience. That will do, Mason. You can bring tea.   785

Exit MASON

LADY MARKBY
Well, I must say it is most annoying to lose anything. I remember once at Bath, years ago, losing in the Pump Room an exceedingly handsome cameo bracelet that Sir John had given   790
me. I don't think he has ever given me anything since, I am sorry to say. He has sadly degenerated. Really, this horrid House of Commons quite ruins our husbands for us. I think the Lower House by far the greatest blow to a happy married life that there has been since that terrible thing called the Higher   795
Education of Women was invented.

768   *A diamond snake-brooch with a ruby* first appears in PR. F has 'a diamond snake brooch with ruby eyes' and earlier versions specify 'a rather large eight-pointed star'. Wilde corrected the BLTS typescript to 'brooch' in some lines, but did not carry this revision through systematically. In earlier versions the jewel served only as a pretext for Mrs C's visit to Lady C.

784–5   *You can bring tea* added in MS2. In F tea has already been served, and the directions differ accordingly.

789   *the Pump Room* associated with the spa's social life as much as its medicinal purposes.

791–2   *I am sorry to say* first appears in PR.

795–6   *the Higher Education of Women* the appropriateness of university studies for women was still a matter of dispute, although the establishment of women's colleges in Oxford and Cambridge and the more enlightened policy of London University had advanced the cause.

LADY CHILTERN

Ah! it is heresy to say that in this house, Lady Markby. Robert is a great champion of the Higher Education of Women, and so, I am afraid, am I.   800

MRS CHEVELEY

The higher education of men is what I should like to see. Men need it so sadly.

LADY MARKBY

They do, dear. But I am afraid such a scheme would be quite   805
unpractical. I don't think man has much capacity for development. He has got as far as he can, and that is not far, is it?
With regard to women, well, dear Gertrude, you belong to the
younger generation, and I am sure it is all right if you approve
of it. In my time, of course, we were taught not to understand   810
anything. That was the old system, and wonderfully interesting
it was. I assure you that the amount of things I and my poor
dear sister were taught not to understand was quite extraordinary. But modern women understand everything, I am told.

MRS CHEVELEY   815

Except their husbands. That is the one thing the modern
woman never understands.

LADY MARKBY

And a very good thing too, dear, I daresay. It might break up
many a happy home if they did. Not yours, I need hardly say,   820
Gertrude. You have married a pattern husband. I wish I could
say as much for myself. But since Sir John has taken to
attending the debates regularly, which he never used to do in
the good old days, his language has become quite impossible.
He always seems to think that he is addressing the House, and   825
consequently whenever he discusses the state of the agricultural

---

807   *and that is not far, is it?* om. LC, BLTS; del. from C but restored in F ('and that is not
         very far, is it?').
810–11 *and wonderfully interesting it was* first appears in PR.
819–41 *And a very good thing . . . like that?* a version of this occurs in MS1 at the equivalent
         of I, 207. In F, LC and C 'all over the house' is followed by 'my maid told me
         afterwards'. *The Welsh Church* was the object of a controversial measure proposed by
         Gladstone, who wished to disestablish the Anglican Church in Wales. In revisions to
         C Wilde substituted 'improper' for the typescript's 'uninteresting'. In BLTS he added
         (but later deleted) another sentence, to follow 'an assembly of gentlemen': 'Besides,
         John has never done anything useful in his life. So his place is with his peers.' In the
         1880s and 1890s the Liberals considered a call for the abolition of the upper
         chamber, provoked by the Lords' blocking the Home Rule bill and other items of
         radical legislation.

labourer, or the Welsh Church, or something quite improper of
that kind, I am obliged to send all the servants out of the room.
It is not pleasant to see one's own butler, who has been with one
for twenty-three years, actually blushing at the sideboard, and   830
the footmen making contortions in corners like persons in
circuses. I assure you my life will be quite ruined unless they
send John at once to the Upper House. He won't take any interest
in politics then, will he? The House of Lords is so sensible. An
assembly of gentlemen. But in his present state, Sir John is   835
really a great trial. Why, this morning before breakfast was half
over, he stood up on the hearthrug, put his hands in his
pockets, and appealed to the country at the top of his voice.
I left the table as soon as I had my second cup of tea, I need
hardly say. But his violent language could be heard all over the   840
house! I trust, Gertrude, that Sir Robert is not like that?

LADY CHILTERN
But I am very much interested in politics, Lady Markby. I love
to hear Robert talk about them.

LADY MARKBY   845
Well, I hope he is not as devoted to Blue Books as Sir John is.
I don't think they can be quite improving reading for anyone.

MRS CHEVELEY (*Languidly*)
I have never read a Blue Book. I prefer books . . . in yellow covers.

LADY MARKBY (*Genially unconscious*)   850
Yellow is a gayer colour, is it not? I used to wear yellow a good
deal in my early days, and would do so now if Sir John was not
so painfully personal in his observations, and a man on the
question of dress is always ridiculous, is he not?

MRS CHEVELEY   855
Oh, no! I think men are the only authorities on dress.

846   *as Sir John is* MS1 adds 'Half an hour over a Blue Book is sufficient to make Sir John
a perfect monster'. The reports of parliamentary committees of enquiry, *Blue Books*
were a byword for methodical, fact-filled, dry publications. The books in *yellow
covers* favoured by Mrs C (l. 849) would be French novels, usually sold in yellow
paper wrappers: they are a familiar Wildean prop. In C Wilde changed 'improper'
to the present reading, 'improving'. In F Mrs Cheveley adds 'They are more accurate'
after l. 849.

851–4   *I used to . . . is he not?* Cf. the passage in MS and HTC at the equivalent of I, 209–21
(see note to those lines above).

856   *authorities on dress* an expertise claimed by Wilde, who espoused the cause of
'rational dress' in the 1880s.

LADY MARKBY

Really? One wouldn't say so from the sort of hats they wear, would one?

> *The* BUTLER *enters, followed by the* FOOTMAN. 860
> *Tea is set on a small table close to* LADY CHILTERN

LADY CHILTERN

May I give you some tea, Mrs Cheveley?

MRS CHEVELEY

Thanks. 865

> *The* BUTLER *hands* MRS CHEVELEY *a cup of tea on a salver*

LADY CHILTERN

Some tea, Lady Markby?

LADY MARKBY

No thanks, dear. (*The servants go out*) The fact is, I have promised 870
to go round for ten minutes to see poor Lady Brancaster, who
is in very great trouble. Her daughter, quite a well-brought-up
girl, too, has actually become engaged to be married to a curate
in Shropshire. It is very sad, very sad indeed. I can't understand
this modern mania for curates. In my time we girls saw them, 875
of course, running about the place like rabbits. But we never
took any notice of them, I need hardly say. But I am told that
nowadays country society is quite honeycombed with them. I
think it most irreligious, and then the eldest son has quarrelled
with his father, and it is said that when they meet at the club 880
Lord Brancaster always hides himself behind the money article
in *The Times*. However, I believe that is quite a common occur-
rence nowadays and that they have to take in extra copies of
The Times at all the clubs in St. James's Street; there are so many

---

860   s.d. in F there are s.d. for the removal of tea at this point.

870–9   *No thanks, dear... irreligious* Lady M's remarks on curates were first drafted for Act I
(see note to l. 167). *Lady Brancaster* is the name originally used for Lady Bracknell
in *Earnest*. The overworked, underpaid and attractive young *curate* was a stock
character in Victorian fiction. W.S. Gilbert's *Patience* (1881), in which he made fun
of the aesthetes, was based on his poem 'The Rival Curates', and was to have
concerned the attraction of two churchmen for the lovesick women of a parish:
considerations of taste and the opportunity of more direct satire suggested the
change to poets as a subject.

884–7   *there are so many sons ... regretted* a version of material originally drafted for
Woman. Cf. Appendix I. In the MS draft of *Earnest* a similar passage occurs:
'Mothers, of course, are all right. They pay a chap's bills and don't bother him. But

sons who won't have anything to do with their fathers, and 885
so many fathers who won't speak to their sons. I think, myself,
it is very much to be regretted.

MRS CHEVELEY

So do I. Fathers have so much to learn from their sons
nowadays. 890

LADY MARKBY

Really, dear? What?

MRS CHEVELEY

The art of living. The only really Fine Art we have produced in
modern times. 895

LADY MARKBY (*Shaking her head*)

Ah! I am afraid Lord Brancaster knew a good deal about that.
More than his poor wife ever did. (*Turning to* LADY CHILTERN)
You know Lady Brancaster, don't you, dear?

LADY CHILTERN 900

Just slightly. She was staying at Langton last autumn, when we
were there.

LADY MARKBY

Well, like all stout women, she looks the very picture of happiness, as no doubt you noticed. But there are many tragedies in 905
her family, besides this affair of the curate. Her own sister, Mrs
Jekyll, had a most unhappy life; through no fault of her own, I
am sorry to say. She ultimately was so broken-hearted that she
went into a convent, or on to the operatic stage, I forget which.
No; I think it was decorative art-needlework she took up. I 910
know she had lost all sense of pleasure in life. (*Rising*) And now,

to his father . . . I bet you anything you like that there is not a single chap, of all the
chaps that you and I know, who would be seen walking down St. James's Street with
his own father' (*Earnest*, I, 612–13, note).

889–912 *So do I . . . And now, Gertrude* om. MS1. ll. 899–911 (from 'You know Lady Brancaster
. . .') first appear in additions to C. The confounding of the terms in which 'art' was
evaluated in relation to 'life' was one of Wilde's favourite strategies – notably in 'The
Critic as Artist' and 'The Decay of Lying' and in Lord Henry Wotton's seductive
conversations with Dorian Gray.

901–2 *She was . . . there* om. LC, BLTS.

904–11 *Well, like all . . . in life* the description of Mrs Jekyll's misfortunes first appears as an
addition to C. In PR 'as no doubt you noticed' and 'I am sorry to say' are added. In
F 'besides this affair of the curate' and 'operatic' first appear. In BLTS and LC
'needlework' is not specified. (It was one of the crafts which Wilde, a disciple of
William Morris, took seriously.) If Mrs Jekyll was a relation, through her husband,
of the protagonist of Stevenson's story (published in 1886) her life must have been
unhappy indeed.

Gertrude, if you will allow me, I shall leave Mrs Cheveley in
your charge and call back for her in a quarter of an hour. Or
perhaps, dear Mrs Cheveley, you wouldn't mind waiting in the
carriage while I am with Lady Brancaster. As I intend it to be a   915
visit of condolence, I shan't stay long.

MRS CHEVELEY (*Rising*)

I don't mind waiting in the carriage at all, provided there is
somebody to look at one.

LADY MARKBY   920

Well, I hear the curate is always prowling about the house.

MRS CHEVELEY

I am afraid I am not fond of girl friends.

LADY CHILTERN (*Rising*)

Oh, I hope Mrs Cheveley will stay here a little. I should like to   925
have a few minutes' conversation with her.

MRS CHEVELEY

How very kind of you, Lady Chiltern! Believe me, nothing
would give me greater pleasure.

LADY MARKBY   930

Ah! no doubt you both have many pleasant reminiscences of
your schooldays to talk over together. Good-bye, dear Gertrude!
Shall I see you at Lady Bonar's tonight? She has discovered a
wonderful new genius. He does . . . nothing at all, I believe. That
is a great comfort, is it not?   935

LADY CHILTERN

Robert and I are dining at home by ourselves tonight, and
I don't think I shall go anywhere afterwards. Robert, of course,
will have to be in the House. But there is nothing interesting on.

LADY MARKBY   940

Dining at home by yourselves? Is that quite prudent? Ah, I

913–29   *Or perhaps . . . pleasure* om. MS1.
915   *I intend it to be* PR restores the phrase from C: other versions read 'It is only'.
918–23   *provided . . . girl friends* this crude remark, suggesting Mrs C's dislike for the
         competition of younger women, first appears in PR.
933–4   *a wonderful new genius* Doing nothing was claimed by Wilde to be an art in itself,
         cf. the sub-title of 'The Critic as Artist': 'With some Remarks upon the Importance
         of Doing Nothing'. In that dialogue Gilbert insists that 'to do nothing at all is the
         most difficult thing in the world, the most difficult and the most intellectual'
         (*Intentions*, p. 176/*CW*, p. 1039). The last three sentences of this speech and the two
         speeches following first appear in F.
941   *Dining at home* F has the s.d. '*Start lowering sun*', presumably referring to the lights
         behind the windows of the room.

forgot, your husband is an exception. Mine is the general rule, and nothing ages a woman so rapidly as having married the general rule.

Exit LADY MARKBY   945

MRS CHEVELEY

Wonderful woman, Lady Markby, isn't she? Talks more and says less than anybody I ever met. She is made to be a public speaker. Much more so than her husband, though he is a typical Englishman, always dull and usually violent.   950

LADY CHILTERN (*Makes no answer, but remains standing. There is a pause. Then the eyes of the two women meet.* LADY CHILTERN *looks stern and pale.* MRS CHEVELEY *seems rather amused*)

Mrs Cheveley, I think it is right to tell you quite frankly that, had I known who you really were, I should not have invited you   955
to my house last night.

MRS CHEVELEY (*With an impertinent smile*)

Really?

LADY CHILTERN

I could not have done so.   960

MRS CHEVELEY

I see that after all these years you have not changed a bit, Gertrude.

LADY CHILTERN

I never change.   965

MRS CHEVELEY (*Elevating her eyebrows*)

Then life has taught you nothing?

LADY CHILTERN

It has taught me that a person who has once been guilty of a dishonest and dishonourable action may be guilty of it a second   970
time, and should be shunned.

MRS CHEVELEY

Would you apply that rule to everyone?

LADY CHILTERN

Yes, to everyone, without exception.   975

MRS CHEVELEY

Then I am sorry for you, Gertrude, very sorry for you.

LADY CHILTERN

You see now, I am sure, that for many reasons any further

947–8   *Talks more . . . usually violent* The first sentence does not appear until F; the rest in
PR. The s.d. first appears in PR.

973–81   *Would you apply . . . impossible?* First appears in MS2.

acquaintance between us during your stay in London is quite   980
impossible?

MRS CHEVELEY (*Leaning back in her chair*)
Do you know, Gertrude, I don't mind your talking morality a
bit. Morality is simply the attitude we adopt towards people
whom we personally dislike. You dislike me. I am quite aware of   985
that. And I have always detested you. And yet I have come here
to do you a service.

LADY CHILTERN (*Contemptuously*)
Like the service you wished to render my husband last night,
I suppose. Thank heaven, I saved him from that.   990

MRS CHEVELEY (*Starting to her feet*)
It was you who made him write that insolent letter to me? It
was you who made him break his promise?

LADY CHILTERN
Yes.   995

MRS CHEVELEY
Then you must make him keep it. I give you till tomorrow
morning – no more. If by that time your husband does not
solemnly bind himself to help me in this great scheme in which
I am interested –   1000

LADY CHILTERN
This fraudulent speculation –

MRS CHEVELEY
Call it what you choose. I hold your husband in the hollow
of my hand, and if you are wise you will make him do what I   1005
tell him.

LADY CHILTERN (*Rising and going towards her*)
You are impertinent. What has my husband to do with you?
With a woman like you?

MRS CHEVELEY (*With a bitter laugh*)   1010
In this world like meets with like. It is because your husband is
himself fraudulent and dishonest that we pair so well together.
Between you and him there are chasms. He and I are closer

983–4   *Do you know . . . a bit* Cf. ll. 249–50, above.
  986   *And I have always detested you* MS1 reads:
          LADY CHILTERN
            Yes, I know your true character.
          MRS CHEVELEY
            Perhaps one's true character is what one wishes to be more than what
            one is. But let that pass. You dislike me. I hate you. I have always hated you.
            And yet . . .

than friends. We are enemies linked together. The same sin
binds us. 1015

LADY CHILTERN

How dare you class my husband with yourself? How dare you
threaten him or me? Leave my house. You are unfit to enter it.

> SIR ROBERT CHILTERN *enters from behind.*
> *He hears his wife's last words, and sees to whom* 1020
> *they are addressed. He grows deadly pale*

MRS CHEVELEY

Your house! A house bought with the price of dishonour.
A house, everything in which has been paid for by fraud.
(*Turns round and sees* SIR ROBERT CHILTERN) Ask him what 1025
the origin of his fortune is! Get him to tell you how he sold to
a stockbroker a Cabinet secret. Learn from him to what you
owe your position.

LADY CHILTERN

It is not true! Robert! It is not true! 1030

MRS CHEVELEY (*Pointing at him with outstretched finger*)
Look at him! Can he deny it? Does he dare to?

SIR ROBERT CHILTERN

Go! Go at once. You have done your worst now.

MRS CHEVELEY 1035

My worst? I have not yet finished with you, with either of you.
I give you both till tomorrow at noon. If by then you don't do
what I bid you to do, the whole world shall know the origin of
Robert Chiltern.

> SIR ROBERT CHILTERN *strikes the bell. Enter* MASON 1040

SIR ROBERT CHILTERN

Show Mrs Cheveley out.

1024 *fraud* in F this is the cue for '*Warning for Curtain*'.
1036–42 *My worst? . . . out* Mrs C's exit-speech needed some adjustment. It is possible that Sir
Robert's line 'Show Mrs Cheveley out' (added to C) was intended to restore his 'face'
and transfer control of the moment to the actor-manager playing the role. In MS1
ll. 1032–9 are one speech, with no interruption, and begin: 'Look at him! He does
not have the courage even to lie about it. I give you both till tomorrow morning . .
.' In MS2 'I have not yet finished with you' is added as answer to the new line for Sir
Robert (l. 1034). In PR 'with either of you' appears. MS1 omits the somewhat
melodramatic defiance, 'the whole world shall know the origin of Robert Chiltern'.
'My worst?' first appears in BLTS.

MRS CHEVELEY *starts; then bows with somewhat exaggerated politeness to* LADY CHILTERN, *who makes no sign of response. As she passes by* SIR ROBERT CHILTERN, *who is standing close*   1045
to the door, she pauses for a moment and looks him straight in the face. She then goes out, followed by the servant, who closes the door after him. The husband and wife are left alone.
LADY CHILTERN *stands like someone in a dreadful dream. Then she turns round and looks at her husband. She looks*   1050
at him with strange eyes, as though she was seeing him for the first time

LADY CHILTERN

You sold a Cabinet secret for money! You began your life with fraud! You built up your career on dishonour! Oh, tell me it is   1055
not true! Lie to me! Lie to me! Tell me it is not true!

SIR ROBERT CHILTERN

What this woman said is quite true. But, Gertrude, listen to me. You don't realize how I was tempted. Let me tell you the
whole thing.   *Goes towards her*   1060

LADY CHILTERN

Don't come near me. Don't touch me. I feel as if you had soiled me for ever. Oh! what a mask you have been wearing all these years! A horrible painted mask! You sold yourself for money. Oh! a common thief were better. You put yourself up to sale to   1065
the highest bidder! You were bought in the market. You lied to the whole world. And yet you will not lie to me.

SIR ROBERT CHILTERN (*Rushing towards her*)
Gertrude! Gertrude!

LADY CHILTERN (*Thrusting him back with outstretched hands*)   1070
No, don't speak! Say nothing! Your voice wakes terrible memories – memories of things that made me love you – memories of words that made me love you – memories that now are

1044   s.d. first appears in PR, replacing a simple '*exit*'.
1062–3 *I feel as if... for ever* in MS1 the idea is expressed more crudely: 'I feel as if you have
       touched me too much, you have soiled me forever.' In F the line does not appear
       and the speech begins 'Don't. Oh! what a mask ...'. The horrible *painted mask* recalls
       a number of instances of the theme in Wilde's work, including Mrs Erlynne's
       description of her life as an 'outcast': 'afraid every moment lest the mask should be
       stripped from one's face' (*LWF*, III, 149–50). Cf. also 'The Decay of Lying': 'In point
       of fact what is interesting about people in "good society" ... is the mask that each
       one of them wears, not the reality that lies behind the mask'. (*Intentions*, p. 15/*CW*,
       p. 975.)
1071   *No, don't speak* MS1 precedes this with 'Life becomes bitter in one's mouth'.

horrible to me. And how I worshipped you! You were to me
something apart from common life, a thing pure, noble, 1075
honest, without stain. The world seemed to me finer because
you were in it, and goodness more real because you lived. And
now – oh, when I think that I made of a man like you my ideal!
the ideal of my life!

SIR ROBERT CHILTERN 1080

There was your mistake. There was your error. The error all
women commit. Why can't you women love us, faults and all?
Why do you place us on monstrous pedestals? We have all feet
of clay, women as well as men; but when we men love women,
we love them knowing their weaknesses, their follies, their 1085
imperfections, love them all the more, it may be, for that reason.
It is not the perfect, but the imperfect, who have need of love.
It is when we are wounded by our own hands, or by the hands
of others, that love should come to cure us – else what use is
love at all? All sins, except a sin against itself, Love should for- 1090
give. All lives, save loveless lives, true Love should pardon. A
man's love is like that. It is wider, larger, more human than a
woman's. Women think that they are making ideals of men.
What they are making of us are false idols merely. You made
your false idol of me, and I had not the courage to come down, 1095
show you my wounds, tell you my weaknesses. I was afraid that
I might lose your love, as I have lost it now. And so, last night
you ruined my life for me – yes, ruined it! What this woman
asked of me was nothing compared to what she offered to me.
She offered security, peace, stability. The sin of my youth, that 1100
I had thought was buried, rose up in front of me, hideous,
horrible, with its hands at my throat. I could have killed it for
ever, sent it back into its tomb, destroyed its record, burned the
one witness against me. You prevented me. No one but you, you

1078–9   *the ideal of my life!* first appears in PR.
1081–1111   *There was your mistake . . . have ruined mine!* very few changes were made in this
speech after MS1. Versions before PR read 'humane' for 'human' (l. 1092); MS1 has
'from the altar on which your vanity had placed me. I had not the courage to show
you my wounds' after 'come down' (l. 1095); 'terrible' in PR replaces the earlier
'horrible'; LC simplifies 'terrible shame, the mockery of the world, a lonely
dishonoured death' to 'horrible death'. In LC and earlier versions 'Let women make
no more ideals of men' is followed by 'in your life' and the next verb and its subject
are in the second person ('Don't put them . . . or you may ruin . . . '). 'You whom I
have so wildly loved' first appears in PR. In F 'some day' (l. 1107) is followed by the
s.d. '(*Pause, goes up stage, then turns to Lady C*)'. The final s.d. first appears in PR,
replacing the simple exit marked in earlier versions.

know it. And now what is there before me but public disgrace,   1105
ruin, terrible shame, the mockery of the world, a lonely dishonoured life, a lonely dishonoured death, it may be, some day?
Let women make no more ideals of men! let them not put them
on altars and bow before them, or they may ruin other lives as
completely as you – you whom I have so wildly loved – have   1110
ruined mine!

> *He passes from the room.* LADY CHILTERN *rushes*
> *towards him, but the door is closed when she reaches it.*
> *Pale with anguish, bewildered, helpless, she sways like a plant*
> *in the water. Her hands, outstretched, seem to tremble*   1115
> *in the air like blossoms in the wind. Then she flings herself*
> *down beside a sofa and buries her face. Her sobs*
> *are like the sobs of a child*

ACT-DROP

ACT III

The Library in LORD GORING'*s house. An Adam room.*
On the right is the door leading into the hall. On the left,
the door of the smoking-room. A pair of folding doors
at the back open into the drawing-room. The fire is lit.
PHIPPS, *the butler, is arranging some newspapers*   5
on the writing-table. The distinction of PHIPPS *is*
his impassivity. He has been termed by enthusiasts
the Ideal Butler. The Sphinx is not so incommunicable.
He is a mask with a manner. Of his intellectual or
emotional life history knows nothing. He represents   10
the dominance of form.

Enter LORD GORING *in evening dress with a buttonhole.*
He is wearing a silk hat and Inverness cape. White-gloved,
he carries a Louis Seize cane. His are all the delicate fopperies
of Fashion. One sees that he stands in immediate relation   15
to modern life, makes it indeed, and so masters it. He is
the first well-dressed philosopher in the history of thought

LORD GORING
  Got my second buttonhole for me, Phipps?

---

1 s.d. first appears in PR, with details added to the proof. In LC the s.d. is 'LORD GORING'*s*
   rooms, PHIPPS *discovered. Enter* LORD GORING.' In F there is business establishing
   Phipps' ascendancy over his fellow servant:
     PHIPPS and HAROLD discovered – Business. HAROLD opens blotter on table, moves
     cigarette stand on table table, R., also arranges papers on table, L. PHIPPS shuts
     blotter, puts cigarette stand in former position, rearranges papers.
   There is a warning: '*Note* Brooch in drawer of table, R.' Wilde added '*by enthusiasts*'
   and '*White-gloved . . . thought*' to PR. The room is decorated by *Robert Adam* (corrected
   from 1st ed's 'Adams') (1728–92), British architect and interior designer. On *the Sphinx*
   cf. note to *Woman*, I, 439–40. Wilde himself affected a *Louis Seize* cane and claimed in
   De Profimdis to have 'stood in symbolic relations to the art and culture of my age'. It
   is difficult not to see this s.d. as the author's comment on himself as he was before his
   downfall.
     MS begins with a short soliloquy by Lord G, who is reading a letter on pink paper.
   Lord C enters and remarks that he usually finds his son 'lolling about other people's
   houses.' His son replies: 'I don't loll, father. I don't know how to loll. But I prefer other
   people's houses to my own. I prefer everything that other people have to what I have.
   I am afraid, father that I have terrible communistic tendencies in me. It comes from
   my never having had time to study the question of property'. MS then moves to l. 115.
   In BLTS the passage is deleted and transferred to l. 113.

PHIPPS   20
  Yes, my lord.

Takes his hat, cane and cape, and presents
new buttonhole on salver

LORD GORING
  Rather distinguished thing, Phipps. I am the only person of   25
  the smallest importance in London at present who wears a
  buttonhole.
PHIPPS
  Yes, my lord. I have observed that.
LORD GORING (*Taking out old buttonhole*)   30
  You see, Phipps, Fashion is what one wears oneself. What is
  unfashionable is what other people wear.
PHIPPS
  Yes, my lord.
LORD GORING   35
  Just as vulgarity is simply the conduct of other people.
PHIPPS
  Yes, my lord.
LORD GORING (*Putting in new buttonhole*)
  And falsehoods the truths of other people.   40
PHIPPS
  Yes, my lord.
LORD GORING
  Other people are quite dreadful. The only possible society is
  oneself.   45
PHIPPS
  Yes, my lord.
LORD GORING
  To love oneself is the beginning of a life-long romance, Phipps.
PHIPPS   50
  Yes, my lord.
LORD GORING (*Looking at himself in the glass*)
  Don't think I quite like this buttonhole, Phipps. Makes me look

22   s.d. *cane* added to PR.
25–9 *Rather. . . Yes, my lord* the sequence first appears in F (which om. ll. 40–41, 49–50).
      On *button-holes*, cf. 'Phrases and Philosophies for the Use of the Young' (*CW*, pp.
      1205–6): 'A really well-made button-hole is the only link between Art and Nature';
      in *Earnest* Algernon tells Cecily: 'I never have any appetite unless I have a button-
      hole first' (II, 172–3).
49   *To love oneself . . . Phipps* Cf. note to l. 475–8.

a little too old. Makes me almost in the prime of life, eh, Phipps? 55

PHIPPS

I don't observe any alteration in your lordship's appearance.

LORD GORING

You don't, Phipps?

PHIPPS 60

No, my lord.

LORD GORING

I am not quite sure. For the future a more trivial buttonhole, Phipps, on Thursday evenings.

PHIPPS 65

I will speak to the florist, my lord. She has had a loss in her family lately, which perhaps accounts for the lack of triviality your lordship complains of in the buttonhole.

LORD GORING

Extraordinary thing about the lower classes in England – they 70 are always losing their relations.

PHIPPS

Yes, my lord! They are extremely fortunate in that respect.

LORD GORING (*Turns round and looks at him.* PHIPPS *remains impassive*) 75

Hum! Any letters, Phipps?

PHIPPS

Three, my lord. *Hands letters on a salver*

LORD GORING (*Takes letters*)

Want my cab round in twenty minutes. 80

PHIPPS

Yes, my lord. *Goes towards door*

LORD GORING (*Holds up letter in pink envelope*)

Ahem! Phipps, when did this letter arrive?

PHIPPS 85

It was brought by hand just after your lordship went to the Club.

---

54   *in the prime of life* in BLTS Wilde altered 'look quite middle-aged' to 'middle-aged', which was adopted in C and LC. The present phrase first appears in F.

66–76   *I will speak . . . Phipps?* added to BLTS.

70   *lower classes* (lower middle classes LC; middle classes C, BLTS.)

74   s.d. *Turns . . . impassive* first appears in PR.

LORD GORING

That will do. (*Exit* PHIPPS) Lady Chiltern's handwriting on Lady
Chiltern's pink notepaper. That is rather curious. I thought   90
Robert was to write. Wonder what Lady Chiltern has got to say
to me? (*Sits at bureau and opens letter, and reads it*) 'I want you.
I trust you. I am coming to you. Gertrude.' (*Puts down the letter
with a puzzled look. Then takes it up, and reads it again slowly*)
'I want you. I trust you. I am coming to you.' So she has found   95
out everything! Poor woman! Poor woman! (*Pulls out watch
and looks at it.*) But what an hour to call! Ten o'clock! I shall
have to give up going to the Berkshires'. However, it is always
nice to be expected, and not to arrive. I am not expected at the
Bachelors', so I shall certainly go there. Well, I will make her stand   100
by her husband. That is the only thing for her to do. That is the
only thing for any woman to do. It is the growth of the moral
sense in women that makes marriage such a hopeless, one-sided
institution. Ten o'clock. She should be here soon. I must tell
Phipps I am not in to anyone else.   *Goes towards bell*   105

Enter PHIPPS

PHIPPS

Lord Caversham.

LORD GORING

Oh, why will parents always appear at the wrong time? Some   110
extraordinary mistake in nature, I suppose.

Enter LORD CAVERSHAM

Delighted to see you, my dear father.   *Goes to meet him*
LORD CAVERSHAM
Take my cloak off.   115
LORD GORING
Is it worth while, father?

89–105   *That will do . . . anyone else* LC and earlier versions of this speech are simpler, without
         the repetition of the letter's contents and the reflections on the 'growth of moral
         sense in women'. In LC Lord G anticipates giving Lady C 'a good lecture'. In C he
         (somewhat incongruously) speaks of her having 'stepped right into the little trap
         [he] laid for her' and intends 'teaching her a salutary lesson when she arrives' (derives
         from additions to BLTS). He also remarks that he will not try any more 'psycho-
         logical experiments' – 'At least not on women, they are far too clever for me'.
110–11   *Some . . . suppose* first appears in C, which adds material from the beginning of the
         act in MS; F om. this sentence.

LORD CAVERSHAM
Of course it is worth while, sir. Which is the most comfortable
chair?   120
LORD GORING
This one, father. It is the chair I use myself, when I have visitors.
LORD CAVERSHAM
Thank ye. No draught, I hope, in this room?
LORD GORING   125
No, father.
LORD CAVERSHAM (*Sitting down*)
Glad to hear it. Can't stand draughts. No draughts at home.
LORD GORING
Good many breezes, father.   130
LORD CAVERSHAM
Eh? Eh? Don't understand what you mean. Want to have a
serious conversation with you, sir.
LORD GORING
My dear father! At this hour?   135
LORD CAVERSHAM
Well, sir, it is only ten o'clock. What is your objection to the
hour? I think the hour is an admirable hour!
LORD GORING
Well, the fact is, father, this is not my day for talking seriously.   140
I am very sorry, but it is not my day.
LORD CAVERSHAM
What do you mean, sir?
LORD GORING
During the season, father, I only talk seriously on the first   145
Tuesday in every month, from four to seven.
LORD CAVERSHAM
Well, make it Tuesday, sir, make it Tuesday.
LORD GORING
But it is after seven, father, and my doctor says I must not have   150
any serious conversation after seven. It makes me talk in my
sleep.

130   *breezes* quarrels, disagreements (slang).
138   *an admirable hour!* in MS Lord C proposes his own company for his son – 'much
         more profitable for you, much more improving for your character'. Lord G replies
         'I don't want my character improved, I am perfectly satisfied with it as it is'.
140   *not my day for talking seriously* analogous to the practice of appointing a regular day
         on which a hostess would be 'at home' to receive afternoon visitors. (Cf. I, 89–90
         'You know we are always at home on Wednesdays'.)

LORD CAVERSHAM

Talk in your sleep, sir? What does that matter? You are not
married.   155

LORD GORING

No, father, I am not married.

LORD CAVERSHAM

Hum! That is what I have come to talk to you about, sir. You
have got to get married, and at once. Why, when I was your age,   160
sir, I had been an inconsolable widower for three months, and
was already paying my addresses to your admirable mother.
Damme, sir, it is your duty to get married. You can't be always
living for pleasure. Every man of position is married nowadays.
Bachelors are not fashionable any more. They are a damaged   165
lot. Too much is known about them. You must get a wife, sir.
Look where your friend Robert Chiltern has got to by probity,
hard work, and a sensible marriage with a good woman. Why
don't you imitate him, sir? Why don't you take him for your
model?   170

LORD GORING

I think I shall, father.

LORD CAVERSHAM

I wish you would, sir. Then I should be happy. At present I make
your mother's life miserable on your account. You are heartless,   175
sir, quite heartless.

LORD GORING

I hope not, father.

LORD CAVERSHAM

And it is high time for you to get married. You are thirty-four   180
years of age, sir.

159–70   *Hum!... model?* in MS Lord C had been 'divorced twice'. The reference to his being
a widower first appears in C, where the mother of Lord G is 'sainted' rather than
'admirable'. The customary period of mourning for a widower was one year, during
which black clothes would be worn. In MS and BLTS the reasons for urging marriage
on Lord G are frankly selfish:
> You don't suppose I want the property to go to my damned nephew, do you? You
> don't suppose I want your idiotic cousin to have the title. I hate all my relations.
> It is only human nature to hate one's relations. A man who doesn't hate his relations
> has no regard for his own flesh and blood ...

Lord G insists that 'pleasure, or the prospect of it, is the only thing that would induce
[him] to marry at all', and resists his father's appeal to his 'duty to [his] name and
race'. The passage was abbreviated in revisions to BLTS; the reference to 'name and
race' does not appear after C.

180 etc.   In LC Lord G is 36, but admits to 33½; in C he is 36 (34¼); and in MS and BLTS he
is 38 (34½).

LORD GORING

Yes, father, but I only admit to thirty-two – thirty-one and a
half when I have a really good buttonhole. This buttonhole is
not . . . trivial enough.   185

LORD CAVERSHAM

I tell you you are thirty-four, sir. And there is a draught in your
room, besides, which makes your conduct worse. Why did you
tell me there was no draught, sir? I feel a draught, sir, I feel it
distinctly.   190

LORD GORING

So do I, father. It is a dreadful draught. I will come and see you
tomorrow, father. We can talk over anything you like. Let me
help you on with your cloak, father.

LORD CAVERSHAM   195

No, sir; I have called this evening for a definite purpose, and I
am going to see it through at all costs to my health or yours. Put
down my cloak, sir.

LORD GORING

Certainly, father. But let us go into another room. (*Rings bell*)   200
There is a dreadful draught here. (*Enter* PHIPPS) Phipps, is
there a good fire in the smoking-room?

PHIPPS

Yes, my lord.

LORD GORING   205

Come in there, father. Your sneezes are quite heart-rending.

LORD CAVERSHAM

Well, sir, I suppose I have a right to sneeze when I choose?

LORD GORING (*Apologetically*)

Quite so, father. I was merely expressing sympathy.   210

LORD CAVERSHAM

Oh, damn sympathy. There is a great deal too much of that sort
of thing going on nowadays.

LORD GORING

I quite agree with you, father. If there was less sympathy in the   215
world there would be less trouble in the world.

215–30   *If there was . . . puppy!* first appears in F (which om. the last speech and reads 'sorrow'
for 'trouble' in l. 216); ll. 224–6 ('Do you always . . . attentively') were transferred
from the drafts of *Earnest*, Act I (l. 276). The lines may have been spoken in performances of *Earnest*; they do not appear in Smithers' edition of the play and the
promptbook compiled by Alexander, but are found in the licensing copy and earlier
versions.

LORD CAVERSHAM (*Going towards the smoking-room*)
That is a paradox, sir. I hate paradoxes.

LORD GORING
So do I, father. Everybody one meets is a paradox nowadays. It   220
is a great bore. It makes society so obvious.

LORD CAVERSHAM (*Turning round, and looking at his son beneath
his bushy eyebrows*)
Do you always really understand what you say, sir?

LORD GORING (*After some hesitation*)   225
Yes, father, if I listen attentively.

LORD CAVERSHAM (*Indignantly*)
If you listen attentively! . . . Conceited young puppy!
                    Goes off grumbling into the smoking-room

                    PHIPPS *enters*   230

LORD GORING
Phipps, there is a lady coming to see me this evening on
particular business. Show her into the drawing-room when she
arrives. You understand?

PHIPPS   235
Yes, my lord.

LORD GORING
It is a matter of the gravest importance, Phipps.

PHIPPS
I understand, my lord.   240

LORD GORING
No one else is to be admitted, under any circumstances.

PHIPPS
I understand, my lord.   *Bell rings*

LORD GORING   245
Ah! that is probably the lady. I shall see her myself.

            Just as he is going towards the door
        LORD CAVERSHAM *enters from the smoking-room*

LORD CAVERSHAM
Well, sir? am I to wait attendance on you?   250

---

246 *Ah! . . . myself in* F Lord G remarks 'For a lady she is wonderfully punctual'. In
     versions before F the badinage with Lord C is longer.

LORD GORING (*Considerably perplexed*)

In a moment, father. Do excuse me. (LORD CAVERSHAM *goes back*) Well, remember my instructions, Phipps – into that room.

PHIPPS

Yes, my lord.   255

> LORD GORING *goes into the smoking-room.*
> HAROLD, *the footman, shows* MRS CHEVELEY *in.*
> *Lamia-like, she is in green and silver. She has a cloak*
> *of black satin, lined with dead rose-leaf silk*

HAROLD   260

What name, madam?

MRS CHEVELEY (*To* PHIPPS, *who advances towards her*)

Is Lord Goring not here? I was told he was at home?

PHIPPS

His lordship is engaged at present with Lord Caversham,   265
madam.

> *Turns a cold, glassy eye on* HAROLD, *who at once retires*

MRS CHEVELEY (*To herself*)

How very filial!

PHIPPS   270

His lordship told me to ask you, madam, to be kind enough to
wait in the drawing-room for him. His lordship will come to
you there.

MRS CHEVELEY (*With a look of surprise*)

Lord Goring expects me?   275

PHIPPS

Yes, madam.

MRS CHEVELEY

Are you quite sure?

---

255   *Yes, my lord* in MS and BLTS Phipps has a brief soliloquy:
> Wonder who the lady coming to see him on important business is? Hope he is not
> going to be married. Hate women about a home. They are so inquisitive.

In BLTS Wilde deleted this and drafted an alternative:
> Hope he is going to be married. I like a well-dressed woman about the house.
> They set off a dinner table so well. Besides, if a man is married he doesn't dine
> at home quite so often. Bachelors nowadays are far too domestic.

This was also deleted.

256   s.d. *Lamia-like* Cf. the woman in serpent's shape of Keats' poem 'Lamia': 'a gordian
shape of dazzling hue/Vermilion-spotted, golden, green and blue' and covered in
'silver mail, and golden brede' (I, 48–9; 158).

269   *How very filial* first appears in PR: another jibe at social institutions (Cf. I, 344–50).

92

PHIPPS   280

His lordship told me that if a lady called I was to ask her to wait
in the drawing-room. (*Goes to the door of the drawing-room and
opens it*) His lordship's directions on the subject were very
precise.

MRS CHEVELEY (*To herself*)   285

How thoughtful of him! To expect the unexpected shows a
thoroughly modern intellect. (*Goes towards the drawing-room
and looks in*) Ugh! How dreary a bachelor's drawing-room always
looks. I shall have to alter all this.

              PHIPPS *brings the lamp from the writing-table*   290

No, I don't care for that lamp. It is far too glaring. Light some
candles.

PHIPPS (*Replaces lamp*)

Certainly, madam.

MRS CHEVELEY   295

I hope the candles have very becoming shades.

PHIPPS

We have had no complaints about them, madam, as yet.

    Passes into the drawing-room and begins to light the candles

MRS CHEVELEY (*To herself*)   300

I wonder what woman he is waiting for tonight. It will be
delightful to catch him. Men always look so silly when they are
caught. And they are always being caught. (*Looks about room and
approaches the writing-table*) What a very interesting room! What
a very interesting picture! Wonder what his correspondence is   305
like. (*Takes up letters*) Oh, what a very uninteresting correspondence! Bills and cards, debts and dowagers! Who on earth

---

286–7   *To expect . . . intellect* first appears in F ('a good deal of intellect').
287   s.d. in F the s.d. specifies *'lights down in drawing-room'* when the door is opened
      and *'White lights up in drawing-room'* as the candles are lit. After the shades have
      been put on there is *'Rose pink light in drawing-room'.*
288   *dreary* altered from 'horrid' in revision to BLTS.
298   *as yet* added to PR.
301–18   *I wonder . . . coming to you.'* F and LC om. 'Bills and cards, debts and dowagers'. It
      derives from an addition to BLTS (adopted in C): 'Poor Arthur, he is always being
      scrambled for by creditors and countesses. With all his faults he is still remarkably
      modern (*Takes up looking-glass.*) and he wears well, too. Almost as well as I do.'
      LC and earlier versions add 'some romantic girl, I suppose' after 'who . . . pink
      paper?' 'Romance . . . settlement' first appears in F. In LC, C, BLTS and MS 'How I
      detest that woman' is followed by: 'She separated us once. I suppose she is trying to
      separate us again. I think I had better read it. I hate reading horrid things about
      myself, and I am invariably doing it. How perverse we all are nowadays.'

writes to him on pink paper? How silly to write on pink paper!
It looks like the beginning of a middle-class romance. Romance
should never begin with sentiment. It should begin with science 310
and end with a settlement. (*Puts letter down, then takes it up
again*) I know that handwriting. That is Gertrude Chiltern's. I
remember it perfectly. The ten commandments in every stroke
of the pen, and the moral law all over the page. Wonder what
Gertrude is writing to him about? Something horrid about me, 315
I suppose. How I detest that woman! (*Reads it*) 'I trust you. I
want you. I am coming to you. Gertrude.' 'I trust you. I want
you. I am coming to you.'

> *A look of triumph comes over her face.*
> *She is just about to steal the letter, when* PHIPPS *comes in* 320

PHIPPS
The candles in the drawing-room are lit, madam, as you directed.
MRS CHEVELEY
Thank you.

> *Rises hastily, and slips the letter under a large silver-cased* 325
> *blotting-book that is lying on the table*

PHIPPS
I trust the shades will be to your liking, madam. They are the
most becoming we have. They are the same as his lordship uses
himself when he is dressing for dinner. 330
MRS CHEVELEY (*With a smile*)
Then I am sure they will be perfectly right.
PHIPPS (*Gravely*)
Thank you, madam.

> MRS CHEVELEY *goes into the drawing-room.* 335
> PHIPPS *closes the door and retires. The door is then*
> *slowly opened, and* MRS CHEVELEY *comes out and creeps*
> *stealthily towards the writing-table. Suddenly voices are heard*
> *from the smoking-room.* MRS CHEVELEY *grows pale, and stops.*

325–6   s.d. *and slips ... table* first appears in PR: F notes '*places pink letter on table and closes
the lid of the blotter over it, down stage, so as to hide it, the pink envelope is left on
corner of table below blotter*'.
336–41   s.d. PHIPPS ... *biting her lip* Wilde added a speech to BLTS making the motives and
actions clear: 'I should like to have that letter! It might be useful when Lady Chiltern
arrives. (Hears *voices and and retreats*) I can't! What a disappointment!' This does not
appear in LC or F.

The voices grow louder, and she goes back into the drawing-room, 340
biting her lip. Enter LORD GORING *and* LORD CAVERSHAM

LORD GORING (*Expostulating*)
  My dear father, if I am to get married, surely you will allow me
  to choose the time, place, and person? Particularly the person.
LORD CAVERSHAM (*Testily*) 345
  That is a matter for me, sir. You would probably make a very
  poor choice. It is I who should be consulted, not you. There is
  property at stake. It is not a matter for affection. Affection
  comes later on in married life.
LORD GORING 350
  Yes. In married life affection comes when people thoroughly
  dislike each other, father, doesn't it?
                    Puts on LORD CAVERSHAM*'s cloak for him*
LORD CAVERSHAM
  Certainly, sir. I mean certainly not, sir. You are talking very 355
  foolishly tonight. What I say is that marriage is a matter for
  common sense.
LORD GORING
  But women who have common sense are so curiously plain,
  father, aren't they? Of course I only speak from hearsay. 360
LORD CAVERSHAM
  No woman, plain or pretty, has any common sense at all, sir.
  Common sense is the privilege of our sex.
LORD GORING
  Quite so. And we men are so self-sacrificing that we never use 365
  it, do we, father?
LORD CAVERSHAM
  I use it, sir. I use nothing else.
LORD GORING
  So my mother tells me. 370

---

346   *That this a matter for me, sir* usually a mother's prerogative with regard to her
      daughter. Cf. Lady Bracknell's insistence on it (*Earnest*, I, 465–470 and III, 71 etc.).
347–7 *a very poor choice* F indicates '*First coat business*' and has s.d. throughout the
      exchange for this, but does not describe the action.
348–57 *Affection ... common sense* first appears, in a slightly different form (with 'sentiment'
      for 'affection') in F.
360   *Of course ... hearsay* BLTS reads 'There is always something wrong about their
      complexions', to which Wilde added in manuscript 'They always look like second-
      hand dictionaries'. The second sentence survived into LC and F.

LORD CAVERSHAM

It is the secret of your mother's happiness. You are very heartless, sir, very heartless.

LORD GORING

I hope not, father.   375

Goes out for a moment [with LORD CAVERSHAM]. *Then returns,
looking rather put out, with* SIR ROBERT CHILTERN

SIR ROBERT CHILTERN

My dear Arthur, what a piece of good luck meeting you on the
doorstep! Your servant had just told me you were not at home.   380
How extraordinary!

LORD GORING

The fact is, I am horribly busy tonight, Robert, and I gave
orders I was not at home to anyone. Even my father had a
comparatively cold reception. He complained of a draught the   385
whole time.

SIR ROBERT CHILTERN

Ah! you must be at home to me, Arthur. You are my best friend.
Perhaps by tomorrow you will be my only friend. My wife has
discovered everything.   390

LORD GORING

Ah! I guessed as much!

SIR ROBERT CHILTERN (*Looking at him*)

Really! How?

LORD GORING (*After some hesitation*)   395

Oh, merely by something in the expression of your face as you
came in. Who told her?

SIR ROBERT CHILTERN

Mrs Cheveley herself. And the woman that I love knows that I
began my career with an act of low dishonesty, that I built up   400

372–3   *It is . . . heartless* MS has a longer version. In BLTS Wilde added the reminder: 'You
were engaged once to a charming girl and jilted her after a week' – adopted in C
('someone' for 'a charming girl') but not in LC.

376   s.d. Wilde corrects an erroneous s.d. in PR ('*Enter* MRS CHEVELEY. *Then enter* LORD
GORING *and* SIR ROBERT CHILTERN').

384–6   *Even . . . time* first appears in PR.

392   *Ah! I guessed as much!* F has '*business with envelope*' before this line and '*Lord G. puts
pink envelope in his pocket*' after it.

400   *low dishonesty* 1st ed., PR, F (dishonour LC, BLTS, C; dishonesty MS). Earlier
versions include an account by Sir Robert of the circumstances under which his wife
learned the secret from Mrs C; Wilde (or Waller) evidently decided that this was
unnecessary, since the audience witnessed the incident in Act II.

my life upon sands of shame – that I sold, like a common huckster, the secret that had been intrusted to me as a man of honour. I thank heaven poor Lord Radley died without knowing that I betrayed him. I would to God I had died before I had been so horribly tempted, or had fallen so low.   405

Burying his face in his hands

LORD GORING (*After a pause*)

You have heard nothing from Vienna yet, in answer to your wire?

SIR ROBERT CHILTERN (*Looking up*)   410

Yes; I got a telegram from the first secretary at eight o'clock tonight.

LORD GORING

Well?

SIR ROBERT CHILTERN   415

Nothing is absolutely known against her. On the contrary, she occupies a rather high position in society. It is a sort of open secret that Baron Arnheim left her the greater portion of his immense fortune. Beyond that I can learn nothing.

LORD GORING   420

She doesn't turn out to be a spy, then?

SIR ROBERT CHILTERN

Oh! spies are of no use nowadays. Their profession is over. The newspapers do their work instead.

LORD GORING   425

And thunderingly well they do it.

SIR ROBERT CHILTERN

Arthur, I am parched with thirst. May I ring for something? Some hock and seltzer?

408–18   *You have heard . . . learn nothing* first appears in F.
416–17   *Nothing . . . in society* PR (All that is known about her is . . . F).
421–6   *She doesn't . . . they do it* first appears in PR. There may be an oblique reference to the conduct of *The Times* (known as 'The Thunderer') in the Parnell Case (1887). Letters, later shown to be forged, had been procured which purported to show that the Irish politician Charles Stuart Parnell approved of the Phoenix Park murders.
429   *hock and seltzer* the mixture of hock and soda-water was a favourite restorative, used by Dorian Gray (*DG*, p. 149 / *CW*, p. 116) and Lord Byron:
And for the future - (But I write this reeling,
Having got drunk exceedingly today.
So that I seem to stand upon the ceiling)
I say – the future is a serious matter –
And so – for God's sake – hock and soda-water!'
(*Don Juan*, fragment on the back of the MS of Canto I).

LORD GORING   430
    Certainly. Let me.   *Rings the bell*
SIR ROBERT CHILTERN
    Thanks! I don't know what to do, Arthur, I don't know what to
    do, and you are my only friend. But what a friend you are – the
    one friend I can trust. I can trust you absolutely, can't I?   435

                        Enter PHIPPS

LORD GORING
    My dear Robert, of course. Oh! (*To* PHIPPS) Bring some hock
    and seltzer.
PHIPPS   440
    Yes, my lord.
LORD GORING
    And Phipps!
PHIPPS
    Yes, my lord.   445
LORD GORING
    Will you excuse me for a moment, Robert? I want to give some
    directions to my servant.
SIR ROBERT CHILTERN
    Certainly.   450
LORD GORING
    When that lady calls, tell her that I am not expected home this
    evening. Tell her that I have been suddenly called out of town.
    You understand?
PHIPPS   455
    The lady is in that room, my lord. You told me to show her into
    that room, my lord.
LORD GORING
    You did perfectly right. (*Exit* PHIPPS) What a mess I am in. No;
    I think I shall get through it. I'll give her a lecture through the   460
    door. Awkward thing to manage, though.
SIR ROBERT CHILTERN
    Arthur, tell me what I should do. My life seems to have
    crumbled about me. I am a ship without a rudder in a night
    without a star.   465

---

    434   *my only friend. But what a friend you are* this, and the final sentence of the speech,
           first appear in PR.
    459–61 *What a mess . . . manage, though* added to BLTS and included in C and LC; om. F.
    464   *a ship without a rudder* F and MS read 'as a ship without a rudder'.

LORD GORING

Robert, you love your wife, don't you?

SIR ROBERT CHILTERN

I love her more than anything in the world. I used to think
ambition the great thing. It is not. Love is the great thing in the 470
world. There is nothing but love, and I love her. But I am
defamed in her eyes. I am ignoble in her eyes. There is a wide
gulf between us now. She has found me out, Arthur, she has
found me out.

LORD GORING 475

Has she never in her life done some folly – some indiscretion
– that she should not forgive your sin?

SIR ROBERT CHILTERN

My wife! Never! She does not know what weakness or
temptation is. I am of clay like other men. She stands apart as 480
good women do – pitiless in her perfection – cold and stern
and without mercy. But I love her, Arthur. We are childless, and
I have no one else to love, no one else to love me. Perhaps if
God had sent us children she might have been kinder to me.
But God has given us a lonely house. And she has cut my heart 485
in two. Don't let us talk of it. I was brutal to her this evening.
But I suppose when sinners talk to saints they are brutal always.
I said to her things that were hideously true, on my side, from
my standpoint, from the standpoint of men. But don't let us
talk of that. 490

LORD GORING

Your wife will forgive you. Perhaps at this moment she is
forgiving you. She loves you, Robert. Why should she not
forgive?

SIR ROBERT CHILTERN 495

God grant it! God grant it! (*Buries his face in his hands*) But
there is something more I have to tell you, Arthur.

Enter PHIPPS *with drinks*

PHIPPS (*Hands hock and seltzer to* SIR ROBERT CHILTERN)

Hock and seltzer, sir. 500

SIR ROBERT CHILTERN

Thank you.

473–4   *She ... out* om. F.
476–7   *Has she ... sin?* F and LC transpose ll. 492–6 to this point. MS, C read 'or worse than
  folly' for 'some indiscretion'.
481–2   *cold and stern and without mercy* om. F.

LORD GORING
Is your carriage here, Robert?

SIR ROBERT CHILTERN   505
No; I walked from the club.

LORD GORING
Sir Robert will take my cab, Phipps.

PHIPPS
Yes, my lord.   *Exit*   510

LORD GORING
Robert, you don't mind my sending you away?

SIR ROBERT CHILTERN
Arthur, you must let me stay for five minutes. I have made up
my mind what I am going to do tonight in the House. The   515
debate on the Argentine Canal is to begin at eleven. (*A chair
falls in the drawing-room*) What is that?

LORD GORING
Nothing.

SIR ROBERT CHILTERN   520
I heard a chair fall in the next room. Someone has been
listening.

LORD GORING
No, no; there is no one there.

SIR ROBERT CHILTERN   525
There is someone. There are lights in the room, and the door is
ajar. Someone has been listening to every secret of my life.
Arthur, what does this mean?

LORD GORING
Robert, you are excited, unnerved. I tell you there is no one in 530
that room. Sit down, Robert.

SIR ROBERT CHILTERN
Do you give me your word that there is no one there?

LORD GORING
Yes.   535

SIR ROBERT CHILTERN
Your word of honour?   *Sits down*

LORD GORING
Yes.

SIR ROBERT CHILTERN (*Rises*)   540
Arthur, let me see for myself.

515–16   *I have made up . . . eleven* first appears in F; LC, C, BLTS and MS provide another
reference to the information expected from Lord Berkshire (cf. note to II, 289–91,
above) and to Mrs C's 'confession'.

LORD GORING
No, no.

SIR ROBERT CHILTERN
If there is no one there why should I not look in that room?   545
Arthur, you must let me go into that room and satisfy myself.
Let me know that no eavesdropper has heard my life's secret.
Arthur, you don't realise what I am going through.

LORD GORING
Robert, this must stop. I have told you that there is no one in   550
that room – that is enough.

SIR ROBERT CHILTERN (*Rushes to the door of the room*)
It is not enough. I insist on going into this room. You have told
me there is no one there, so what reason can you have for
refusing me?   555

LORD GORING
For God's sake, don't! There is someone there. Someone whom
you must not see.

SIR ROBERT CHILTERN
Ah, I thought so!   560

LORD GORING
I forbid you to enter that room.

SIR ROBERT CHILTERN
Stand back. My life is at stake. And I don't care who is there. I
will know who it is to whom I have told my secret and my   565
shame.   *Enters room*

LORD GORING
Great Heavens! his own wife!

SIR ROBERT CHILTERN *comes back,*
with a look of scorn and anger on his face   570

SIR ROBERT CHILTERN
What explanation have you to give me for the presence of that
woman here?

LORD GORING
Robert, I swear to you on my honour that that lady is stainless   575
and guiltless of all offence towards you.

SIR ROBERT CHILTERN
She is a vile, an infamous thing!

553–93   *It is not enough . . . word of honour* F has a simpler version of the sequence,
          culminating in Lord G's protest: 'But Robert, you know perfectly well that Lady
          Chiltern –' and the angry reply, 'I think, sir, that we had better leave my wife's name
          out of the question'. PR seems closer to BLTS than to F in this passage.

LORD GORING

Don't say that, Robert! It was for your sake she came here. 580
It was to try and save you she came here. She loves you and no
one else.

SIR ROBERT CHILTERN

You are mad. What have I to do with her intrigues with you? Let
her remain your mistress! You are well suited to each other. She, 585
corrupt and shameful – you, false as a friend, treacherous as an
enemy even –

LORD GORING

It is not true, Robert. Before heaven, it is not true. In her
presence and in yours I will explain all. 590

SIR ROBERT CHILTERN

Let me pass, sir. You have lied enough upon your word of
honour.

> SIR ROBERT CHILTERN *goes out.*
> LORD GORING *rushes to the door of the* 595
> *drawing-room, when* MRS CHEVELEY
> *comes out, looking radiant and much amused*

MRS CHEVELEY (*With a mock curtsey*)

Good evening, Lord Goring!

LORD GORING 600

Mrs Cheveley! Great Heavens! . . . May I ask what you were
doing in my drawing-room?

MRS CHEVELEY

Merely listening. I have a perfect passion for listening through
keyholes. One always hears such wonderful things through 605
them.

590   *I will explain all* LC and earlier versions add a further exchange in which Lord G
      insists on the woman's being 'pure and good and gentle' and Sir Robert tells him
      that he hopes never to see either of them again.

604–6   *Merely listening . . . through them* MS reads:
        We often pay after dinner calls in Vienna. It is quite the thing to do. So I thought
        I would pay you one, and your servant asked me to wait in your drawing-room,
        so I waited. I was so sorry Gertrude Chiltern did not join me. It would have been
        a delightful meeting. I was bored to death till you and the admirable Sir Robert
        began to talk about me – then I listened.
        Lord G replies, 'What do you mean by saying Lady Chiltern didn't join you?'. This is
        followed by a note asking the typist to leave a space. In BLTS this instruction is
        followed, and Wilde has filled in the gap with manuscript additions, including
        ll. 608–10 'Doesn't that . . . by this time'). The MS equivalent of the scene that
        follows differs considerably from the present edition. Goring trades Mrs C's written
        'confession' of dishonesty for the incriminating letter, and burns them both. There
        is no mention of the brooch, which does not appear until the F typescript.

102

LORD GORING

Doesn't that sound rather like tempting Providence?

MRS CHEVELEY

Oh! surely Providence can resist temptation by this time.　　610

Makes a sign to him to take her cloak off, which he does

LORD GORING

I am glad you have called. I am going to give you some good
advice.

MRS CHEVELEY　　615

Oh! pray don't. One should never give a woman anything that
she can't wear in the evening.

LORD GORING

I see you are quite as wilful as you used to be.

MRS CHEVELEY　　620

Far more! I have greatly improved. I have had more experience.

LORD GORING

Too much experience is a dangerous thing. Pray have a
cigarette. Half the pretty women in London smoke cigarettes.
Personally I prefer the other half.　　625

MRS CHEVELEY

Thanks. I never smoke. My dressmaker wouldn't like it, and a
woman's first duty in life is to her dressmaker, isn't it? What the
second duty is, no one has as yet discovered.

LORD GORING　　630

You have come here to sell me Robert Chiltern's letter, haven't
you?

MRS CHEVELEY

To offer it to you on conditions. How did you guess that?

LORD GORING　　635

Because you haven't mentioned the subject. Have you got it
with you?

MRS CHEVELEY (*Sitting down*)

Oh, no! A well-made dress has no pockets.

LORD GORING　　640

What is your price for it?

621–9　*I have had . . . discovered* Cf. Appendix I for revisions to this passage. The epigram
on the two duties of women ('and a woman's . . . discovered') adapts a *bon mot* that
appears in F's version of Act II (see note to II. 615–40).

In MS and BLTS Lord G announces his intention of showing the 'confession' of
Mrs C to his uncle (at the embassy in Vienna) and Lady M, thus ensuring that Mrs
C will be ostracised there. She accuses him directly of being Lady C's lover.

MRS CHEVELEY

How absurdly English you are! The English think that a cheque-book can solve every problem in life. Why, my dear Arthur, I have very much more money than you have, and quite 645 as much as Robert Chiltern has got hold of. Money is not what I want.

LORD GORING

What do you want then, Mrs Cheveley?

MRS CHEVELEY 650

Why don't you call me Laura?

LORD GORING

I don't like the name.

MRS CHEVELEY

You used to adore it. 655

LORD GORING

Yes: that's why.

> MRS CHEVELEY *motions to him to sit down beside her.*
> *He smiles, and does so*

MRS CHEVELEY 660

Arthur, you loved me once.

LORD GORING

Yes.

MRS CHEVELEY

And you asked me to be your wife. 665

LORD GORING

That was the natural result of my loving you.

MRS CHEVELEY

And you threw me over because you saw, or said you saw, poor old Lord Mortlake trying to have a violent flirtation with me in 670 the conservatory at Tenby.

651   *Why don't you call me Laura?* an intimacy appropriate only between close relatives, married couples and those engaged to be married: Mrs C is taunting him with a reference to their engagement.

663   *Yes* LC adds 'I have done many foolish things in my life. That was the most foolish'.

669–71   *because . . . Tenby* om. F. In LC she accuses Lord G of throwing her over 'without a word of warning', of giving no explanation and refusing to see her. Later in this version we are given more circumstantial details of the flirtation in question, including the rather crude admonition: 'Mrs Cheveley, you had not quite realized that conservatories have glass walls. They are not like boudoirs. They are not so convenient.' In the subsequent description of Tenby, C (following revisions to BLTS) included remarks on the English country house later transferred to Act I (ll. 646–9). Mrs C had been seen sitting on Lord Mortlake's knees, kissing him; she offers flippant reasons for this behaviour ('And I never could live without at least one flirtation a day').

LORD GORING
　I am under the impression that my lawyer settled that matter
　with you on certain terms . . . dictated by yourself.
MRS CHEVELEY　　　　　　　　　　　　　　　　　　　675
　At that time I was poor; you were rich.
LORD GORING
　Quite so. That is why you pretended to love me.
MRS CHEVELEY (*Shrugging her shoulders*)
　Poor old Lord Mortlake, who had only two topics of　680
　conversation, his gout and his wife! I never could quite make
　out which of the two he was talking about. He used the most
　horrible language about them both. Well, you were silly, Arthur.
　Why, Lord Mortlake was never anything more to me than
　an amusement. One of those utterly tedious amusements one　685
　only finds at an English country house on an English country
　Sunday. I don't think anyone at all morally responsible for what
　he or she does at an English country house.
LORD GORING
　Yes. I know lots of people think that.　　　　　　　　　　690
MRS CHEVELEY
　I loved you, Arthur.
LORD GORING
　My dear Mrs Cheveley, you have always been far too clever to
　know anything about love.　　　　　　　　　　　　　　695
MRS CHEVELEY
　I did love you. And you loved me. You know you loved me; and
　love is a very wonderful thing. I suppose that when a man has
　once loved a woman, he will do anything for her, except
　continue to love her?　　　　　　　　　　　　　　　　700
　　　　　　　　　　　　　　　　　　　Puts her hand on his
LORD GORING (*Taking his hand away quietly*)
　Yes: except that.

673–4　　*my lawyer . . . terms* too honourable to let it be thought that a lady had given grounds
　　　　for the breaking-off of an engagement, Lord Goring took the responsibility upon
　　　　himself. The 'terms' would be a financial settlement to avoid the possibility of his
　　　　being sued for breach of promise of marriage.
687–8　　*I don't think . . . country house* first appears in F. The tedium of English country life
　　　　is a theme of the first act of *Woman*.

MRS CHEVELEY (*After a pause*)
  I am tired of living abroad. I want to come back to London. 705
  I want to have a charming house here. I want to have a salon. If
  one could only teach the English how to talk, and the Irish how
  to listen, society here would be quite civilised. Besides, I have
  arrived at the romantic stage. When I saw you last night at the
  Chilterns', I knew you were the only person I had ever cared for, 710
  if I ever have cared for anybody, Arthur. And so, on the morn-
  ing of the day you marry me, I will give you Robert Chiltern's
  letter. That is my offer. I will give it to you now, if you promise
  to marry me.
LORD GORING 715
  Now?
MRS CHEVELEY (*Smiling*)
  Tomorrow.
LORD GORING
  Are you really serious? 720
MRS CHEVELEY
  Yes, quite serious.
LORD GORING
  I should make you a very bad husband.
MRS CHEVELEY 725
  I don't mind bad husbands. I have had two. They amused me
  immensely.
LORD GORING
  You mean that you amused yourself immensely, don't you?
MRS CHEVELEY 730
  What do you know about my married life?
LORD GORING
  Nothing: but I can read it like a book.
MRS CHEVELEY
  What book? 735

---

705   *I am tired of living abroad* ... LC's version of the remainder of this act, which is
        based on C, includes some of the material printed here but om. ll. 705–20 ('I am
        tired ... really serious?'), 739–68 ('Do you think ... true character') and 789–937
        (Well, Arthur, ... With pleasure'). F's version approximates to that of PR.
706–11 *I want to have ... And so* om. F. The ideal of a *salon*, in which the hostess would
        attract to her drawing-room the cream of intellectual society, was difficult to achieve.
        Wilde said of the rich, homosexual Russian emigré André Raffalovich that he came
        to London intending to found a *salon* and only succeeded in founding a saloon
        (*Letters*, p. 173, note).

LORD GORING (*Rising*)
The Book of Numbers.

MRS CHEVELEY
Do you think it quite charming of you to be so rude to a
woman in your own house?   740

LORD GORING
In the case of very fascinating women, sex is a challenge, not a
defence.

MRS CHEVELEY
I suppose that is meant for a compliment. My dear Arthur,   745
women are never disarmed by compliments. Men always are.
That is the difference between the two sexes.

LORD GORING
Women are never disarmed by anything, as far as I know them.

MRS CHEVELEY (*After a pause*)   750
Then you are going to allow your greatest friend, Robert
Chiltern, to be ruined, rather than marry someone who really
has considerable attractions left. I thought you would have
risen to some great height of self-sacrifice, Arthur. I think you
should. And the rest of your life you could spend in contem-   755
plating your own perfections.

LORD GORING
Oh! I do that as it is. And self-sacrifice is a thing that should be
put down by law. It is so demoralizing to the people for whom
one sacrifices oneself. They always go to the bad.   760

MRS CHEVELEY
As if anything could demoralize Robert Chiltern! You seem to
forget that I know his real character.

LORD GORING
What you know about him is not his real character. It was an   765
act of folly done in his youth, dishonourable, I admit, shameful,
I admit, unworthy of him, I admit, and therefore . . . not his true
character.

MRS CHEVELEY
How you men stand up for each other!   770

739–49 *Do you think . . . as I know them* first appears in PR. Lines 742–3 ('In the case of
a very fascinating woman . . . ') are adapted from material originally drafted for
Act II.

758–60 *And self-sacrifice . . . sacrifices oneself* this anticipates Lord G's interview with Lady C
near the end of Act IV (ll. 624–75).

LORD GORING

How you women war against each other!

MRS CHEVELEY (*Bitterly*)

I only war against one woman, against Gertrude Chiltern. I hate
her. I hate her now more than ever.   775

LORD GORING

Because you have brought a real tragedy into her life, I suppose.

MRS CHEVELEY (*With a sneer*)

Oh, there is only one real tragedy in a woman's life. The fact
that her past is always her lover, and her future invariably her   780
husband.

LORD GORING

Lady Chiltern knows nothing of the kind of life to which you
are alluding.

MRS CHEVELEY   785

A woman whose size in gloves is seven and three-quarters never
knows much about anything. You know Gertrude has always
worn seven and three-quarters? That is one of the reasons why
there was never any moral sympathy between us . . . Well,
Arthur, I suppose this romantic interview may be regarded as at   790
an end. You admit it was romantic, don't you? For the privilege
of being your wife I was ready to surrender a great prize, the
climax of my diplomatic career. You decline. Very well. If Sir
Robert doesn't uphold my Argentine scheme, I expose him.
Voilà tout.   795

LORD GORING

You mustn't do that. It would be vile, horrible, infamous.

MRS CHEVELEY (*Shrugging her shoulders*)

Oh! don't use big words. They mean so little. It is a commercial
transaction. That is all. There is no good mixing up sentimen-   800
tality in it. I offered to sell Robert Chiltern a certain thing. If he
won't pay me my price, he will have to pay the world a greater
price. There is no more to be said. I must go. Good-bye. Won't
you shake hands?

777–88   *Because . . . seven and three-quarters?* added to BLTS with variations of detail. In a line
deleted from C Mrs C remarks that 'I don't mind her having a large heart, but I can't
stand large hands'. After l. 789 both BLTS and C move to the equivalent of l. 935: the
letters have been burned, and the bracelet incident is absent.

791–3   *You admit . . . Very well* first appears in PR.

795   *Voilà tout* altered in PR from its English equivalent 'That is all'.

797   *You mustn't* altered from 'Don't' in PR.

799–803 *It is a commercial . . . I must go* first appears in PR.

LORD GORING   805

With you? No. Your transaction with Robert Chiltern may pass
as a loathsome commercial transaction of a loathsome commercial age; but you seem to have forgotten that you who came
here tonight to talk of love, you whose lips desecrated the word
love, you to whom the thing is a book closely sealed, went this   810
afternoon to the house of one of the most noble and gentle
women in the world to degrade her husband in her eyes, to try
and kill her love for him, to put poison in her heart, and
bitterness in her life, to break her idol and, it may be, spoil her
soul. That I cannot forgive you. That was horrible. For that   815
there can be no forgiveness.

MRS CHEVELEY

Arthur, you are unjust to me. Believe me, you are quite unjust
to me. I didn't go to taunt Gertrude at all. I had no idea of
doing anything of the kind when I entered. I called with Lady   820
Markby simply to ask whether an ornament, a jewel, that I lost
somewhere last night, had been found at the Chilterns'. If you
don't believe me, you can ask Lady Markby. She will tell you it
is true. The scene that occurred happened after Lady Markby
had left, and was really forced on me by Gertrude's rudeness   825
and sneers. I called, oh! – a little out of malice if you like – but
really to ask if a diamond brooch of mine had been found. That
was the origin of the whole thing.

LORD GORING

A diamond snake-brooch with a ruby?   830

MRS CHEVELEY

Yes. How do you know?

LORD GORING

Because it is found. In point of fact, I found it myself, and
stupidly forgot to tell the butler anything about it as I was   835
leaving. (*Goes over to the writing-table and pulls out the drawers*)
It is in this drawer. No, that one. This is the brooch, isn't it?

Holds up the brooch

806–10   *Your transaction . . . sealed* first appears in PR (F begins 'You went this afternoon . . .'),
         as do ll. 812–15 ('to try . . . her soul'), 815–16 ('That I cannot . . . forgiveness'), 818
         (you are unjust to me') and 822–8 ('If you don't . . . the whole thing'). These
         differences between PR and F might indicate that copy for PR was based on a fuller
         version predating F (and simplified for performance by the compiler of F) or that Wilde
         added to the rhetorical intensity of the passage in 1898–99 when he prepared it for the
         printer. Only the last of the additions seems designed to clarify the play's action.
830   *with a ruby* (with ruby eyes F)

MRS CHEVELEY

    Yes. I am so glad to get it back. It was . . . a present.   840

LORD GORING

    Won't you wear it?

MRS CHEVELEY

    Certainly, if you pin it in. (LORD GORING *suddenly clasps it on her arm*) Why do you put it on as a bracelet? I never knew it   845
could be worn as a bracelet.

LORD GORING

    Really?

MRS CHEVELEY (*Holding out her handsome arm*)

    No; but it looks very well on me as a bracelet, doesn't it?   850

LORD GORING

    Yes; much better than when I saw it last.

MRS CHEVELEY

    When did you see it last?

LORD GORING (*Calmly*)   855

    Oh, ten years ago, on Lady Berkshire, from whom you stole it.

MRS CHEVELEY (*Starting*)

    What do you mean?

LORD GORING

    I mean that you stole that ornament from my cousin, Mary   860
Berkshire, to whom I gave it when she was married. Suspicion
fell on a wretched servant, who was sent away in disgrace. I
recognized it last night. I determined to say nothing about it till
I had found the thief. I have found the thief now, and I have
heard her own confession.   865

MRS CHEVELEY (*Tossing her head*)

    It is not true.

LORD GORING

    You know it is true. Why, thief is written across your face at this
moment.   870

MRS CHEVELEY

    I will deny the whole affair from beginning to end. I will say
that I have never seen this wretched thing, that it was never in
my possession.

---

849   s.d. *Holding . . . arm* added to PR.
866   s.d. added to PR by Wilde together with subsequent s.d. at ll. 875 (*Her thin . . . from her*), 889, 896 and 901.

MRS CHEVELEY *tries to get the bracelet off her arm,*   875
but fails. LORD GORING *looks on amused. Her thin fingers*
tear at the jewel to no purpose. A curse breaks from her

LORD GORING
The drawback of stealing a thing, Mrs Cheveley, is that one
never knows how wonderful the thing that one steals is. You   880
can't get that bracelet off, unless you know where the spring
is. And I see you don't know where the spring is. It is rather
difficult to find.

MRS CHEVELEY
You brute! You coward!   885

She tries again to unclasp the bracelet, but fails

LORD GORING
Oh! don't use big words. They mean so little.

MRS CHEVELEY (*Again tears at the bracelet in a paroxysm of rage,*
with inarticulate sounds. Then stops, and looks at LORD GORING)   890
What are you going to do?

LORD GORING
I am going to ring for my servant. He is an admirable servant.
Always comes in the moment one rings for him. When he
comes I will tell him to fetch the police.   895

MRS CHEVELEY (*Trembling*)
The police? What for?

LORD GORING
Tomorrow the Berkshires will prosecute you. That is what the
police are for.   900

MRS CHEVELEY (*Is now in an agony of physical terror. Her face is*
distorted. Her mouth awry. A mask has fallen from her. She is,
for the moment, dreadful to look at)
Don't do that. I will do anything you want. Anything in the
world you want.   905

LORD GORING
Give me Robert Chiltern's letter.

MRS CHEVELEY
Stop! Stop! Let me have time to think.

LORD GORING   910
Give me Robert Chiltern's letter.

879–80   *The drawback . . . steals is* added in manuscript to F.
894–900 *Always . . . are for* (And have you given in charge for theft F).

MRS CHEVELEY

I have not got it with me. I will give it to you tomorrow.

LORD GORING

You know you are lying. Give it to me at once. 915

MRS CHEVELEY *pulls the letter out, and hands it to him.*
She is horribly pale.

This is it?

MRS CHEVELEY (*In a hoarse voice*)

Yes. 920

LORD GORING (*Takes the letter, examines it, sighs, and burns it*
over the lamp)

For so well-dressed a woman, Mrs Cheveley, you have moments
of admirable common sense. I congratulate you.

MRS CHEVELEY (*Catches sight of* LADY CHILTERN'*s letter, the* 925
cover of which is just showing from under the blotting-book)

Please get me a glass of water.

LORD GORING

Certainly.

Goes to the corner of the room and pours out a glass of water. 930
While his back is turned MRS CHEVELEY *steals* LADY CHILTERN'*s*
letter. When LORD GORING *returns with the glass*
she refuses it with a gesture

MRS CHEVELEY

Thank you. Will you help me on with my cloak? 935

LORD GORING

With pleasure. *Puts her cloak on*

MRS CHEVELEY

Thanks. I am never going to try to harm Robert Chiltern again.

LORD GORING 940

Fortunately you have not the chance, Mrs Cheveley.

MRS CHEVELEY

Well, even if I had the chance, I wouldn't. On the contrary, I am
going to render him a great service.

913–20 *I have not . . . Yes* F has 'Yes! yes!' followed by the s.d. '*Bus. – gives letter. Lord G. takes*
bracelet off'.

930 s.d. F has a practical, prompter's version of this s.d.: '*Show by her expression that she*
remembers the pink letter under the blotter'.

939 *Thanks . . .* from this point LC, BLTS, C and MS differ only in minor details from F,
PR and 1st ed.

LORD GORING   945
    I am charmed to hear it. It is a reformation.
MRS CHEVELEY
    Yes. I can't bear so upright a gentleman, so honourable an
    English gentleman, being so shamefully deceived, and so –
LORD GORING   950
    Well?
MRS CHEVELEY
    I find that somehow Gertrude Chiltern's dying speech and
    confession has strayed into my pocket.
LORD GORING   955
    What do you mean?
MRS CHEVELEY (*With a bitter note of triumph in her voice*)
    I mean that I am going to send Robert Chiltern the love letter
    his wife wrote to you tonight.
LORD GORING   960
    Love letter?
MRS CHEVELEY (*Laughing*)
    'I want you. I trust you. I am coming to you. Gertrude.'

        LORD GORING *rushes to the bureau and takes up*
            the envelope, finds it empty, and turns round   965

LORD GORING
    You wretched woman, must you always be thieving? Give me
    back that letter. I'll take it from you by force. You shall not leave
    my room till I have got it.

        He rushes towards her, but MRS CHEVELEY *at once*   970
        puts her hand on the electric bell that is on the table.
        The bell sounds with shrill reverberations, and PHIPPS *enters*

MRS CHEVELEY (*After a pause*)
    Lord Goring merely rang that you should show me out. Good-
    night, Lord Goring!   975

951–4   *Well? . . . pocket* om. F, LC. The lines are found in BLTS and MS ('What do you mean?'
        for 'Well?') and are deleted in C. The phrase 'dying speech and confession' recalls
        the 'confession' of Mrs C that figures in early drafts.
961–3   *Love Letter? . . . Gertrude* om. BLTS, MS. In F Lord G has put the pink envelope in
        his pocket. He examines it now and finds it to be empty.
    967 *You wretched woman* om. BLTS, MS; in C 'miserable' is del. and 'unfortunate'
        substituted; *must you . . . thieving?* om. F.
968–9   *You shall not . . . got it* om. F.
    972 s.d. *The bell . . . reverberations* added to PR.

Goes out, followed by PHIPPS. *Her face is illumined with
evil triumph. There is joy in her eyes. Youth seems to have
come back to her. Her last glance is like a swift arrow.*
LORD GORING *bites his lip, and lights a cigarette*

ACT-DROP   980

978   s.d. *Her face . . . a swift arrow* added to PR.

ACT IV

Scene – Same as Act II.
LORD GORING *is standing by the fireplace with his hands*
in his pockets. He is looking rather bored

LORD GORING (*Pulls out his watch, inspects it, and rings the bell*)
    It is a great nuisance. I can't find anyone in this house to talk to.   5
    And I am full of interesting information. I feel like the latest
    edition of something or other.

Enter SERVANT

JAMES
    Sir Robert is still at the Foreign Office, my lord.   10
LORD GORING
    Lady Chiltern not down yet?
JAMES
    Her ladyship has not yet left her room. Miss Chiltern has just
    come in from riding.   15
LORD GORING (*To himself*)
    Ah! that is something.
JAMES
    Lord Caversham has been waiting some time in the library for
    Sir Robert. I told him your lordship was here.   20
LORD GORING
    Thank you. Would you kindly tell him I've gone?
JAMES (*Bowing*)
    I shall do so, my lord.   *Exit* SERVANT
LORD GORING   25
    Really, I don't want to meet my father three days running. It is a
    great deal too much excitement for any son. I hope to goodness

  1   s.d. *Scene* in F, LC, C and MS the act begins with a different sequence and is set in
       Lady C's boudoir. Mabel tells Lady C about Sir Robert's speech (ll. 81–5 in the
       present text) and complains that Lord G failed to keep his appointment with her.
       When he arrives, Lord G is reproached with his discourtesy. He asks to speak to Lady
       C alone. She tells him that she has decided to stand by her husband, and is assured
       that the incriminating letter has been burned (l. 321 etc.). The present arrangement
       appears in BLTS and PR. In BLTS the first sentence only of the s.d. is included.
  5   *this house* (this extraordinary house BLTS).
 5–7   *to talk . . . or other* om. BLTS.
 10   *Sir Robert . . . Office* In BLTS this is a question, to which James replies 'Yes, my lord'.

he won't come up. Fathers should be neither seen nor heard.
That is the only proper basis for family life. Mothers are
different. Mothers are darlings.   30

> *Throws himself down into a chair, picks up a paper*
> *and begins to read it. Enter* LORD CAVERSHAM

LORD CAVERSHAM
Well, sir, what are you doing here? Wasting your time as usual,
I suppose?   35

LORD GORING (*Throws down paper and rises*)
My dear father, when one pays a visit it is for the purpose of
wasting other people's time, not one's own.

LORD CAVERSHAM
Have you been thinking over what I spoke to you about last   40
night?

LORD GORING
I have been thinking about nothing else.

LORD CAVERSHAM
Engaged to be married yet?   45

LORD GORING (*Genially*)
Not yet: but I hope to be before lunch-time.

LORD CAVERSHAM (*Caustically*)
You can have till dinner-time if it would be of any convenience
to you.   50

LORD GORING
Thanks awfully, but I think I'd sooner be engaged before lunch.

LORD CAVERSHAM
Humph! Never know when you are serious or not.
                                                                     55
LORD GORING
Neither do I father.   *A pause*

LORD CAVERSHAM
I suppose you have read *The Times* this morning?

LORD GORING (*Airily*)
The Times? Certainly not. I only read *The Morning Post*. All that 60

28–30   *Fathers . . . different* om. BLTS.
60   *The Times*? om. BLTS, which continues: 'Certainly not, father. Nothing ages one so
        rapidly as reading the *Times*'. In LC and earlier texts these opinions are relayed by
        Mabel, who attributes them to Lord G. As she leafs through the paper she remarks:
        Wish there were not so many pages in *The Times* –I can never find anything but
        the letters from the country clergy, and the reports of the university extension
        scheme, and they are so demoralizing for a young girl.
        A manuscript s.d. in F has her '*sitting on couch, L. throwing sheets of the paper about
        in vain endeavour to find the speech.*'

one should know about modern life is where the Duchesses are;
anything else is quite demoralizing.

LORD CAVERSHAM

Do you mean to say you have not read *The Times'* leading
article on Robert Chiltern's career?   65

LORD GORING

Good heavens! No. What does it say?

LORD CAVERSHAM

What should it say, sir? Everything complimentary, of course.
Chiltern's speech last night on this Argentine Canal Scheme   70
was one of the finest pieces of oratory ever delivered in the
House since Canning.

LORD GORING

Ah! Never heard of Canning. Never wanted to. And did . . . did
Chiltern uphold the scheme?   75

LORD CAVERSHAM

Uphold it, sir? How little you know him! Why, he denounced it
roundly, and the whole system of modern political finance.
This speech is the turning-point in his career, as *The Times*
points out. You should read this article, sir. (*Opens* The Times)   80
'Sir Robert Chiltern . . . most rising of all our young statesmen
. . . Brilliant orator . . . Unblemished career . . . Well-known
integrity of character . . . Represents what is best in English
public life . . . Noble contrast to the lax morality so common
among foreign politicians.' They will never say that of you, sir.   85

LORD GORING

I sincerely hope not, father. However, I am delighted at what
you tell me about Robert, thoroughly delighted. It shows he has
got pluck.

LORD CAVERSHAM   90

He has got more than pluck, sir, he has got genius.

LORD GORING

Ah! I prefer pluck. It is not so common, nowadays, as genius is.

---

74 *Canning* George Canning (1770–1827), statesman and orator. The references to
Canning first appear in PR.

77–85 *Uphold . . . of you, sir* in LC and earlier versions, Mabel reads the excerpts from the
report, including '"ethical something" . . . Ah! that is too long a word for me. Besides,
I don't know what ethical means'. In BLTS Lord C is more emphatic in his denunciation of the canal scheme: 'Why, he didn't leave a drop of water in the whole
damned concern. The thing is a fraud, and a very infamous fraud, and he denounced
it roundly . . .' See Appendix I for the BLTS continuation of the dialogue after this
speech.

LORD CAVERSHAM
I wish you would go into Parliament. 95
LORD GORING
My dear father, only people who look dull ever get into the
House of Commons, and only people who are dull ever succeed
there.
LORD CAVERSHAM 100
Why don't you try to do something useful in life?
LORD GORING
I am far too young.
LORD CAVERSHAM (*Testily*)
I hate this affectation of youth, sir. It is a great deal too 105
prevalent nowadays.
LORD GORING
Youth isn't an affectation. Youth is an art.
LORD CAVERSHAM
Why don't you propose to that pretty Miss Chiltern? 110
LORD GORING
I am of a very nervous disposition, especially in the morning.
LORD CAVERSHAM
I don't suppose there is the smallest chance of her accepting
you. 115
LORD GORING
I don't know how the betting stands today.
LORD CAVERSHAM
If she did accept you she would be the prettiest fool in England.

105　*this affectation of youth* Wilde frequently expressed his preference for the company
of the young, statements which sometimes touched dangerously on his sexual
preferences and which were turned against him at his trials. Cf., for example, among
his 'Phrases and Philosophies for the Use of the Young': 'The old believe everything;
the middle-aged suspect everything; the young know everything' (*CW*, p. 1206). A
similar collection, 'A Few Maxims for the Instruction of the Over-educated'
(*Saturday Review*, 1891), includes 'Those whom the gods love grow young'. Asked in
cross-examination 'What enjoyment was it to you to entertain grooms and
coachmen [to expensive meals]?' Wilde replied: 'The pleasure to me was being with
those who are young, bright, happy, careless, and free. I do not like the sensible and
I do not like the old' (H. Montgomery Hyde, *The Trials of Oscar Wilde*, New York,
1973, p. 127). See also Lord Illingworth's praise of the virtues of youth in *Woman*
(III, 12–20).
117　*I don't . . . today* BLTS adds 'I have not been to the club today', which may have
seemed to imply too strongly that Mabel's name really is bandied about the club
world in an ungentlemanly fashion.

LORD GORING 120
    That is just what I should like to marry. A thoroughly sensible wife would reduce me to a condition of absolute idiocy in less than six months.

LORD CAVERSHAM
    You don't deserve her, sir. 125

LORD GORING
    My dear father, if we men married the women we deserved, we should have a very bad time of it.

Enter MABEL CHILTERN

MABEL CHILTERN 130
    Oh! . . . How do you do, Lord Caversham? I hope Lady Caversham is quite well?

LORD CAVERSHAM
    Lady Caversham is as usual, as usual.

LORD GORING 135
    Good morning, Miss Mabel!

MABEL CHILTERN (*Taking no notice at all of* LORD GORING, *and addressing herself exclusively to* LORD CAVERSHAM)
    And Lady Caversham's bonnets . . . are they at all better?

LORD CAVERSHAM 140
    They have had a serious relapse, I am sorry to say.

LORD GORING
    Good morning, Miss Mabel!

MABEL CHILTERN (*To* LORD CAVERSHAM)
    I hope an operation will not be necessary. 145

LORD CAVERSHAM (*Smiling at her pertness*)
    If it is we shall have to give Lady Caversham a narcotic. Otherwise she would never consent to have a feather touched.

LORD GORING (*With increased emphasis*)
    Good morning, Miss Mabel! 150

MABEL CHILTERN (*Turning round with feigned surprise*)
    Oh, are you here? Of course you understand that after your

---

119–23 *If she did . . . six months* used later in the act in LC and earlier versions.

141–52 *They have had . . . Oh, are you here?* om. BLTS, which (with MS and C) has a different version of the conversation. Lord G, told by Mabel that she 'got a great deal of sympathy, especially from Mr Trafford' on account of her fruitless wait for him in the Park, excuses himself.

    . . . I was terribly engaged this morning. I was asleep, in fact, till ten. And when I woke up, I found that my horse had gone lame. I went a little lame myself. Everything, in fact, went quite lame.

breaking your appointment I am never going to speak to you again.

LORD GORING   155

Oh, please don't say such a thing. You are the one person in London I really like to have to listen to me.

MABEL CHILTERN

Lord Goring, I never believe a single word that either you or I say to each other.   160

LORD CAVERSHAM

You are quite right, my dear, quite right . . . as far as he is concerned, I mean.

MABEL CHILTERN

Do you think you could possibly make your son behave a little   165
better occasionally? Just as a change.

LORD CAVERSHAM

I regret to say, Miss Chiltern, that I have no influence at all over my son. I wish I had. If I had, I know what I would make him do.   170

MABEL CHILTERN

I am afraid that he has one of those terribly weak natures that are not susceptible to influence.

LORD CAVERSHAM

He is very heartless, very heartless.   175

LORD GORING

It seems to me that I am a little in the way here.

MABEL CHILTERN

It is very good for you to be in the way, and to know what people say of you behind your back.   180

LORD GORING

I don't at all like knowing what people say of me behind my back. It makes me far too conceited.

LORD CAVERSHAM

After that, my dear, I really must bid you good morning.   185

MABEL CHILTERN

Oh! I hope you are not going to leave me all alone with Lord Goring? Especially at such an early hour in the day.

LORD CAVERSHAM

I am afraid I can't take him with me to Downing Street. It is not   190
the Prime Minister's day for seeing the unemployed.

190–1   *I am afraid . . . unemployed* BLTS follows up Lord G's reference (later deleted) to his
horse, at ll. 141–52. Concern about the *unemployed* as a group, and as a political

Shakes hands with MABEL CHILTERN, *takes up his hat
and stick, and goes out, with a parting glare of indignation
at* LORD GORING

MABEL CHILTERN (*Takes up roses and begins to arrange them in*   195
a bowl on the table)
People who don't keep their appointments in the Park are
horrid.
LORD GORING
Detestable.   200
MABEL CHILTERN
I am glad you admit it. But I wish you wouldn't look so pleased
about it.
LORD GORING
I can't help it. I always look pleased when I am with you.   205
MABEL CHILTERN (*Sadly*)
Then I suppose it is my duty to remain with you?
LORD GORING
Of course it is.
MABEL CHILTERN   210
Well, my duty is a thing I never do, on principle. It always
depresses me. So I am afraid I must leave you.
LORD GORING
Please don't, Miss Mabel. I have something very particular to
say to you.   215
MABEL CHILTERN (*Rapturously*)
Oh! is it a proposal?
LORD GORING (*Somewhat taken aback*)
Well, yes, it is – I am bound to say it is.
MABEL CHILTERN (*With a sigh of pleasure*)   220
I am so glad. That makes the second today.
LORD GORING (*Indignantly*)
The second today? What conceited ass has been impertinent
enough to dare to propose to you before I had proposed to you?

force, had come to a head in the Trafalgar Square riot in 1886. It was a commonplace
of the conservative press (including *Punch*) that only workshy ne'er-do-wells took
part, and *The Times* used inverted commas for the collective noun – 'the
unemployed' – in its report of the disturbance. The s.d. after this speech, and at
l. 195, first appear in PR.

207   *Then . . . you?* (In that case, I will certainly leave you BLTS). The s.d. here, and at
ll. 216, 218, 222 and 248 first appear in PR.

MABEL CHILTERN   225

Tommy Trafford, of course. It is one of Tommy's days for proposing. He always proposes on Tuesdays and Thursdays, during
the season.

LORD GORING

You didn't accept him, I hope?   230

MABEL CHILTERN

I make it a rule never to accept Tommy. That is why he goes on
proposing. Of course, as you didn't turn up this morning, I very
nearly said yes. It would have been an excellent lesson both for
him and for you if I had. It would have taught you both better   235
manners.

LORD GORING

Oh! bother Tommy Trafford. Tommy is a silly little ass. I love
you.

MABEL CHILTERN   240

I know. And I think you might have mentioned it before. I am
sure I have given you heaps of opportunities.

LORD GORING

Mabel, do be serious. Please be serious.

MABEL CHILTERN   245

Ah! that is the sort of thing a man always says to a girl before
he has been married to her. He never says it afterwards.

LORD GORING (*Taking hold of her hand*)

Mabel, I have told you that I love you. Can't you love me a little
in return?   250

MABEL CHILTERN

You silly Arthur! If you knew anything about . . . anything,
which you don't, you would know that I adore you. Everyone in
London knows it except you. It is a public scandal the way I
adore you. I have been going about for the last six months tell-   255
ing the whole of society that I adore you. I wonder you consent

226–8   *It is . . . season* Cf. note to Act III, l. 140. The last three words do not appear in BLTS.
246–7   *Ah! . . . afterwards* BLTS adds: 'I wish you wouldn't say those sort of things to me.
         They don't come well from you at all'. The revision concentrates attention on the
         references to marriage and 'seriousness', without the distracting reference to Lord
         G's reputation.
   252   *Anything about . . . anything* (Anything about women BLTS).
   254   *a public scandal* This phrase, present in all versions of the proposal sequence (which
         LC, C, F and MS place at the end of the act) reiterates the comic variation on the
         scandal theme (cf. Lady M's speech at II, 745, etc., Mabel's references to the *tableaux
         vivants*, etc.). The s.d. at l. 263 first appears in PR.

to have anything to say to me. I have no character left at all. At least, I feel so happy that I am quite sure I have no character left at all.

LORD GORING (*Catches her in his arms and kisses her. Then there is a pause of bliss*)   260

Dear! Do you know I was awfully afraid of being refused!

MABEL CHILTERN (*Looking up at him*)

But you never have been refused yet by anybody, have you Arthur? I can't imagine anyone refusing you.   265

LORD GORING (*After kissing her again*)

Of course I'm not nearly good enough for you, Mabel.

MABEL CHILTERN (*Nestling close to him*)

I am so glad, darling. I was afraid you were.

LORD GORING (*After some hesitation*)   270

And I'm . . . I'm a little over thirty.

MABEL CHILTERN

Dear, you look weeks younger than that.

LORD GORING (*Enthusiastically*)

How sweet of you to say so! . . . And it is only fair to tell you   275
frankly that I am fearfully extravagant.

MABEL CHILTERN

But so am I, Arthur. So we're sure to agree. And now I must go and see Gertrude.

LORD GORING   280

Must you really?   *Kisses her*

MABEL CHILTERN

Yes.

LORD GORING

Then do tell her I want to talk to her particularly. I have been   285
waiting here all the morning to see either her or Robert.

MABEL CHILTERN

Do you mean to say you didn't come here expressly to propose to me?

LORD GORING (*Triumphantly*)   290

No; that was a flash of genius.

MABEL CHILTERN

Your first.

LORD GORING (*With determination*)

My last.   295

275–6   *And it is . . . extravagant* om. BLTS, which has an extended version of the dialogue. See Appendix I.

MABEL CHILTERN

I am delighted to hear it. Now don't stir. I'll be back in five
minutes. And don't fall into any temptations while I am away.

LORD GORING

Dear Mabel, while you are away, there are none. It makes me   300
horribly dependent on you.

Enter LADY CHILTERN

LADY CHILTERN

Good morning, dear! How pretty you are looking!

MABEL CHILTERN   305

How pale you are looking, Gertrude! It is most becoming!

LADY CHILTERN

Good morning, Lord Goring!

LORD GORING (*Bowing*)

Good morning, Lady Chiltern!   310

MABEL CHILTERN (*Aside to* LORD GORING)

I shall be in the conservatory, under the second palm tree on
the left.

LORD GORING

Second on the left?   315

MABEL CHILTERN (*With a look of mock surprise*)

Yes; the usual palm tree.

> *Blows a kiss to him, unobserved by* LADY CHILTERN,
> *and goes out*

LORD GORING   320

Lady Chiltern, I have a certain amount of very good news to tell
you. Mrs Cheveley gave me up Robert's letter last night, and I
burned it. Robert is safe.

---

297   *I am delighted to hear it* BLTS has a longer version of this speech:
I am very glad to hear it. I certainly don't want to marry a man of genius. I'd be
very unhappy with him. I like you. You have no past: and no future. You are a
perfect darling. Just the sort of man every girl should marry.
Lord G replies: 'I hope they won't, darling. I don't want to marry anyone but you'.
Mabel's next speech begins, 'I'll take very great precautions that you don't', and picks
up with 'I'll be back in five minutes . . .'.

310   *Good morning, Lady Chiltern* in BLTS Lord G asks Mabel to leave the room, and she
complies. The s.d. at ll. 311, 316, 318–9 first appear in PR. With the interview
between Lord G and Lady C the printed version and its close antecedents (F, BLTS)
begin to agree with LC, C and MS.

312   *second palm tree* in l. 605 it has become the third.

321, etc.   *Lady Chiltern . . .* LC and earlier versions have a different beginning to this sequence,
including variant speeches for Lady C. See Appendix I.

124

LADY CHILTERN (*Sinking on the sofa*)

Safe! Oh! I am so glad of that. What a good friend you are to 325
him – to us!

LORD GORING

There is only one person now that could be said to be in any
danger.

LADY CHILTERN 330

Who is that?

LORD GORING (*Sitting down beside her*)

Yourself.

LADY CHILTERN

I! In danger? What do you mean? 335

LORD GORING

Danger is too great a word. It is a word I should not have used.
But I admit I have something to tell you that may distress you,
that terribly distresses me. Yesterday evening you wrote me a
very beautiful, womanly letter, asking me for my help. You 340
wrote to me as one of your oldest friends, one of your husband's oldest friends. Mrs Cheveley stole that letter from my
rooms.

LADY CHILTERN

Well, what use is it to her? Why should she not have it? 345

LORD GORING (*Rising*)

Lady Chiltern, I will be quite frank with you. Mrs Cheveley puts
a certain construction on that letter and proposes to send it to
your husband.

LADY CHILTERN 350

But what construction could she put on it? . . . Oh! not that! not
that! If I in – in trouble, and wanting your help, trusting you,
propose to come to you . . . that you may advise me . . . assist
me . . . Oh! are there women so horrible as that . . . ? And she

---

351   *But what . . . on it?* in F this is followed by a manuscript s.d.: '*They look fixedly at each
other a moment. Lady C. falls back on chair horrified*'.

354–6   *Oh! . . . happened* texts before PR have a longer version of this, far more
melodramatic in tone:

> Oh! what have I done? What did you make me do? Why did you let her take it? You
> should have killed her first. Why didn't you kill her? You have killed me instead!
> . . . No, no, what have I to fear? I am innocent of anything . . . Robert could not
> believe such a thing of me, any more than I before yesterday could have believed
> of him what I now know to be true. Ah! he will believe it! It will be his revenge!
> (BLTS, later deleted in manuscript revision.) In F there are appropriate manuscript
> s.ds. for this: she moves '*wildly R. to C. and down L.*', sinks on the couch, rises '*with
> a cry*' ('Ah! he will believe it!') and falls back on the couch.

125

proposes to send it to my husband? Tell me what happened. Tell   355
me all that happened.

LORD GORING

Mrs Cheveley was concealed in a room adjoining my library,
without my knowledge. I thought that the person who was
waiting in that room to see me was yourself. Robert came in   360
unexpectedly. A chair or something fell in the room. He forced
his way in, and he discovered her. We had a terrible scene. I still
thought it was you. He left me in anger. At the end of everything Mrs Cheveley got possession of your letter – she stole it,
when or how, I don't know.   365

LADY CHILTERN

At what hour did this happen?

LORD GORING

At half-past ten. And now I propose that we tell Robert the
whole thing at once.   370

LADY CHILTERN (*Looking at him with amazement that is almost
terror*)

You want me to tell Robert that the woman you expected was
not Mrs Cheveley, but myself? That it was I whom you thought
was concealed in a room in your house, at half-past ten o'clock   375
at night? You want me to tell him that?

LORD GORING

I think it is better that he should know the exact truth.

LADY CHILTERN (*Rising*)

Oh, I couldn't, I couldn't!   380

LORD GORING

May I do it?

LADY CHILTERN

No.

LORD GORING (*Gravely*)   385

You are wrong, Lady Chiltern.

LADY CHILTERN

No. The letter must be intercepted. That is all. But how can
I do it? Letters arrive for him every moment of the day. His
secretaries open them and hand them to him. I dare not ask the   390
servants to bring me his letters. It would be impossible. Oh!
why don't you tell me what to do?

LORD GORING

Pray be calm, Lady Chiltern, and answer the questions I am
going to put to you. You said his secretaries open his letters.   395

LADY CHILTERN
  Yes.
LORD GORING
  Who is with him today? Mr Trafford, isn't it?
LADY CHILTERN   400
  No. Mr Montfort, I think.
LORD GORING
  You can trust him?
LADY CHILTERN (*With a gesture of despair*)
  Oh! how do I know?   405
LORD GORING
  He would do what you asked him, wouldn't he?
LADY CHILTERN
  I think so.
LORD GORING   410
  Your letter was on pink paper. He could recognize it without
  reading it, couldn't he? By the colour?
LADY CHILTERN
  I suppose so.
LORD GORING   415
  Is he in the house now?
LADY CHILTERN
  Yes.
LORD GORING
  Then I will go and see him myself, and tell him that a certain   420
  letter, written on pink paper, is to be forwarded to Robert today,
  and that at all costs it must not reach him. (*Goes to the door, and
  opens it*) Oh! Robert is coming upstairs with the letter in his
  hand. It has reached him already.
LADY CHILTERN (*With a cry of pain*)   425
  Oh! you have saved his life; what have you done with mine?

        Enter SIR ROBERT CHILTERN. *He has the letter
    in his hand, and is reading it. He comes towards his wife,
            not noticing* LORD GORING'*s presence*

---

399   *Mr Trafford* earlier versons have 'Mr Montfort' (Cf. note to 'The Persons of the Play)
       and om. l. 401
420–26 *Then I will go . . . mine!* the present arrangement first appears in BLTS. F, LC and
       earlier versions have Mabel enter at the equivalent of l. 421, overhear the reference
       to a letter on pink paper, and inform them that she has seen Chiltern coming
       upstairs, reading such a letter. Lady C's exclamation (l. 426) is simply 'I am lost!'.

127

SIR ROBERT CHILTERN   430

'I want you. I trust you. I am coming to you. Gertrude.' Oh, my
love! Is this true? Do you indeed trust me, and want me? If so,
it was for me to come to you, not for you to write of coming to
me. This letter of yours, Gertrude, makes me feel that nothing
that the world may do can hurt me now. You want me,   435
Gertrude?

> LORD GORING, *unseen by* SIR ROBERT CHILTERN,
> *makes an imploring sign to* LADY CHILTERN *to accept
> the situation and* SIR ROBERT*'s error*

LADY CHILTERN   440
Yes.

SIR ROBERT CHILTERN
You trust me, Gertrude?

LADY CHILTERN
Yes.   445

SIR ROBERT CHILTERN
Ah! why did you not add you loved me?

LADY CHILTERN (*Taking his hand*)
Because I loved you.

> LORD GORING *passes into the conservatory*   450

SIR ROBERT CHILTERN (*Kisses her*)
Gertrude, you don't know what I feel. When Montfort passed
me your letter across the table – he had opened it by mistake,
I suppose, without looking at the handwriting on the envelope
– and I read it – oh! I did not care what disgrace or punishment 455
was in store for me, I only thought you loved me still.

LADY CHILTERN
There is no disgrace in store for you, nor any public shame. Mrs
Cheveley has handed over to Lord Goring the document that
was in her possession, and he has destroyed it.   460

SIR ROBERT CHILTERN
Are you sure of this, Gertrude?

LADY CHILTERN
Yes; Lord Goring has just told me.

SIR ROBERT CHILTERN   465
Then I am safe! Oh! what a wonderful thing to be safe! For two

---

437 s.d. First appears in PR.
452 In versions before PR, the speech begins 'My wife! my wife!'.
454 *without . . . envelope* first appears in PR.

days I have been in terror. I am safe now. How did Arthur
destroy my letter? Tell me.

LADY CHILTERN

He burned it. 470

SIR ROBERT CHILTERN

I wish I had seen that one sin of my youth burning to ashes.
How many men there are in modern life who would like to see
their past burning to white ashes before them! Is Arthur still
here? 475

LADY CHILTERN

Yes; he is in the conservatory.

SIR ROBERT CHILTERN

I am so glad now I made that speech last night in the House, so
glad. I made it thinking that public disgrace might be the result. 480
But it has not been so.

LADY CHILTERN

Public honour has been the result.

SIR ROBERT CHILTERN

I think so. I fear so, almost. For although I am safe from detec- 485
tion, although every proof against me is destroyed, I suppose,
Gertrude . . . I suppose I should retire from public life?

He looks anxiously at his wife

LADY CHILTERN (*Eagerly*)

Oh yes, Robert, you should do that. It is your duty to do that. 490

SIR ROBERT CHILTERN

It is much to surrender.

LADY CHILTERN

No; it will be much to gain.

472–4 *I wish . . . before them* cf. the vivid personification of the 'sin' in Act II (ll. 1100–102).
At the climax of *Dorian Gray* the hero attempts to kill his past:

> He looked round, and saw the knife that had stabbed Basil Hallward, He had
> cleaned it many times, till there was no stain left upon it. It was bright, and
> glistened. As it has killed the painter, so it would kill the painter's work, and all that
> that meant. It would kill the past, and when that was dead he would be free. It
> would kill this monstrous soul-life, and, without its hideous warnings, he would
> be at peace. He seized the thing, and stabbed the picture with it.

(*DG*, p. 223 / *CW*, pp. 166–7.) The phrase 'in modern life' first appears in BLTS; in
versions before PR 'white ashes before them' is simply 'ashes'.

485 *I think so* see Appendix I for an additional passage from texts before PR.

494 *No . . . gain* in versions before PR this is followed by four additional speeches:

SIR ROBERT

It is a just punishment, but all punishment is bitter in one's mouth.

SIR ROBERT CHILTERN *walks up and down the room*   495
with a troubled expression. Then comes over to his wife,
and puts his hand on her shoulder

SIR ROBERT CHILTERN
And you would be happy living somewhere alone with me,
abroad perhaps, or in the country away from London, away from   500
public life? You would have no regrets?

LADY CHILTERN
Oh! none, Robert.

SIR ROBERT CHILTERN (*Sadly*)
And your ambition for me? You used to be ambitious for me.   505

LADY CHILTERN
Oh, my ambition! I have none now, but that we two may love
each other. It was your ambition that led you astray. Let us not
talk about ambition.

LORD GORING *returns from the conservatory,*   510
looking very pleased with himself, and with an entirely
new buttonhole that someone has made for him

SIR ROBERT CHILTERN (*Going towards him*)
Arthur, I have to thank you for what you have done for me. I
don't know how I can repay you.   515

Shakes hands with him

LORD GORING
My dear fellow, I'll tell you at once. At the present moment,
under the usual palm tree . . . I mean in the conservatory . . .

Enter MASON   520

MASON
Lord Caversham.

LADY CHILTERN
Don't say that, Robert. It seems to me that the people one should pity most in
life are those who are not punished for the wrong they have done. They should
be pitied, not the others.
SIR ROBERT
Then I shall send in my resignation this afternoon.
LADY CHILTERN
My husband! my husband!
(LC version).
500   *abroad . . . country* first appears in PR.
514–19   *Arthur . . . conservatory* in texts before PR, Lord G enters with Mabel and begins to
ask permission to marry her. Lord C interrupts.

130

LORD GORING

That admirable father of mine really makes a habit of turning
up at the wrong moment. It is very heartless of him, very heart-   525
less indeed.

Enter LORD CAVERSHAM. MASON *goes out*

LORD CAVERSHAM

Good morning, Lady Chiltern! Warmest congratulations to
you, Chiltern, on your brilliant speech last night. I have just left   530
the Prime Minister, and you are to have the vacant seat in the
Cabinet.

SIR ROBERT CHILTERN (*With a look of joy and triumph*)
A seat in the Cabinet?

LORD CAVERSHAM   535

Yes; here is the Prime Minister's letter.   *Hands letter*

SIR ROBERT CHILTERN (*Takes letter and reads it*)
A seat in the Cabinet!

LORD CAVERSHAM

Certainly, and you well deserve it too. You have got what we   540
want so much in political life nowadays – high character, high
moral tone, high principles. (*To* LORD GORING) Everything
that you have not got, sir, and never will have.

LORD GORING

I don't like principles, father. I prefer prejudices.
                                                              545

525–6   *It is . . . indeed* (I must remonstrate with him F, LC, C). BLTS om. this line and
        substitutes: 'Fathers should be neither seen nor heard. That is the only proper basis
        of family life'.
531–2   *the vacant seat in the Cabinet* in MS Wilde originally had Lord C bring news of an
        under-secretaryship, with the 'promise' of the next vacant cabinet post. He also
        provided a reason for anticipating this as an imminent possibility: a cabinet reshuffle
        was on the way, partly on account of a certain member's being unable to get a wink
        of sleep in the House of Commons and so seeking elevation to the Lords. This was
        deleted from the MS. Wilde evidently felt unsure about Lord C's indiscretion in
        bringing the news, and the convenience of his intimacy with the premier. In F and
        C Sir Robert is told that the Prime Minister 'was very much impressed':
            In fact, I am deputed by him to certain degree, informally, you understand, to
            offer you the vacant seat in the Cabinet.
  545   *I don't . . . prejudices* (om. F, LC, C; I am afraid so, father BLTS). Most texts before
        PR include at this point a sequence which incorporates material later redeployed to
        the scene which opens the act in BLTS, PR and the 1st ed. (including ll. 40–56). Lord
        G is rebuked by his father for lacking the ambition that drives Sir Robert: 'Look at
        Chiltern; there is where ambition brings man'. The s.d. following the speech first
        appears in PR.

*SIR ROBERT CHILTERN is on the brink of accepting
the Prime Minister's offer, when he sees his wife
looking at him with her clear, candid eyes. He then
realizes that it is impossible*

SIR ROBERT CHILTERN   550
  I cannot accept this offer, Lord Caversham. I have made up my
  mind to decline it.

LORD CAVERSHAM
  Decline it, sir!

SIR ROBERT CHILTERN   555
  My intention is to retire at once from public life.

LORD CAVERSHAM (*Angrily*)
  Decline a seat in the Cabinet, and retire from public life? Never
  heard such damned nonsense in the whole course of my existence. I beg your pardon, Lady Chiltern. Chiltern, I beg your   560
  pardon. (*To* LORD GORING) Don't grin like that, sir.

LORD GORING
  No, father.

LORD CAVERSHAM
  Lady Chiltern, you are a sensible woman, the most sensible   565
  woman in London, the most sensible woman I know. Will you
  kindly prevent your husband from making such a . . . from
  talking such . . . Will you kindly do that, Lady Chiltern?

LADY CHILTERN
  I think my husband is right in his determination, Lord Caver-   570
  sham. I approve of it.

LORD CAVERSHAM
  You approve of it? Good Heavens!

LADY CHILTERN (*Taking her husband's hand*)
  I admire him for it. I admire him immensely for it. I have never 575
  admired him so much before. He is finer than even I thought
  him. (*To* SIR ROBERT CHILTERN) You will go and write your
  letter to the Prime Minister now, won't you? Don't hesitate
  about it, Robert.

SIR ROBERT CHILTERN (*With a touch of bitterness*)   580
  I suppose I had better write it at once. Such offers are not
  repeated. I will ask you to excuse me for a moment, Lord
  Caversham.

LADY CHILTERN
  I may come with you, Robert, may I not?   585

SIR ROBERT CHILTERN
Yes, Gertrude.

LADY CHILTERN *goes out with him*

LORD CAVERSHAM
What is the matter with this family? Something wrong here, eh?   590
(*Tapping his forehead*) Idiocy? Hereditary, I suppose. Both of
them, too. Wife as well as husband. Very sad. Very sad indeed!
And they are not an old family. Can't understand it.

LORD GORING
It is not idiocy, father, I assure you.   595

LORD CAVERSHAM
What is it then, sir?

LORD GORING (*After some hesitation*)
Well, it is what is called nowadays a high moral tone, father.
That is all.   600

LORD CAVERSHAM
Hate these new-fangled names. Same thing as we used to call
idiocy fifty years ago. Shan't stay in this house any longer.

LORD GORING (*Taking his arm*)
Oh! just go in here for a moment, father. Third palm tree to the   605
left, the usual palm tree.

LORD CAVERSHAM
What, sir?

LORD GORING
I beg your pardon, father, I forgot. The conservatory, father, the   610
conservatory – there is someone there I want you to talk to.

LORD CAVERSHAM
What about, sir?

LORD GORING
About me, father.   615

---

593 *And . . . understand it* first appears in PR.

599 *a high moral tone* cf. *Earnest*, I, 205, etc.: 'When one is placed in the position of a
guardian, one has to adopt a very high moral tone on all subjects. It's one's duty to
do so . . . '.

603 *any longer* texts before PR add: 'I'll go back to the Prime Minister and tell him that
Chiltern is the damnedest fool I ever knew' ('is off his head' BLTS). At this point
Mabel emerges from the conservatory, only to be sent back in so that Lord Goring
might speak to Lady Chiltern alone. (She observes that she doesn't like knowing
what people say about her behind her back – 'It makes me too conceited'; cf. ll.
181–2, above).

610–20 *I beg . . . loud* om. F, BLTS. Earlier texts have a longer exchange, incorporating
material later used in the opening of the act (including ll. 119–23), followed by the
conversation beginning at l. 624 of the present edition.

LORD CAVERSHAM (*Grimly*)
Not a subject on which much eloquence is possible.

LORD GORING
No, father; but the lady is like me. She doesn't care much for
eloquence in others. She thinks it a little loud. 620

> LORD CAVERSHAM *goes into the conservatory.*
> LADY CHILTERN *enters*

LORD GORING
Lady Chiltern, why are you playing Mrs Cheveley's cards?

LADY CHILTERN (*Startled*) 625
I don't understand you.

LORD GORING
Mrs Cheveley made an attempt to ruin your husband. Either
to drive him from public life, or to make him adopt a dishonourable position. From the latter tragedy you saved him.
The former you are now thrusting on him. Why should you do 630
him the wrong Mrs Cheveley tried to do and failed?

LADY CHILTERN
Lord Goring?

LORD GORING (*Pulling himself together for a great effort, and showing the philosopher that underlies the dandy*) 635
Lady Chiltern, allow me. You wrote me a letter last night in
which you said you trusted me and wanted my help. Now is the
moment when you really want my help, now is the time when
you have got to trust me, to trust in my counsel and judgment.
You love Robert. Do you want to kill his love for you? What sort 640
of existence will he have if you rob him of the fruits of his
ambition, if you take him from the splendour of a great political
career, if you close the doors of public life against him, if you
condemn him to sterile failure, he who was made for triumph
and success? Women are not meant to judge us, but to forgive 645
us when we need forgiveness. Pardon, not punishment, is their
mission. Why should you scourge him with rods for a sin done
in his youth, before he knew you, before he knew himself?
A man's life is of more value than a woman's. It has larger 650

635   s.d. first appears in PR.
645–6   *triumph and success* texts before PR add:
> What sort of love will he keep for you when he is soured, disappointed, baffled,
> unhappy? When he sits alone, thinking over a ruined past, mourning over a lost
> future? He will have no love for you. He will grow to hate you. You will be horrible
> in his eyes. (BLTS version, marked for deletion.)

issues, wider scope, greater ambitions. A woman's life revolves
in curves of emotions. It is upon lines of intellect that a man's
life progresses. Don't make any terrible mistake, Lady Chiltern.
A woman who can keep a man's love, and love him in return, has
done all the world wants of women, or should want of them.   655

LADY CHILTERN (*Troubled and hesitating*)
But it is my husband himself who wishes to retire from public
life. He feels it is his duty. It was he who first said so.

LORD GORING
Rather than lose your love, Robert would do anything, wreck   660
his whole career, as he is on the brink of doing now. He is making for you a terrible sacrifice. Take my advice, Lady Chiltern,
and do not accept a sacrifice so great. If you do, you will live to
repent it bitterly. We men and women are not made to accept
such sacrifices from each other. We are not worthy of them.   665
Besides, Robert has been punished enough.

LADY CHILTERN
We have both been punished. I set him up too high.

LORD GORING (*With deep feeling in his voice*)
Do not for that reason set him down now too low. If he has   670
fallen from his altar, do not thrust him into the mire. Failure to
Robert would be the very mire of shame. Power is his passion.

---

652   *in curves of emotions* (on curves of emotions F, etc.) Presumably intended as an
       example of Lord Goring's 'psychology', but in fact a restatement of the classic theory
       of the 'complementarity' of the sexes. Cf. John Ruskin, 'Of Queens' Gardens' (*Sesame
       and Lilies*, 1865):
       > The man's power is active, progressive, defensive. He is eminently the doer, the
       > creator, the discoverer, the defender. His intellect is for speculation and
       > invention; his energy for adventure, for war, and for conquest, wherever war is
       > just, wherever conquest necessary. But the woman's power is for rule, not for
       > battle, – and her intellect is not for invention or creation, but for sweet ordering,
       > arrangement, and decision . . . Her great function is Praise: she enters into no
       > conquest, but infallibly adjudges the crown of contest. (Section 68.)

       This view had already been challenged by a number of dramatists and novelists, as
       well as by behavioural psychologists (including Havelock Ellis). For a discussion of
       Ruskin's ideas in their context, see Kate Millett, *Sexual Politics* (1971), ch. 3.
654–5 *A woman . . . of them* see Appendix I for additional passage from texts before PR.
665   *worthy of them* texts before PR add:
       > LADY CHILTERN
       > You think that Robert wishes to continue in public life, having done what he has
       > done?
       > LORD GORING
       > A strong man thinks only about his future. A weak man about his past.
       > (BLTS version, marked for deletion).

He would lose everything, even his power to feel love. Your
husband's life is at this moment in your hands, your husband's
love is in your hands. Don't mar both for him.   675

Enter SIR ROBERT CHILTERN

SIR ROBERT CHILTERN
Gertrude, here is the draft of my letter. Shall I read it to you?
LADY CHILTERN
Let me see it.   680

SIR ROBERT *hands her the letter. She reads it, and then,*
with a gesture of passion, tears it up

SIR ROBERT CHILTERN
What are you doing?
LADY CHILTERN   685
A man's life is of more value than a woman's. It has larger issues,
wider scope, greater ambitions. Our lives revolve in curves of
emotions. It is upon lines of intellect that a man's life
progresses. I have just learnt this, and much else with it, from
Lord Goring. And I will not spoil your life for you, nor see you   690
spoil it as a sacrifice to me, a useless sacrifice!
SIR ROBERT CHILTERN
Gertrude! Gertrude!
LADY CHILTERN
You can forget. Men easily forget. And I forgive. That is how   695
women help the world. I see that now.
SIR ROBERT CHILTERN (*Deeply overcome by emotion, embraces*
her)
My wife! my wife! (*To* LORD GORING) Arthur, it seems that
I am always to be in your debt.   700
LORD GORING
Oh dear no, Robert. Your debt is to Lady Chiltern, not to me!
SIR ROBERT CHILTERN
I owe you much. And now tell me what you were going to ask
me just now as Lord Caversham came in.   705

678   *Shall . . . you?* texts before PR read:
        Gertrude, here is the draft of the letter I am going to send to the Prime Minister.
        I will see one of the whips this evening and tell him to make arrangements for my
        resigning my seat.
        Lady C takes the letter and tears it up, without speaking. Her husband asks 'Gertrude,
        what do you mean?'.
691   *a useless sacrifice* texts before PR add: 'I love you all the same, and not with blind eyes
        now!'

LORD GORING
  Robert, you are your sister's guardian, and I want your consent
  to my marriage with her. That is all.
LADY CHILTERN
  Oh, I am so glad! I am so glad!   710
                          Shakes hands with LORD GORING
LORD GORING
  Thank you, Lady Chiltern.
SIR ROBERT CHILTERN (*With a troubled look*)
  My sister to be your wife?   715
LORD GORING
  Yes.
SIR ROBERT CHILTERN (*Speaking with great firmness*)
  Arthur, I am very sorry, but the thing is quite out of the ques-
  tion. I have to think of Mabel's future happiness. And I don't 720
  think her happiness would be safe in your hands. And I cannot
  have her sacrificed!
LORD GORING
  Sacrificed!
SIR ROBERT CHILTERN   725
  Yes, utterly sacrificed. Loveless marriages are horrible. But there
  is one thing worse than an absolutely loveless marriage. A
  marriage in which there is love, but on one side only; faith, but
  on one side only; devotion, but on one side only, and in which
  of the two hearts one is sure to be broken.   730
LORD GORING
  But I love Mabel. No other woman has any place in my life.
LADY CHILTERN
  Robert, if they love each other, why should they not be
  married?   735
SIR ROBERT CHILTERN
  Arthur cannot bring Mabel the love that she deserves.
LORD GORING
  What reason have you for saying that?
SIR ROBERT CHILTERN (*After a pause*)   740
  Do you really require me to tell you?

---

707   *guardian* (natural guardian, her parents being dead F, etc.).
719–22 *Arthur . . . sacrificed!* F and earlier texts have a a longer version, in which Lord G
       reminds Sir Robert that he is under some obligation to him.
726   *horrible* in BLTS he adds 'They are the stain upon our age!' (marked for deletion).

LORD GORING

Certainly I do.

SIR ROBERT CHILTERN

As you choose. When I called on you yesterday evening I found   745
Mrs Cheveley concealed in your rooms. It was between ten and
eleven o'clock at night. I do not wish to say anything more.
Your relations with Mrs Cheveley have, as I said to you last
night, nothing whatsoever to do with me. I know you were
engaged to be married to her once. The fascination she exer-   750
cised over you then seems to have returned. You spoke to me
last night of her as of a woman pure and stainless, a woman
whom you respected and honoured. That may be so. But I cannot give my sister's life into your hands. It would be wrong of
me. It would be unjust, infamously unjust to her.   755

LORD GORING

I have nothing more to say.

LADY CHILTERN

Robert, it was not Mrs Cheveley whom Lord Goring expected
last night.   760

SIR ROBERT CHILTERN

Not Mrs Cheveley! Who was it then?

LORD GORING

Lady Chiltern!

LADY CHILTERN   765

It was your own wife. Robert, yesterday afternoon Lord Goring
told me that if ever I was in trouble I could come to him for
help, as he was our oldest and best friend. Later on, after that
terrible scene in this room, I wrote to him telling him that I
trusted him, that I had need of him, that I was coming to him   770
for help and advice. (SIR ROBERT CHILTERN *takes the letter out
of his pocket*) Yes, that letter. I didn't go to Lord Goring's after
all. I felt that it is from ourselves alone that help can come.
Pride made me think that. Mrs Cheveley went. She stole my

---

755   F and earlier texts add further expostulation on both sides, ending with a 'false exit'
      for Lord Goring.
768   *Later on* texts before PR continue:
      wounded in my pride, wounded in my monstrous pride at what you had said to
      me in that terrible scene in this room I wrote to Lord Goring, telling him . . .
      (BLTS version, marked for deletion.) Wilde removed this and other passages
      suggesting that her approaching Lord Goring was indeed reprehensible, and
      motivated by her reaction *against* her husband. Cf. Appendix I for sequence omitted
      from the interview between Lady C and Lord G (ll. 654–5, above).

letter and sent it anonymously to you this morning, that you   775
should think ... Oh! Robert, I cannot tell you what she wished
you to think ...

SIR ROBERT CHILTERN

What! Had I fallen so low in your eyes that you thought that even
for a moment I could have doubted your goodness? Gertrude,   780
Gertrude, you are to me the white image of all good things, and
sin can never touch you. Arthur, you can go to Mabel, and you
have my best wishes! Oh! stop a moment. There is no name at
the beginning of this letter. The brilliant Mrs Cheveley does not
seem to have noticed that. There should be a name.   785

LADY CHILTERN

Let me write yours. It is you I trust and need. You and none else.

LORD GORING

Well, really, Lady Chiltern, I think I should have back my own
letter.   790

LADY CHILTERN (*Smiling*)

No; you shall have Mabel.

> *Takes the letter and writes her husband's name on it*

LORD GORING

Well, I hope she hasn't changed her mind. It's nearly twenty   795
minutes since I saw her last.

> *Enter* MABEL CHILTERN *and* LORD CAVERSHAM

MABEL CHILTERN

Lord Goring, I think your father's conversation much more improving than yours. I am only going to talk to Lord Caversham   800
in the future, and always under the usual palm tree.

LORD GORING

Darling!   *Kisses her*

776–7   *wished you to think* F, LC and the BLTS typescript have an additional passage which
         first appears in revisions to C:
> ... I was afraid. I did not dare to tell you the truth!
>
> SIR ROBERT
>
> You should have told me, Arthur.
>
> LADY CHILTERN
>
> He wanted to, I would not let him.
>
> SIR ROBERT
>
> My child! my poor child! Well, upon my word, Arthur, Mrs Cheveley turns out
> after all to be an extremely stupid woman. (BLTS version, marked for deletion.)
> The dialogue then continues with 'You can go to Mabel ...'.

782   *go to Mabel* a survival from the earliest drafts, in which at this point the proposal had
        yet to take place.

LORD CAVERSHAM (*Considerably taken aback*)

What does this mean, sir? You don't mean to say that this   805
charming, clever young lady has been so foolish as to accept
you?

LORD GORING

Certainly, father! And Chiltern's been wise enough to accept the
seat in the Cabinet.   810

LORD CAVERSHAM

I am very glad to hear that, Chiltern . . . I congratulate you, sir.
If the country doesn't go to the dogs or the Radicals, we shall
have you Prime Minister, some day.

Enter MASON   815

MASON

Luncheon is on the table, my Lady!

MASON *goes out*

LADY CHILTERN

You'll stop to luncheon, Lord Caversham, won't you?   820

LORD CAVERSHAM

With pleasure, and I'll drive you down to Downing Street
afterwards, Chiltern. You have a great future before you, a great
future. Wish I could say the same for you, sir. (*To* LORD GORING)
But your career will have to be entirely domestic.   825

LORD GORING

Yes, father, I prefer it domestic.

LORD CAVERSHAM

And if you don't make this young lady an ideal husband, I'll cut
you off with a shilling.   830

MABEL CHILTERN

An ideal husband! Oh, I don't think I should like that. It sounds
like something in the next world.

LORD CAVERSHAM

What do you want him to be then, dear?   835

MABEL CHILTERN

He can be what he chooses. All I want is to be . . . to be . . . oh!
a real wife to him.

LORD CAVERSHAM
>Upon my word, there is a good deal of common sense in that,   840
>Lady Chiltern.

>*They all go out except* SIR ROBERT CHILTERN.
>*He sinks into a chair, wrapt in thought. After a little time*
>LADY CHILTERN *returns to look for him*

LADY CHILTERN (*Leaning over the back of the chair*)   845
>Aren't you coming in, Robert?
SIR ROBERT CHILTERN (*Taking her hand*)
>Gertrude, is it love you feel for me, or is it pity merely?
LADY CHILTERN (*Kisses him*)
>It is love, Robert. Love, and only love. For both of us a new life   850
>is beginning.

CURTAIN

841   *Lady Chiltern* (my dear F, LC etc.) In MS the play now moves to its conclusion with
the single line, spoken by Lady C: 'There is love in it, and that is better'. In C this
becomes 'Ah! There is love, and that is everything!' (derived from a manuscript
addition to the typescript acquired by the Clark library at the Prescott Collection
Sale), to which Wilde added 'father', at the same time changing the speaker to Lord G.
The final three speeches appear as an addition to BLTS, and the s.d. accompanying
them first appear in PR. In F a manuscript s.d. following the final words reads '*Exit*
CAVERSHAM – GORING *and* SIR ROBERT *meet c. shaking hands as Curtain falls*'. This
may well have been the practice of the first production: it is not unlikely that Wilde's
original intention to give Lady Chiltern the curtain-line was set aside in the interests
of the actor-manager, then modified to give Hawtrey the 'tag', and finally changed
in the published edition to return it to Lady C when the more elaborate and intimate
ending was added.

APPENDIX I

I, 554–60
She is . . . to make, too
After the report of Mrs Cheveley's opinion of the opera audience,
MS and HTC have the following dialogue:

LORD G
> Then you and Lady Marchmont could not have been there!

MRS M
> Of course we were not. It was not a Wagner night!

LADY B
> We only go on Wagner nights.

LORD G
> Ah! I only go to talk. Best place for talking I know, the Opera. One can say what one likes!

LADY B
> Then you must never come to my box, Lord Goring. You had better go with Mrs Cheveley. I hear she talked the whole time last night at the top of her voice!

MISS C
> Who talked the whole time last night at the top of her voice? I am sure I should like her!

LADY B
> Mrs Cheveley!

(HTC version, marked for deletion.)

I, 783
You thought that letter had been destroyed
In MS this is part of a long speech, without
the interruptions from Sir Robert. It continues:

I know the Baron told you so. How foolish of you to believe him. No sensible person – and in business the Baron was always sensible – ever destroys a dangerous letter, or writes a compromising one. The Baron kept it, not to harm you, but to make himself secure. Now the Baron and I were great friends. I would have done anything in

143

the world for him, except love him. He would have done anything in the world for me, except marry me – so we remained simply friends. For ten years we were great friends. The Baron died quite suddenly as you know. His wealth he left to his nephew. To me he left as a memento a little villa he had in Hungary – with some Boucher tapestries and nice Louis Seize furniture – the sort of background that just suits me. One day in the drawer of an inlaid escritoire I found a large sealed packet marked 'to be destroyed after my death' – you know what a woman's curiosity is – almost as great as a man's. I opened it of course. The secret history of the nineteenth century was in it. Letters from great ladies offering their favours for money. Letters from kings who had lost their thrones. Letters from demagogues who wanted to be kings. And a letter from you on the top of which, in that delicate small hand of his that you must remember, the Baron had written 'The [origin] of Robert Chiltern' – and on the back of it the sum, £50,000.

It is interesting that, at this early stage, Wilde connected the taste for Boucher and Louis Seize furnishings with the desire for power and wealth.

I, 810–39
My dear . . . this scheme
After 'you would be hounded out of public life'
MS continues:

and all the people who had done the same sort of thing themselves, or something much worse, would of course be the loudest against you. When a victim is offered up to public respectability it counts as a general whitewashing all round and every thief has the opportunity of dilating on the enormous importance of honesty.

'You have a splendid position' is elaborated as follows:

you are undersecretary for Foreign Affairs: you will have the next vacant seat in the Cabinet: everybody tells me that you have brilliant social position. You have wealth that you have doubled, trebled by judicious investment: and you have a wife of the highest possible moral principles.

I, 911
He has had . . . career
In MS and HTC Lady M observes that Lord Radley
placed great trust in Sir Robert:

And got him his first seat in Parliament and everything of that
kind . . . And I should fancy helped him in other ways, though I
don't really know of course. Sir Robert is well born, on one side, at
any rate – his mother was Lady Adeliza Gillray, but there was not a
penny of money in the family. I remember Lady Adeliza always went
about in a plain black silk dress, which is a great confession of
failure, and it is said that she used to pay her visits in omnibuses,
though perhaps that is only a malicious scandal.

Wilde may have thought this too reminiscent of Mrs Arbuthnot's im-
poverishment and black dress: the earlier play was too fresh in the public
mind for him to risk implying that Sir Robert was a Gerald, come to
mature years under Lord Radley's kind (and perhaps fatherly) protection.

II, 131–49
One night after dinner . . . possessed it
MS1 has a cancelled opening to this speech
in which Sir Robert's early poverty is referred to:

Arthur, *you* don't know what want of money means. You have never
known it. I have. My father was poor all his life. The result was that
he was an utterly disappointed man. The position he was entitled
to hold he was never able to attain. He was baffled and trammelled
at every point. It soured his nature and [?cramped] his mind. I grew
up in a sordid atmosphere of ways and means where every penny
was counted and every pound haggled over. The rich people who
lived near us laughed at my father for his absurd pride, at my mother
for her shabby dresses – I used to see them do it. It enraged me.
I knew the humiliation of being poor myself when I was a boy. At
school I was always in shabby clothes. At Oxford I had not enough
to live on. I could not accept hospitality that I could not return. So
I lived apart from the others. I was lonely and in my loneliness and
bitterness I determined to be rich. When I left Oxford Lord Radley
who was a cousin of my mother's offered me the post of his secretary. I accepted it with joy. I felt a chance was open to me at last.

A number of details were changed in the remainder of the speech. In MS1
'modern', 'quiet' and 'preached to us' are absent, and the gospel taught is

'tragic' rather than 'marvellous'. There is no reference to Arnheim's 'jewels' and 'carved ivories' and the sequence moves directly from 'the luxury in which he lived' (l. 144) to 'six weeks later I wrote him the letter...'(l. 189). MS2 gives the development of his philosophy more or less as printed, including the curious image of luxury as 'a background, a painted scene in a play'. The Baron's teaching might be compared with the reflections of Lord Henry Wotton in Dorian Gray, who wonders whether 'we could ever make psychology so absolute a science that each little spring of life would be revealed to us'. To him the hero appears 'like one of those gracious figures in a pageant or play, whose joys seem to be remote from one, but whose sorrows stir one's sense of beauty, and whose wounds are like red roses' (*DG*, pp. 57–8 / *CW*, p. 56).

I, 242
MS and C have the following passage, before
'*The English can't stand . . .*'

Well, a man who know[s] the House of Commons very well said once that if one of the Members had murdered his mother-in-law, and got up in the House and asked leave to make a personal explanation, and frankly admitted that in a moment of irritation which no one regretted more than himself, he *had* brained the aged lady with the drawing room poker, and threw himself on the mercy of the House, and appealed to other honourable members as to whether his general conduct had not been uniformly courteous and humane – well, the man who knew the temper of the astounding assembly at Westminster said that the member in question would sit down amidst a perfect storm of applause, and that any further reference to the manner in which he had treated his aged relative would be regarded by both sides as being in extremely bad taste.

(Marked for omission in C.)

II, 262 etc.
That I will not do . . .
MSI contains a longer version of this dialogue, including
the following cancelled exchanges after the equivalent of l. 226:

SIR R
But this woman? How can I defend myself against her?
LORD G
She has learned the gospel of gold. Bribe her.

SIR R

I will give her half of my fortune.

LORD G

And how much would that be?

SIR R

Two hundred thousand pounds.

LORD G

And if she asked for all your fortune?

SIR R

Rather than lose my wife's love I would give it all.

LORD G

Then the gospel of gold breaks down sometimes.

SIR R

Rather than lose the woman I love I would strip myself of everything I have. Rather than lose her love I would make myself an outcast. But if she knew of this thing that I have done she would turn from me. Her very virtues make her pitiless. Her perfections mar her –

It is interesting that this passage, subsequently rejected, includes the notion of self-sacrifice – with its Biblical associations of the naked penitent – that fascinated Wilde. The rearrangement takes away some of the less convincing, melodramatic touches and focuses attention on Mrs Cheveley – with Sir Robert's marriage as background.

III, 623–9

Pray have . . . discovered

The point of the reference to smoking changed
in the course of revision. The BLTS typescript reads:

MRS C

Thanks. May I smoke a cigarette? I can never talk business unless I am smoking a cigarette.

LORD G

Certainly. You don't mind my smoking? Thanks. Well, Mrs Cheveley?

This derives (with one slight alteration) from MS. After revision in manuscript to BLTS, Wilde produced the version in the C typescript:

MRS C

Thanks. I'd sooner walk about. May I smoke a cigarette? I never can talk business unless I am smoking cigarettes. All the pretty women in Vienna smoke cigarettes.

LORD G

And half the pretty women in London. Well, Mrs Cheveley?

In revising C, Wilde changed the second speech to:

And half our pretty women in London. Personally I prefer the other half. Well, Mrs Cheveley.

LC is close to the revised C; F has a hybrid of the early drafts and the text as printed.

IV, 85

They will never say that of you, sir
This is added to the BLTS typescript, from which the following passage of dialogue has been deleted:

LORD G

It is quite wonderful, father, I have nothing to say, except that he deserves it all.

LORD C

Mark my words, sir. Robert Chiltern will be Prime Minister some day.

LORD G

I don't mind. *I* am not going to compete, father.

LORD C

You haven't got the necessary ambition.

LORD G

No, that is the only thing that is wanting.

LORD C

It is not the only thing, sir. You have not got the high principles that are requisite.

LORD G

I don't like principles. I prefer prejudices. There is much more to be said in favour of people's prejudices than there is in favour of people's principles.

LORD C

Well, you have got to acquire ambition and principles at once. I am going to put you into politics, sir. You have got to stand for Parliament at the next election.

LORD G

My dear father, that would be quite impossible. Why, only people who look dull ever get into the House of Commons, and only people who are dull ever succeed there.

IV, 275–6

And it is . . . extravagant

The BLTS typescript om. this, and continues
with a passage marked for omission:

LORD G

How nice of you to say so! And now, when shall we get married?

MABEL

Well, today is Thursday, isn't it? I suppose you have any amount of engagements till the end of the season haven't you?

LORD G

Only one that I care twopence about.

MABEL

Dear, how sweet you are! Of course, you have got to see Robert. He is my guardian.

LORD G

Oh! that won't take five minutes, at the most.

MABEL

And I have got to see my dressmaker. That will take about six months at the least, and we must give people time to get their presents. And then I want the thing to be a dead secret for a little while.

LORD G

A dead secret? Why?

MABEL

Oh! how silly you are! Of course I should like to tell everyone about our engagement, and it is not very nice to tell a person anything that is not a great secret. What is the use of telling people things that they know already? One might just as well write for the papers.

LORD G

Well, it will be a dead secret till I get Robert's consent.

MABEL

Yes: and after he has given his consent we will deny the whole thing.

LORD G

Why? I certainly won't.

MABEL

Well, I will. I'll say I've been driven into it. And everybody will be most sympathetic. I love people to be sympathetic. Ah! but I love love better.

LORD G

Darling!

The most elaborate of the earlier versions of this scene (all of which are placed nearer the end of the act, after Sir Robert's permission has been granted) is contained in the draft acquired by the Clark Library at the Prescott Collection sale. The typescript leaves, ff. 27–8, which include the sequence do not correspond to the subsequent typescript (C) which otherwise derives directly from the Prescott version. Mabel's response to Lord Goring's fear of being refused is more extreme in this draft:

> MABEL (*Looking up at him*)
> But you never have been refused yet by anybody, have you, Arthur? I can't imagine anyone refusing you. (*Smiling*) It would create a sensation. It would give you a sensation. It would give me a sensation. (*Solemnly*) I feel that I am going to refuse you.
> LORD G (*Drawing back: showing a human emotion for the first time*)
> What! You adore me, and you are going to refuse me?
> MABEL (*Sadly*)
> That is the trouble. I love you. I adore you. To have you would be perfect – too perfect. You hate perfection. I fear perfection. It cannot last – it wouldn't be, if it did. (*Rapturously*) It would be nicer to create a sensation than to have you for a husband. All London would thank me. The season has been frightfully dull. (*Archly*) And it would be good for you. (*As if to herself*) I shall miss you … but … I shall accept the other proposal. How delightful! that makes the second today.

This is Tommy Trafford's, made as usual on one of his days for proposing:

> LORD G
> Oh! bother Tommy Trafford!
> MABEL (*Dismally*)
> I shall. I shall marry him. Bother him! Of course! That is the business of wives. But it will improve his manners. Yours are beyond improvement. They are charming! (LORD GORING *smiles deprecatingly*) They are perfectly scandalous! Lord Caversham says so. Every one says so. (*Sighs*) Poor Tommy!

After admitting that he is extravagant, Lord Goring adds that he has been 'terribly irregular' (implicitly, in his bachelordom). Mabel counters: 'Dearest! So am I! Irregularity is the thief of boredom. So we'll never quarrel'. (It should be noted that these pages are remarkable for the fullness of their stage directions – rare in Wilde's drafts.)

IV, 321 etc.
Lady Chiltern . . .
In MS this sequence begins as follows:

LADY C

Lord Goring, what can you think of me? I dare not look you in the face. (LORD GORING *approaches and kisses her hand*) In a moment of folly I wrote to you a foolish letter. It was Violet who by telling me what she thought I am, what I know I should be, prevented me from coming to your house at night. Oh why did you, my friend, our friend, suggest so mad, so wrong a thing to me, whom you should have protected rather, knowing what you did about my husband, whom I love, and whose love I fear I have lost[?]

LORD G

I wished to teach you a lesson, Lady Chiltern, a lesson in charity. I wished you to realise how weak we all are, and how kind we should be to those who have done weak or foolish things.

C's version does not imply that Lord Goring's letter was intended to have such an effect, or that anything improper might be thought to have taken place:

LADY C

Lord Goring, I am afraid I must have kept you in yesterday evening, waiting for me. Do excuse me. But at the last moment I felt that no real help comes to any one of us, except from ourselves, and that when we stand face to face with a great tragedy we have to solve it for ourselves and by ourselves. The tragedy that has come on me so suddenly, so horribly, I have solved as I think it should be solved. Whatever public disgrace comes on Robert, I will share with him, if he will let me. It is my duty!

LORD G

How good! how wise you are! But there will be no public disgrace. Mrs Cheveley gave up Robert's letter to me last night, and I burned it. Robert is safe.

This also appears in LC and F, but is deleted in BLTS.

IV, 485
I think so
BLTS continues with a passage
marked for omission:

... But, oh! why is it that you women are so much finer than we are? When I look into your eyes, I see truth there. When I kiss your hands, I feel truth in them. Your lips are eloquent of truth. You women are made of finer material than we are. We are soiled with the mire and the battle. You are our proper ideals.

LADY C

Oh, don't say those things to me, Robert. Don't ever say those things to me.

SIR R

What else should I say to the woman I worship?

LADY C

We are not made for worship.

SIR R

For love, then, which is better. And now, Gertrude, although I am safe from detection ...

IV, 654–5
all the world wants of women
BLTS reads 'all we want of women',
and continues with a passage marked for omission:

... Be content if you can keep your husband's love. Don't sacrifice him to gratify the vanity of a high moral tone!

LADY C

Is this the philosophy you are going to teach your wife when you marry[?]

LORD G

Certainly. I am idle, and my father tells me I am good-for-nothing. That may be so. But I think that women are simply made to love and to be loved, and if I ever do some weak or wrong thing, I will expect from my wife pity, gentleness, kindness, forgiveness.

LADY C

You think me hard and unwomanly, then?

LORD G

I think you hard but not unwomanly.

This may have been removed on the grounds of its prolixity, but it is a purely conventional view of woman as forgiving angel, and may have seemed too blatantly orthodox for a supposedly 'original' speaker. The 'curves of emotion' speech has at least an air of originality.

APPENDIX II

This extract from 'Dress at the Theatres' by 'Florence' (in *The Sketch*, 9 January 1895) gives lady readers an account of costume in *An Ideal Husband*. It suggests the elaboration and expense of fashionable dress in the period – effects difficult to reproduce now economically, because of the amount of material involved. It will be seen that Wilde's description of Mrs Gieveley in his stage direction (I, 111) corresponds to the magazine's description of her dress. The columnist begins with an account of eighteenth-century costumes in Henry James' play *Guy Domville*.

So much for these fascinating last-century costumes; and now, if for a change you would like some eminently up-to-date gowns which are full of good ideas, you had better let me tell you about the dresses in the new Haymarket piece, 'An Ideal Husband', for they are distinctly worthy of notice. I have nothing but admiration for Miss Julia Neilson's three beautiful gowns; but then, when the wearer is so perfectly and grandly beautiful herself, she makes the gown instead of the gown making her. In Act II, then, Miss Neilson [as Lady Chiltern] wears a white satin gown, brocaded with a large conventional floral design, the skirt and the whole of the long train being bordered with small bunches of Neapolitan violets, set at regular distances apart, while great trails of the same flowers pass over the shoulders and fall on to the loosely hanging sleeves of white chiffon, which fall away from the arm in front in a fashion most becoming to anyone with such lovely arms as Miss Neilson's. The bodice itself is draped across with the chiffon, a great bunch of violets being placed on the right side of the corsage, and another at the left side of the waist, where the chiffon is tied into long, broad sash-ends, sprinkled over with a shower of violets. Miss Neilson wears long strings of pearls, caught up on the bodice in festoons, together with a diamond tiara and sundry diamond ornaments. Her next dress has a perfectly plain skirt of white satin foulard, brocaded with a Pompadour design of shadowy pink roses nestling in tender green leaves, the bodice being veiled with accordian-pleated pink chiffon, held in in front by two broad braces of the brocade, tapering to a point at the waist, which is encircled by a twist of chiffon. Miss Julia Neilson, like Mrs. Patrick Campbell, abjures collars, and the chiffon is softly shirred beneath the throat, which is left perfectly free, the puffed sleeves of brocade having deep transparent cuffs – also of the shirred chiffon. Miss Neilson does not come on in Act III, but she reappears in the last act in a wonderfully handsome dress with a perfectly plain trained skirt of buttercup-yellow satin, the bodice, which is a most elaborately beautiful one, having a vest arrangement of golden tissue, through which there gleams a suggestion of blue, the deep shoulder-capes, which fall in soft, graceful folds and taper to a point at each side of the waist, being of the yellow satin, lined with pinkish mauve. A band of gold passementerie, glittering with stones which reproduce the various colours, outlines the neck and encircles the waist, and the sleeves are composed of draperies of brocade and golden gauze, the cuffs being of blue glacé, covered with the pinkish-mauve chiffon, while at the back, below the neck, there is a butterfly bow of the gauze, edged with jewelled passementerie.

Next comes the turn of Miss Florence West, who, as the scheming adventuress of the piece, has some very striking and elaborate gowns, though two, at least, of them did not by any means meet with my approval. The first – an evening dress – is of dark emerald-green satin, the bodice veiled with gauze of the same colour, glistening here and there with broad streaks of silver and cream. This filmy drapery is continued on the skirt, where it terminates just below the knees in front, and disappears into the long train at the side, beneath a trail of roses in every imaginable shade of pink and crimson. The skirt is bordered in front with festoons of gauze, caught by tiny bunches of pink roses, over each of which hovers a graceful swallow, two more birds being used as trimming, one of them having fluttered on to the centre of the bodice at the back, while the other nestles into the waist in front. I have nothing but disapproval for such a mode of trimming, for, though it may be original and, in a way, effective, it is barbarous and unpleasant, and I only hope that women will show their disapproval of this needless slaughter by refraining from imitation. But to return to the remaining – and unoffending – details of the dress. It is guiltless of sleeves, unless a rope of roses which passes over the shoulders can be said to do duty as such, and a lovely effect is secured by closely set clusters of shaded roses, which line the edge of the skirt and the whole of the enormously long train, every movement disclosing some fresh shade. Certainly a lovely and original gown, but the sight of those birds spoiled it entirely, as far as I was concerned. Miss Florence West's next costume is startling, to put it mildly. It consists of yellow mirror moiré, and has a deep square collar of scarlet velvet, which forms crossed revers in front, fastening over at the left side with a paste button. Both from collar and revers falls a deep frill of mellow-tinted lace, and, in order that there may be plenty of contrast, there is a collar-band of bright-green velvet, with a bunch of violets set at each side. Then the sleeves are of cream-coloured chiné glacé, brocaded with pink roses and foliage, and to crown all there is a hat of green straw, which has masses of orchids in various colours, including purple and red. Then remember that, for this occasion, Miss West has indulged in hair of the fashionable red, or – I apologise – auburn shade, and you may possibly imagine the effect of this combination of colours, which, however, I am bound to say, Miss West carries off exceedingly well. As far as good taste is concerned, her last dress must take first place, for it is simply fashioned of pale tea-rose-yellow satin, brocaded with shadowy roses in the faintest possible shade of pink, the cuffs being turned back with red satin, and a touch of the same colour appearing between the soft falls of lace which adorn the bodice. Round the waist there is a loose golden girdle, the long ends studded with rubies; and Miss West also wears a splendid cloak of black satin, lined with red satin, the cape being cut in battlements over a deep frill of lace, and turned back with red.

Then comes the turn of dainty Miss Maude Millet [as Mabel Chiltern], who has three of the smartest imaginable gowns, in which I immediately recognised a master hand, and eventually found it to be that of Madame Humble, of 19, Conduit Street. The first, which is an ideal evening-gown for a young girl, is of yellow satin, the full skirt perfectly plain, with the exception of a great spray of flowers – white lilac, mauve orchids, and deep-shaded pansies – which is arranged in most artistic fashion at the left side. The bodice is veiled in front with slightly overhanging folds of gold-sequined net, while bands of gold sequins are curved round the sides with excellent effect upon the figure, three diamond buttons being placed down the back. The full puffed sleeves of the satin droop slightly off the shoulders, which are crossed by clusters of the same flowers that adorn the skirt. But for genuine novelty and effectiveness the second dress must take the first place. It is of eau-de-Nil satin, patterned with a tiny spot and an equally diminutive conventional leaf. At each side of the skirt there is a larger bow of orange-coloured velvet, which forms a base for three gracefully curving black ostrich tips – an original method of trimming which is likely to commend itself to most people. The waistband, of black satin ribbon, tied at the back in two smart bows, with a little space between, and the collar, of orange velvet, has two tiny black tips at each side. Then there are square epaulettes of black satin, covered with lace, and, to give a perfect finishing touch, a picture hat of black velvet, the full crown embroidered with steel and trimmed with black ostrich feathers. For the last act,

Miss Millett has a pale-tan crépon gown, the skirt having a tiny pointed panel at each side of turquoise-blue mirror velvet, with an appliqué of white cloth, stitched with gold thread and sequins, and fastened in quaintly to the crépon with little gold buttons on one side and black button-holes on the other, and tied at the top with a black satin bow. The bodice has a blouse front of the velvet, with a wide box-pleat down the centre, and neck and waist bands of black satin, the former covered with lace and adorned at the back with lace ruffles and a butterfly bow of satin. But most charming of all is the zouave of blue satin, enriched with its appliqué of cloth and gold, and I think you will allow that Miss Millett's dresses stand out well from all the others.

Then Miss Fanny Brough [as Lady Markby], in a very becoming grey coiffure, has a ruby-coloured velvet evening dress with a berthe of costly lace, and a day dress of grey and terra-cotta brocade, trimmed with satin ribbon to match, grey velvet, and lace; and the list is concluded by Miss Vane Featherstone in green-and-pink striped chiné silk, brocaded with pink roses with a green velvet bodice, and Miss Helen Forsyth, lovely as ever, in a perfectly cut gown of pink mirror velvet.

Women's costume in An Ideal Husband: *Lady Chiltern in Act IV* (*left*)
and Mabel Chiltern in Act IV (*from* The Sketch, *January 1895*)

APPENDIX III

THE STRUCTURE OF THE PLAY

The numbers in parentheses indicate the beginning of each section, according to the line numbering of the present edition. Scenes containing major elements of the main plot's development are indicated with an asterisk.

Act I (*Octagon Room in Sir Robert Chiltern's House*)

a   Party guests (1–).
b* Arrival of Lady Markby, Mrs Cheveley (111–).
c* Sir Robert enters: conversation with Mrs Cheveley (in Lady Markby's presence) (173–).
d   Lord Goring enters: conversation with Mabel (353–).
e   Lord Caversham and Goring; then conversations between Goring and Lady Marchmont and Lady Basildon and finally Mabel (459–).
f* Sir Robert's private conversation with Mrs Cheveley: request for help, threat of blackmail (641–).
g   Lady Markby returns (902–).
h* Mrs Cheveley speaks to Lady Chiltern: refers to Sir Robert's intention to support canal project (936–).
i* Conversation between Mabel and Goring: finding of bracelet (980–).
j   Mabel, Goring and Lady Chiltem: leave taking (1035–).
k* Lady Chiltem and Sir Robert alone: she insists that he must refuse to support the canal project (1069–1248).

Act II (*Morning-room in Sir Robert Chiltern's House*)

a* Goring and Sir Robert: the story of his career (1–).
b   Lady Chiltem returns (375–).
c* Goring speaks to Lady Chiltern: if she ever needs his help, she must contact him (445–).
d   Mabel enters (536–).
e   Mabel and Lady Chiltern: talk of Mabel's suitor Tommy Trafford (609).
f   Lady Markby arrives with Mrs Cheveley (679–).
g* Mrs Cheveley left alone with Lady Chiltern: the threat made explicit; Sir Robert enters at 1089 (946–).
h* Lady Chiltern and Sir Robert alone again: he rebukes her for idealising him (1048–1119).

Act III (*Library of Lord Goring's House*)

(N.B. Sections a–d contain elements necessary to set up situation for what follows.)

a   Phipps and Goring. Letter arrives from Lady Chiltern, asking for Goring's help (1–).

b   Caversham arrives: after conversation, is shown into smoking-room. Phipps told to show lady who is expected into drawing-room (112–).

c   Mrs Cheveley arrives and is shown into drawing-room (257–).

d   Caversham leaves (342–).

e* Sir Robert arrives. After discussion with Goring, discovers that Mrs Cheveley is in drawing-room – after Goring, assuming she is Lady Chiltern, has defended her honour (377–).

f* Mrs Cheveley and Goring: confronted with bracelet, she gives up incriminating letter, steals Lady Chiltern's note to Goring (589–980).

Act IV (*Morning-room in Sir Robert's House as in Act II*)

a   Goring and Caversham (1–).

b   Mabel joins them (129–).

c   Mabel and Goring (151–).

d* Lady Chiltern and Goring (321–).

e* Sir Robert arrives, with 'compromising' letter, but assumes it is intended for him (Goring leaves them alone at 451) (427–).

f   Goring returns, evidently having proposed to Mabel; Caversham brings news of Prime Minister's offer (511–).

g   Caversham and Goring conversation (590–).

h* Goring and Lady Chiltern: he persuades her not to stand in her husband's way (623–).

i* Sir Robert returns; she insists that he must now accept offer (677–).

j* Mabel and Caversham return; Sir Robert refuses to allow Goring to marry her, but Lady Chiltern explains the misunderstanding over Mrs Cheveley's presence in Goring's house. Conclusion, with Sir Robert and Lady Chiltern left alone on stage (798–853).